THE HIDDEN INNS OF

THE SOUTH OF ENGLAND

including Berkshire, Buckinghamshire, Hertfordshire, Isle of Wight, Oxfordshire and Wiltshire

By Peter Long

© Travel Publishing Ltd.

Regional Hidden Places

Cambs & Lincolnshire
Chilterns
Cornwall
Derbyshire
Devon
Dorset, Hants & Isle of Wight
East Anglia
Gloucs, Wiltshire & Somerset
Heart of England
Hereford, Worcs & Shropshire
Highlands & Islands
Kent
Lake District & Cumbria
Lancashire & Cheshire
Lincolnshire & Nottinghamshire
Northumberland & Durham
Sussex
Yorkshire

National Hidden Places

England
Ireland
Scotland
Wales

Hidden Inns

East Anglia
Heart of England
Lancashire & Cheshire
North of England
South
South East
South and Central Scotland
Wales
Welsh Borders
West Country
Yorkshire
Wales

Country Living
Rural Guides

East Anglia
Heart of England
Ireland
North East of England
North West of England
Scotland
South
South East
Wales
West Country

Published by: Travel Publishing Ltd, 7a Apollo House, Calleva Park, Aldermaston, Berks, RG7 8TN

ISBN 1-904-43405-3

© Travel Publishing Ltd

First published 2000, second edition 2004

Printing by: Scotprint, Haddington

Maps by: © Maps in Minutes ™ (2004)
© Crown Copyright, Ordnance Survey 2004

Editor: Peter Long

Cover Design: Lines & Words, Aldermaston

Cover Photograph: The Saye and Sele Arms, Broughton, nr Banbury, Oxfordshire

Text Photographs: © www.britainonview.com

FOREWORD

The *Hidden Inns* series originates from the enthusiastic suggestions of readers of the popular *Hidden Places* guides. They want to be directed to traditional inns "off the beaten track" with atmosphere and character which are so much a part of our British heritage. But they also want information on the many places of interest and activities to be found in the vicinity of the inn.

The inns or pubs reviewed in the *Hidden Inns* may have been coaching inns but have invariably been a part of the history of the village or town in which they are located. All the inns included in this guide serve food and drink and some offer the visitor overnight accommodation. A full page is devoted to each inn which contains a coloured photograph, full name, address and telephone number, directions on how to get there, a full description of the inn and its facilities and a wide range of useful information such as opening hours, food served, accommodation provided, credit cards taken and details of entertainment. *Hidden Inns* guides however are not simply pub guides. They provide the reader with helpful information on the many places of interest to visit and activities to pursue in the area in which the inn is based. This ensures that your visit to the area will not only allow you to enjoy the atmosphere of the inn but also to take in the beautiful countryside which surrounds it.

The *Hidden Inns* guides have been expertly designed for ease of use and are now printed in full colour. *The Hidden Inns of the South of England* is divided into six chapters each of which is laid out in the same way. To identify your preferred geographical region refer to the contents page overleaf. To find a pub or inn and details of facilities they offer simply use the index to the rear of the guide or locator map at the beginning of each chapter which refers you, via a page number reference, to a full page dedicated to the specific establishment. To find a place of interest, again use the index to the rear of the book or list found at the beginning of each chapter which will guide you to a descriptive summary of the area that includes details of each place of interest.

We do hope that you will get plenty of enjoyment from visiting the inns, pubs and places of interest contained in this guide. We are always interested in what our readers think of the inns or places covered (or not covered) in our guides so please do not hesitate to write to us. This is a vital way of helping us ensure that we maintain a high standard of entry and that we are providing the right sort of information for our readers. Finally if you are planning to visit any other corner of the British Isles we would like to refer you to the list of Travel Publishing guides to be found at the rear of the book.

Travel Publishing

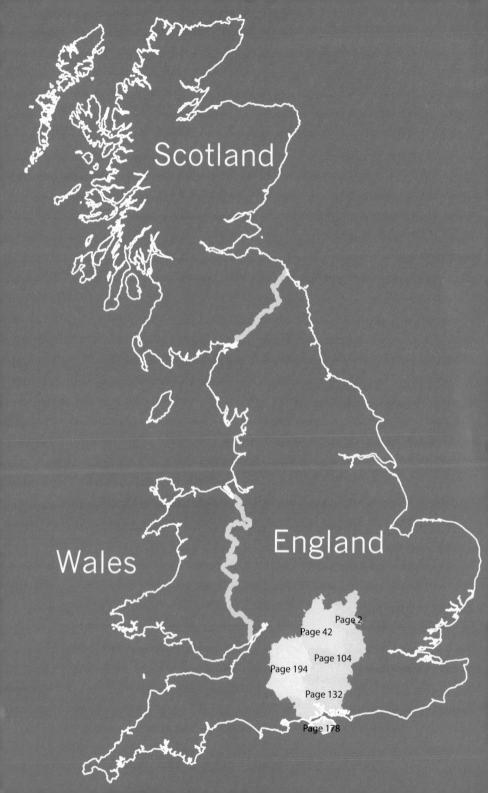

Scotland

England

Wales

CONTENTS

Please note all cross references refer to page numbers

BUCKINGHAMSHIRE

South Buckinghamshire, with the River Thames as its southern county boundary, lies almost entirely within the Chiltern Hills and is a charming and delightful area that has, over the years inspired many writers and artists, including Milton, Shakespeare and Roald Dahl. This chalk range, much of which is classed as an Area of Outstanding Natural Beauty, is particularly noted for its beech woods: Burnham Beeches, with its abundance of deer and birdlife, is a fine example. The conservation of this beautiful area of wood and heathland as a place for wildlife and a recreation area for city residents is an interesting story with many parallels with today's struggles to keep the countryside away from the developers and their bulldozers.

In this charming area there are many places of interest. Chalfont St Giles was the temporary home of John Milton while he was escaping the plague in 17th century London. Other famous residents of this attractive region include Benjamin Disraeli and Sir Francis Dashwood, founder of the infamous Hell Fire Club.

The region centred round Aylesbury, the county town since the 18th century and an ancient market place serving the Vale of Aylesbury, is still largely unspoilt vale, running from the Chilterns in the south to Buckingham

Buckingham Town

in the north. This region offers visitors miles of secluded country walks; a thousand miles of footpaths include the ancient Ridgeway, and the quiet country lanes and gentle undulations make cycling a pleasure - the Vale is at the heart of the National Cycle Network. The attractive rural landscape is littered with bustling market towns and charming villages and has been the inspiration for such writers as Shakespeare and Roald Dahl. This is also an area with a great deal for anyone interested in architecture. Now the home of the University of Natural Law, Mentmore Towers, the first of the Rothschild mansions, was the backdrop in the 19th century of the most glittering of society parties; Waddesdon Manor, another Rothschild mansion, is a magnificent building in the style of a French chateau. Here, too, are a number of stately windmills, including those at Pitstone and Ford End.

Perhaps the least discovered part of the county is the region centred round the ancient county town of Buckingham. It was granted this status as far back as Saxon times, and only relinquished it in the 18th century. Not crossed by any of the county's

Burnham Beeches

Waddesdon Manor

major roads, it has long been a chiefly rural district, with a wealth of attractive villages and old market towns to discover and explore. The wealthy have always found this an excellent place in which to settle and there are many fine houses, including Ascott House in Wing, Stowe (now a school, with magnificent gardens that are open to the public) and Winslow Hall, designed by Sir Christopher Wren. Perhaps the most famous house of all in the area, though certainly not the grandest, is Claydon House, the home of the Verney family; Florence Nightingale was a frequent visitor, particularly in the last years of her life. This area of Buckinghamshire also boasts two very fine churches: All Saints at Wing, with its Saxon nave, Perpendicular roof and memorials to the Dormer family; and St Michael's at Stewkley, whose unspoilt Norman interior is among the finest in the land.

The northern region of Buckinghamshire is dominated by the new town of Milton Keynes. It was developed in the 1960s when there was a general move to provide housing away from the sprawling mass of London, and though the town itself is modern there are numerous ancient villages close by. This is William Cowper's part of the world, and a visit to his museum at Olney tells the story of his life and times. here, too, is a 20th century place of interest: Bletchley Park, the top-secret codebreaking station of the Second World War, where thousands of man and women worked round the clock to decipher the enemy's messages to help bring an earlier end to the war.

Though many of the county's towns and villages have histories going back well before the Norman Conquest, the influence of London is never far away, and several have been linked with the capital for many years by the Metropolitan Railway.

Amersham

The Romans were farming around here in the 3rd and 4th centuries, the Saxons called it Agmodesham and to the Normans it was Elmondesham. So the town has plenty of history, much of which is told in the Museum.

The town's main street has a good mix of fine old buildings, notably the 17th century Market Hall and **Amersham Museum**, housed in part of a medieval hall. Amersham was an important staging post in coaching days and many of the old inns remain, including the **Crown Hotel** that many will recognise from the film *Four Weddings and a Funeral*.

Aylesbury

In the heart of Buckinghamshire and the county town since the 18th century, this ancient town is sheltered by the Chiltern Hills and also gives its name to the broad vale over which it looks. A rich pastureland, where cows where fattened for the tables of London and the famous Aylesbury ducks were raised, this town has held a market here since the 13th century. In the centre of the old part of Aylesbury, the market square has on one side an 18th century County Hall, where the Great Train Robbers were tried.

Much of the character of Aylesbury has been lost in a wave of post-war planning and development but parts of the old town, particularly around the market square, are now a conservation area. Here, are sleepy lanes and cottages, the parish Church of St Mary that was almost completely rebuilt in the 19th century and the King's Head inn where Henry VIII is said to have wooed Anne Boleyn. There are also three large monuments here: to Lord Chesham; to Benjamin Disraeli; and to John Hampden. Hampden, who lived nearby, was famous for making a stand against Charles I in 1635 when he refused to pay Ship Money, believing that the tax would go straight into the King's pocket and not to the navy. During the Civil War, the town was a base for both Cromwell and the King, depending on how well the battle was progressing, and nearby, at Holman's Bridge, saw a bitter blow for the Royalist cause when Prince Rupert of the Rhine suffered a crushing defeat. This period of history is covered in depth in the splendid Georgian building that houses the **County Museum**. There is also an excellent section on Louis XVIII of France who lived at nearby Hartwell House during his years of exile, and those who are familiar with such children's stories as Charlie and the Chocolate Factory will enjoy the display on the life and works of Roald Dahl, who lived and wrote in the Vale of Aylesbury.

Beaconsfield

This is very much a town in two parts: the old town, dating back to medieval times, and the new town which grew up following the construction of the Metropolitan railway line into central London.

One of the glories of the old town is the **Church of St Mary and All Saints** which is considered by many to be one of the finest in the Chilterns. The town also has several literary connections. One of the best known was the poet Edmund Waller, born in the village of Coleshill, just to the north. After getting involved in a Royalist plot in 1643, he was banished from Parliament and spent some time in exile before returning to Beaconsfield after a pardon to concentrate on writing. Somewhat wiser than in his youth, Waller took care to write poems in favour of Cromwell and, after his restoration to the throne, the King. He is buried in the churchyard in a tomb topped by an impressive obelisk. The tomb bears a tribute from fellow poet John Dryden: 'Among the poets of his age he was acknowledged to be the best.' Beaconsfield was also the home of GK Chesterton, author of the popular Father Brown crime stories, the poet Robert Frost and the much loved children's author Enid Blyton.

For a unique step back in time to the 1930s, visitors should seek out the charm of Bekonscot, a rural model village. The oldest model village in the world, **Bekonscot** was begun in the 1920s by Roland Callingham, a London accountant, who started by building models in his garden. As the number of buildings and models grew, Callingham purchased more land and, with the aid of a friend from Ascot who added a model railway, created the village seen today. When the village first opened, people started throwing coins into bucket for charity and, even today, all surplus profits go to charity.

Bletchley

Now more a suburb of Milton Keynes, Bletchley is famous for **Bletchley Park**, also known as Station X, the Victorian mansion which housed the wartime codebreakers. During World War II, 12,000 men and women worked here and in outstations, unable to tell family and friends the nature of their employment, but their work in breaking the Enigma code is thought have helped end the war two years early and to have saved countless lives. It is now a heritage site run by a charitable

Bekonscot Model Village

trust, with historic Victorian and wartime buildings, exhibitions and tours for visitors. There are military vehicles and a mass of war memorabilia, and the **Cryptology Trail** allows visitors to follow the path of a coded message from its interception through decoding to interpretation. Here, too, is the rebuilt Colossus, the world's first electronic valve computer which helped to break Hitler's messages to his generals.

However, though this once thriving country town is now all but merged with its larger neighbour, it still retains a distinctive air. The original village here dates back to Roman times and it was first recorded as a town in 1108.

Buckingham

This pleasant town, whose heart is contained in a loop of the River Ouse, dates back to Saxon times and was once granted a charter by Alfred the Great. Although it became the county town in AD 888, when King Alfred divided the shires, from an early date many of the serious functions of a county town were performed by the more centrally located Aylesbury. According to the Saxon Chronicle, it was Edward the Elder who fortified the town in AD 918 when he brought his army here during his advance on the Danish invaders. The stronghold he built, on which later stood a Norman castle, is now the site of the parish Church of St Peter and St Paul.

At the time of the Domesday Survey, the manor of Buckingham was held by Walter Gifford, later created the Duke of

Buckinghamshire by William the Conqueror, and it remained with the same family until the time of Henry VIII. Notable visitors to this prosperous medieval market town include Catherine of Aragon, who stayed at Castle House in 1514; Edward VI, who founded the Latin School; and Elizabeth I, who dined at the manor house while on her way to Bicester.

In 1725, a disastrous fire destroyed much of the town; many buildings were replaced and there are some fine Georgian houses of which Castle House in West Street is the best example. The town's early-18th century gaol, one of the first to be purpose-built, today houses the **Old Gaol Museum**, which not only reflects the building's history but also has displays on the town's past and the county's military exploits.

One building that did survive the devastating fire is the **Buckingham Chantry Chapel**. Now owned by the National Trust, the chapel was constructed in 1475 on the site of a Norman building whose doorway has been retained. Well worth a visit, the chapel was restored by George Gilbert Scott in 1875.

A much more recent addition to this delightful country market town is the **University of Buckingham**, which was granted its charter in 1983.

Chalfont St Giles

One of the most interesting buildings in this quintessential English village is an Elizabethan mansion, **The Vache**, which

Milton's Cottage

collections of important first editions of Milton's works and a portrait of the poet by Sir Godfrey Kneller. In the churchyard of St Giles is the grave of Bertram Mills, the circus owner. Mills spent much of his childhood on one of his father's farms in Chalfont, and he entered the world of the circus after the First World War.

was the home of friends of Captain Cook; in the grounds is a monument to the famous seafarer. Madame Tussaud, famous for her fascinating exhibitions in London, started her waxworks here in the village.

However, by far the most famous building in Chalfont St Giles, associated with an equally famous resident, is **Milton's Cottage**. John Milton moved to this 16th century cottage (now a Grade I listed building) in 1665 to escape the plague that was sweeping London; the cottage was found for him by fellow Quaker and former pupil Thomas Ellwood. Though the blind poet moved back to London in 1666, Milton wrote *Paradise Lost* and began work on its sequel, *Paradise Regained*, while taking refuge in the village. This is the only house lived in by the poet to have survived, and the cottage and its garden have been preserved as they were when Milton was in residence. The building is now home to a museum which includes

Another fascinating and unusual place to visit in the village is the **Chiltern Open Air Museum** which rescues buildings of historic or architectural importance from across the Chilterns region and re-erects them on its 45 acre site. Though offers of buildings come from many sources, the museum will only accept one that is to be demolished. Once the decision to move a building has been taken the painstaking task of dismantling the structure, piece by piece, is undertaken, followed, finally, by its reconstruction at the museum site. The buildings rescued by the museum are then used to house and display artefacts and implements that are appropriate to the building's original use and history. Also on the museum site is a series of fields farmed using medieval methods where, among the historic crops, organic woad is grow from which indigo dye is extracted for use in dyeing demonstrations.

A mile south of Chalfont St Giles is

the village of **Jordans**, reached down a quiet country lane. Jordans is famous as the burial place of William Penn, Quaker and founder of Pennsylvania. He and members of his family are buried in the graveyard outside the Quaker meeting house. In the grounds of nearby Old Jordans Farm is the Mayflower Barn, said to have been constructed from the timbers of the ship that took the Pilgrim Fathers to America.

Chalfont St Peter

Now a commuter town, Chalfont St Peter dates back to the 7th century and, as its name means 'the spring where the calves come to drink', there is a long history here of raising cattle in the surrounding lush meadows. First mentioned in 1133, the parish Church of St Peter was all but destroyed when its steeple collapsed in 1708. The building seen today dates from that time as it was rebuilt immediately after the disaster.

Housed in a barn at Skippings Farm is the **Hawk and Owl Trust's National Education and Exhibition Centre** Dedicated to conserving wild birds of prey in their natural habitats, the Trust concerns itself with practical research, creative conservation and imaginative educational programmes.

Chenies

This picturesque village, with a pretty green surrounded by an old school, a chapel and a 15th century parish church, is also home to **Chenies Manor**, a fascinating 15th century manor house. Originally the home of the Earls (later Dukes) of Bedford, before they moved to Woburn, this attractive building has stepped gables and elaborately patterned high brick chimneys. Built by the architect who enlarged Hampton Court for Henry VIII, the house has played host not only to the king but also to his daughter Elizabeth. Naturally, there is a ghost here, that of Henry VIII, whose footsteps can be heard as he drags his ulcerated leg around the manor house in an attempt to catch Catherine Howard in the act of adultery with one of his entourage, Tom Culpeper. The house has much to offer, with tapestries, fine furniture and a collection of antique dolls, but the gardens should not be overlooked. Among the delights are a Tudor style

Chenies Manor

sunken garden, a physic garden with a variety of herbs that were used for both medicinal and culinary purposes, and an oak tree that was a favourite of Elizabeth's.

Chesham

A pleasant town situated among wooded hills and for many years a rival to Amersham: in 1454 the Bishop of Lincoln allowed the parishioners here to process around their Church of St Mary at Whitsun to avoid the inevitable fighting associated with their processions at St Mary's Church in Amersham. A successful combination of commuter town, industrial centre and country community, Chesham's growth from a sleepy market town was due to its Metropolitan Railway link with central London. The company began operating the first underground railway in the world in 1863, running trains from Paddington to Farringdon Street, but was never content with being just an urban or suburban railway. So the company pursued its main line ambitions through a policy of acquiring other lines to link into its system as well as building its own. At its high point, the company ran trains as far into Buckinghamshire as Aylesbury and Quainton Road. Today, Chesham still retains its rail link with central London. Chesham was the birthplace of Arthur Liberty, the son of a haberdasher and draper, who went on to found the world-famous Liberty department store in London's Regent Street in 1875. Another notable resident

was Roger Crabbe, who, having suffered head injuries in the Civil War, was sentenced to death by Cromwell. After receiving a pardon, Crabbe opened a hat shop in the town where he is reputed to have worn sackcloth, eaten turnip tops and given his money to the poor. He was eccentric enough to be used by Lewis Carroll as the model for the Mad Hatter in *Alice in Wonderland*.

Chicheley

This attractive village is home of **Chicheley Hall**, a beautiful baroque house that was built in the early 18th century for Sir John Chester and which remains today one of the finest such houses in the country. However, over the years the hall's history has been somewhat uncertain and, after years of use by the military and as a school, it was bought in 1952 by the 2nd Earl Beatty, who restored it to its former glory.

The Earl's father, the 1st Earl, was a particularly courageous naval commander and, as well as receiving the DSO at the age of just 25, he was also a commander at the decisive battle of Jutland in 1916. Mementoes of the 1st Earl's illustrious career at sea can be seen in the study when the hall is occasionally open to the public.

Dadford

Just to the south of the village lies **Stowe School**, a leading public school which occupies an 18th-century mansion that

Stowe School

was once the home of the Dukes of Buckingham. Worked upon by two wealthy owners who both had a great sense of vision, the magnificent mansion house, which was finally completed in 1774, is open to the public during school holidays.

Between 1715 and 1749, the owner Viscount Cobham hired various well known landscape designers to lay out the fantastic gardens that can still be seen around the house. Taking over the house in 1750, Earl Temple, along with his nephew, expanded the grounds and today they remain one of the most original and finest landscape gardens in Europe. Worked on by the best designers of the day, the gardens contain temples, alcoves and rotundas scattered around the landscape that were placed to evoke in the onlooker a romantic and poetic frame of mind.

It is one of the more intriguing quirks of fate that Lancelot Brown, always known as Capability Brown supposedly because he told his clients that their parks had capabilities, was head gardener at Stowe for 10 years. He arrived here in 1741 and began to work out his own style, a more natural style of landscape gardening which was to take over where gardens like the ones at Stowe left off.

Brown's concept was to ensure that the landscape element of the garden, the tree planting, lakes and lawns, should look as natural as possible. **Stowe Landscape Gardens** are now in the hands of the National Trust and are open to the public.

Gayhurst

Built during the reign of Elizabeth I, **Gayhurst House** was given to Sir Francis Drake in recognition of his circumnavigation of the world though the building seen today was not the one that Drake would have lived in. It was later occupied by Sir Everard Digby, one of the conspirators behind the Gunpowder Plot of 1605.

The house can be seen from the village church, which is a perfect Georgian building begun in 1728. Though it has retained many of its original fittings and furnishings, the real eye-catcher inside is a monument to Sir Nathan Wrighte in his robes of Lord Keeper of the Privy Seal, and to his son George.

Great Kimble

Though the village is home to a church with an interesting series of 14th-century wall paintings, its real claim to fame is the nearby 16th-century mansion, **Chequers**, the country residence of the British Prime Minister. Built by William Hawtrey in 1565, but much altered and enlarged in the 18th and 19th centuries, the house was restored to its original form by Arthur Lee in 1912. In 1920, as Lord Lee of Fareham, he gave the house and estate to the nation to be used as the PM's country home.

The first Prime Minister to make use of Chequers was Lloyd George and many who have known the house have since moved, or stayed, in the area: Ramsay MacDonald's daughter lived at nearby Speen; Harold Wilson bought a house in Great Missenden; and Nye Bevan owned a farm in the Chilterns.

Great Linford

Situated on the banks of the Grand Union Canal, this village, which is now more or less a suburb of Milton Keynes, has a 13th-century church, a 17th-century manor house and a **Stone Circle**, one of very few such prehistoric monuments in the county. Despite the encroachment of its much larger neighbour, the village has retained a distinctive air that is all its own.

The central block of the present manor house was built in 1678 by Sir William Pritchard, Lord Mayor of London. As well as making Great Linford his country seat, Pritchard also provided a boys' school and almshouses for six unmarried poor of the parish. The manor house was extended in the 18th century by the Uthwatt family, relatives of the Lord Mayor, and they used various tricks to give an impressive and elegant appearance to the building. The Grand Union Canal, constructed in the mid 19th century, cuts through the estate. Today, the grounds of the manor house are a public park. Brick kilns survive at Great Linford from the days when bricks were in great demand for the new railway towns of Wolverton and New Bradwell.

Great Missenden

Home to one of only two courthouses in the Chiltern Hundreds (the other is at Long Crendon), Great Missenden's **Old Court House** dates from the early 1400s. Also in this attractive village is an attractive flint and stone church and Missenden Abbey, which was founded in 1133 by the Augustinian order. A daughter community of St Nicholas's Abbey in Normandy, the abbey has long since gone and in its place stands a fashionable Gothic mansion dating from 1810.

Among the famous visitors to the village were Robert Louis Stevenson, the author of *Treasure Island*, and the anti-slavery campaigner William Wilberforce. However, Great Missenden is probably best known as being the home of Roald Dahl, the world-renowned author. He lived here for 30 years and the gardens of his home are open the public once a year. He is buried in the churchyard of St Peter and St Paul.

Haddenham

This charming village, with its 12th-century church, is where the original Aylesbury ducks were bred. It was sometimes known as Silly Haddenham because, as the story goes, the villagers thatched the village pond to protect the ducks from the rain.

Here too can be found St Tiggywinkles, one of the world's leading wildlife hospitals, and its visitor centre.

Hambleden

This much filmed village was given to the National Trust by the family of the bookseller WH Smith - who later became Viscount Hambleden. He lived close by at Greenlands, on the banks of the River Thames. The unusually large **Church of St Mary**, known as the cathedral of the Chilterns, dates from the 14th century, and though it has been altered over the years, its size and beauty still dominate the area. Inside the building's 18th-century tower is a fascinating 16th-century panel which is believed to have been the bedhead of Cardinal Wolsey - it certainly bears the cardinal's hat and the Wolsey arms.

The village's other building of interest is **Hambleden Mill**, which dates back at least as far as the 14th century.

High Wycombe

The largest town in Buckinghamshire, High Wycombe is traditionally known for the manufacture of chairs and, in particular, the famous Windsor design. It is still a centre of furniture manufacture, and the **Wycombe Local History and Chair Museum** has displays which give the visitor an excellent idea of the work and crafts of the local people over the years. There is, of course, a superb collection of chairs and other furniture here which are more suited to the houses of ordinary people rather than those of the wealthy. In the grounds of the museum is a medieval motte which would normally indicate that a castle once stood here but, in this case, the structure was probably little more than a wooden tower.

High Wycombe has a number of old buildings of note. The octagonal **Little Market House** was designed by Robert Adams in 1761, and the 18th century Guildhall is the annual venue for a traditional ceremony showing a healthy scepticism for politicians when the mayor and councillors are publicly weighed - to see if they have become fat at the expense of the citizens.

The oldest standing building in the town is All Saints' Church, a large, fine building dating from the 11th century and enlarged in the 13th century.

Hughenden

This village was the home of the great Victorian Prime Minister Benjamin

Hughenden Manor

Disraeli's home in nearby **Bradenham**. The Bradenham Estate includes Bradenham Woods, an area of ancient beech that is among the finest in the whole Chilterns region. Although beech predominates, other trees, including oak, whitebeam, ash and wild cherry, are being encouraged.

Ivinghoe

As the large Church of St Mary would suggest, Ivinghoe was once a market town of some importance. In this now quiet village can be found **Ford End Watermill**, a listed building that, though probably much older, was first recorded in 1767. It is the only working watermill, with its original machinery, left in Buckinghamshire, and the farm on which it stands has also managed to retain the atmosphere of an 18th-century farm.

To the east lies the National Trust's **Ivinghoe Beacon**, a wonderful viewpoint on the edge of the Chiltern Hills. The site of an Iron Age hill fort, the beacon was also the inspiration for Sir Walter Scott's *Ivanhoe*. The Beacon is at one end of the **Ridgeway National Trail**; the other end is the World Heritage Site of Avebury in Wiltshire, and the 85-mile length still follows the same route over the high ground used since prehistoric times..

Disraeli from 1847 to his death in 1881, and he is buried in the estate church. The son of a writer and literary critic, Isaac D'Israeli, who lived for a time in the village of Bradenham on the other side of High Wycombe, Disraeli was also a novelist. He bought **Hughenden Manor** shortly after the publication of his novel *Tancred*. Though not a wealthy man, Disraeli felt that a leading Conservative politician should have a stately home of his own and, in order to finance the purchase, his supporters lent him the money so that he could have this essential characteristic of an English gentleman.

The house and grounds are owned by the National Trust and are open to the public. Also owned by the Trust is Isaac

Lacey Green

Buckinghamshire seems to have more than its fair share of windmills and, here at Lacey Green, is a fine example of a smock mill. Technologically more advanced than post mills, where the body of the mill which carries the sails and all the grinding machinery is mounted on an upright post which can turn through 360 degrees, with a

River Thames at Marlow

smock mill only the cap carrying the sails rotates to meet the wind. As a result the body of the mill, housing the milling machinery, can be bigger, heavier and stronger. Lacey Green's smock mill was first built in the mid 17th century and was moved from Chesham to this site in 1821.

This was also the village where the young poet Rupert Brooke used to spend his weekends in the company of his friends at the quaintly named local pub, the Pink and Lily. The son of a master at Rugby School and a student at Cambridge University, Brooke began writing poetry as a boy and in the years before World War I he travelled widely. He fought in the conflict and died of blood poisoning in 1915 while on his way to the Dardenelles in Turkey. He was buried on the Greek island of Scyros.

Close to the village lies Speen Farm and the **Home of Rest for Horses**. Run by a charitable organisation established in 1886 to care for horses, ponies and

donkeys who had finished their working life, its most famous resident was Sefton, the cavalry horse injured in the Hyde Park bomb blast of the early 1980s.

Little Marlow

In the village cemetery is the grave of the novelist and playwright Edgar Wallace, who died in Hollywood while working on the screenplay for *King Kong*. He lived for many years at nearby Bourne End.

Marlow

An attractive commuter town on the banks of the River Thames. It was at a riverside pub, the Two Brewers, that Jerome K Jerome wrote his masterpiece *Three Men in a Boat*. Other writers to find inspiration here include Mary Shelley, who finished her novel *Frankenstein* after moving here in 1817, TS Eliot and Thomas Love Peacock. Today, Marlow is probably best known for its annual June **Regatta**. Marlow's famous suspension bridge was built in 1832 by Tierney Clarke, who built a similar bridge linking Buda and Pest across the Danube.

Mentmore

The village is home to the first of the Rothschild mansions, **Mentmore Towers**, which was built for Baron Meyer Amschel de Rothschild between 1852 and 1855. A splendid building in the Elizabethan style, it was the work of Sir Joseph Paxton, the designer of Crystal Palace, and is a superb example of grandiose Victorian extravagance. The lavish decoration hides several technologically advanced details for those times, such as central heating, and, as might be expected from Paxton, there are large sheets of glass and a glass roof in the design.

In the late 19th century the house became the home of Lord Rosebery and the magnificent turreted building was the scene of many glittering parties and gatherings of the most wealthy and influential people in the country. In the 1970s the house was put up for auction and, while the furniture and works of art were sold to the four corners of the world, the building was bought by the Maharishi Mahesh Yogi and is now the headquarters of his University of Natural Law. Mentmore Towers is occasionally open to the public.

Middle Claydon

This village is home to **Claydon House**, a historic building that dates from the 17th century but has 19th century additions. The home of the Verney family and now owned by the National Trust, the house contains a number of state rooms with magnificent carved wood and plaster decorations. Particularly delightful are the Chinese rooms which reflect the 18th century enthusiasm for all things Oriental. The house has strong associations with Florence Nightingale: her sister married into the Verney family and the pioneer of modern hospital care spent long periods at the house, especially during her old age. Her bedroom in the house and a museum of her life and experiences during the Crimean War can be seen. Florence died in 1910 after a long career which embraced concerns of public health as well as the training of nurses; the Lady of the Lamp was the first woman to be awarded the Order of Merit.

Claydon House

Milton Keynes

The development corporation that was charged in 1967 with organising the new town of Milton Keynes provided a place of tree-lined boulevards, uncongested roads, spacious surroundings, and acres of parkland. It also has new housing, high-tech industries, modern leisure facilities, and a large covered shopping centre - and it's home to Wimbledon FC! One of the town's most notable buildings is **Christ Church**, built in the style of Christopher Wren. The first purpose-built ecumenical city church in Britain, it was opened in March 1992 by Her Majesty the Queen.

While Milton Keynes is certainly a place of today, it has not altogether forgotten the rural past of the villages which are now incorporated into its suburbs. The **Museum of Industry and Rural Life**, with its large collection of industrial, domestic, and agricultural bygones, is devoted to the lives of the people who lived in the area in the 200 years leading up to the creation of the new town. Exhibitions on art, crafts, local history and social life can be seen at the **Exhibition Gallery**, next to the town's library.

Olney

This pretty town on the banks of the River Ouse is famous for its association with William Cowper, who came to the town to be under the ministry of the Rev. John Newton. Newton was a

reformed slave-trader as well as a fiery preacher; he is buried in the churchyard of St Peter and St Paul, where he was curate.

For over 300 years, Olney was a centre of lace-making by hand, using wooden or bone bobbins. When it was at its most expensive, in the 1700s, only the well-to-do could afford the lace, but the rise in machine-made lace from Nottingham saw a sharp decline in Olney lace. A revival of the trade was attempted by Harry Armstrong when, in 1928, he opened the Lace Factory but, although handmade lace is still produced locally, the factory only lasted until Armstrong's death in 1943.

The town's present day claim to fame is its annual Pancake Race held every

Church of St Peter and St Paul, Olney

Shrove Tuesday. Legend has it that the first 'race' was run in the 15th century when a local housewife heard the Shriving Service bell ringing and she ran to church complete with her frying pan and pancake. Today's re-enactment is open to any lady of Olney over 18 years and she must wear a skirt, an apron, and a scarf as well as carry a frying pan and pancake.

Nearby **Emberton Country Park**, on the site of former gravel pits, is an ideal place to relax. Not only are there four lakes and a stretch of the River Ouse within the park's boundaries but facilities include fishing, sailing, and nature trails.

The house in which Cowper lived from 1768 to 1786 is now the **Cowper and Newton Museum**, an interesting place that not only concentrates on Cowper's life and work but also has some exhibits and collections concerned with times in which he lived and the life of Olney. Each of the rooms of the large early 18th-century town house has been specially themed, and there are numerous displays of Cowper's work, including the 'Olney Hymns'. Cowper wrote 67 of these and the remaining 281 were written by John Newton, whose most famous hymn is *Amazing Grace*. William Cowper was also a keen gardener and the summer house where he wrote can still be seen in the rear garden; it was here, too, that he chose to experiment with plants that were new to 18th century England.

Also at the Museum is the nationally important Lace Collection, and other displays include the finds from local archaeological digs which have unearthed dinosaur bones, Roman coins, medieval fishing weights and Civil War relics.

Pitstone

Though the exact age of **Pitstone Windmill** is not known, it is certainly one of the oldest post mills in Britain. The earliest documentary reference to its existence was made in 1624. It is open to the public on a limited basis. Also in the village is a **Farm Museum**, where all manner of farm and barn machinery, along with domestic bygones, are on display.

Pitstone Windmill

Princes Risborough

Once home to a palace belonging to the Black Prince, the eldest son of Edward III, this attractive place has a host of 17th and 18th century cottages. Nearby is **Princes Risborough Manor House** (National Trust), which is an early example of a redbrick building – it dates from 1670.

Quainton

A pleasant village with the remains of an ancient cross on the green, a number of fine Georgian houses and a row of almshouses built in 1687.

Two major attractions are the 100ft **Quainton Tower Mill** and, at the station, the **Buckinghamshire Railway Centre**, a working steam museum that boasts one of the largest collections of preserved steam and diesel locomotives in the country.

Stewkley

Renowned for being England's longest village, Stewkley is also home to one of the country's finest Norman churches. Dating from around 1150, the Church is a splendid example of Norman architecture and is decorated with zigzag patterns, including a string course which runs all around the building. The tympanum over the west door is carved with dragons and is surrounded by three layers of decorated arches.

Stoke Poges

It was in the churchyard in this surprisingly still rural village that Thomas Gray was inspired to pen his *Elegy Written in a Country Churchyard*. He often visited Stoke Poges to see his mother, who was staying with her sister in a large late-Georgian house that was built for the grandson of the famous Quaker, William Penn. Gray is buried with his mother in the village churchyard, while just east of the churchyard is the massive **Gray Monument**.

The Church of St Giles dates from the 13th century, but perhaps its most interesting feature is the unusual medieval bicycle depicted in one of the stained-glass windows. Behind the church is an Elizabethan manor house where Elizabeth I was entertained and Charles I imprisoned.

Taplow

The name Taplow comes from Taeppa's hlaw (the Old English word for mound) and when the remains of Taeppa's mound, a Saxon burial ground high above the River Thames, were excavated in 1883, archaeologists discovered many artefacts including the arms of the buried hero. The items discovered in his grand burial site are on show at the British Museum, London.

To the north of the village lies the country house of **Cliveden**, once the home of Lady Nancy Astor, the first woman to take her seat as a Member of Parliament. Women were first given the right to vote and also stand for Parliament in 1918, and when in 1919 Lady Astor's husband became a viscount and moved from the Commons to the Lords, she stood as candidate for his Plymouth seat. Subsequently elected,

Cliveden House

Lady Astor concerned herself with social issues of the time during her spell as a Member of Parliament.

Cliveden, now the grandest of grand hotels, is a magnificent 19th century mansion overlooking the River Thames. In the 1930s it was a glittering centre of the social and political scene; it had a darker side, as some of the Cliveden set became associated with the appeasement of both Mussolini and Hitler.

The splendid grounds, which are open to the public, include a great formal parterre, a water garden, a secret rose garden and informal landscapes.

To the south of the village lies Wickenden Vineyards which are open to the public. Wickenden, which was

established in 1976, covers some four acres and has over 5,000 vines.

Thornborough

This lively and attractive village is home to Buckinghamshire's only surviving medieval bridge. Built in the 14th century, the six-arched structure spans Claydon Brook. Close by are two large mounds which were opened in 1839 and revealed a wealth of Roman objects. It is known that there was a Roman temple here, but its location has not been found.

Waddeson

The village is home to another of the county's magnificent country houses, **Waddesdon Manor**. Built between 1874 and 1889 for Baron Ferdinand de Rothschild in the style of a French Renaissance chateau, the house is set in rolling English countryside and makes a lasting impression. The Baron came from the Austrian branch of the great banking family, but he made his home in Britain from the age of 21. In 1874 he bought the Waddesdon and Winchenden estates from the Duke of Marlborough and set about creating his fantastic country house.

The manor's construction was an

immense operation and a steam railway was specially built to move the materials. After 15 years of work, what had been a bare hill was topped with a superb building which borrows elements from several different French chateaux, surrounded by formal gardens and landscaped grounds. The French influence even extended to the carthorses used on the site - powerful Percheron mares that were imported from Normandy.

Now in the hands of the National Trust, the house is home to one of the best collections of 18th century French decorative arts in the world, including Sèvres porcelain, Beauvais tapestries and fine furniture. There are also paintings by Gainsborough, Reynolds and 17th century Dutch and Flemish masters on display.

Wendover

This delightful old market town, situated in a gap in the Chiltern Hills, has an attractive main street of half-timbered

Wendover Cottages

thatched houses and cottages, of which the best examples are **Anne Boleyn's Cottages** A picturesque place, often seen as the gateway to the Chilterns, Wendover also has a fine selection of antique shops, tea rooms and bookshops. On the edge of the Chiltern escarpment lie **Wendover Woods**: created for recreational pursuits as well as for conservation and timber production, these Forestry Commission woods have numerous trails through the coniferous and broadleaved woodland.

West Wycombe

This charming estate village, where many of the houses are owned by the National Trust, has a main street displaying architecture from the 15th century through to the 19th century. Close by is **West Wycombe Park**, the home of the local landowners, the Dashwood family until the 1930s and now a National Trust property. Of the various members of the family, it was Sir Francis Dashwood who had most influence on both the house and the village. West Wycombe house was originally built in the early 18th century but Sir Francis boldly remodelled it several years later, and the grounds and park were landscaped by Thomas Cook, a pupil of Capability Brown. The grounds contain temples and an artificial lake shaped like a swan, and the house has a good collection of tapestries, furniture and paintings.

Hewn out of a nearby hillside are **West Wycombe Caves**, created, possibly from some existing caverns, by Sir Francis as part of a programme of public works. After a series of failed harvests, which created great poverty and distress among the estate workers and tenant farmers, Sir Francis employed the men to extract chalk from the hillside to be used in the construction of the new road between the village and High Wycombe.

The village **Church of St Lawrence** is yet another example of Sir Francis'

West Wycombe Caves

enthusiasm for remodelling old buildings. Situated on the remnants of an Iron Age fort, the church was originally built in the 13th century. Dashwood remodelled the interior in the style of an Egyptian hall and also heightened the tower, adding a great golden ball to the top. There is room in the ball for six people and it was

here that Sir Francis entertained his notorious friends. Sir Francis had a racier side to his character and was the founder of the infamous Hell Fire Club. This group of rakes, who were also known as the Brotherhood of Sir Francis or Dashwood's Apostles, met a couple of times a years to engage in highly colourful and highly dubious activities.

Willen

The Church of St Mary Magdalene, built in the late 17th century, is an elegant building in the style of Sir Christopher Wren, but Willen has a much more modern important building in the shape of the **Peace Pagoda and Buddhist Temple**, opened in 1980. It was built by the monks and nuns of the Nipponsan Myohoji and was the first peace pagoda in the western hemisphere. In this place of great tranquillity and beauty, a thousand cherry trees and cedars, donated by the ancient Japanese town of Yoshino, were planted on the hill surrounding the pagoda, in memory of the victims of all wars.

Wing

The village is famous for its fine Saxon **Church of All Saints** which, although it has undergone much alteration down the centuries, still retains its rare Saxon apse and crypt. Dating from about AD 970, it is one of the most interesting churches of its period left in England. Inside there are numerous brasses and monuments, including one to Sir Robert Dormer, dated 1552, that is in a pure renaissance style and is said to be the finest contemporary example in the country.

Just to the east of the village lies **Ascott House**, another mansion that was owned by a member of the Rothschild dynasty. It was bought in 1874 by Leopold Rothschild, who had the original Jacobean farmhouse essentially rebuilt, though the timber framed core was kept. Now in the hands of the National Trust, and remodelled again in the 1930s, the house is home to Arthur Rothschild's fine collection of paintings as well as some excellent French furniture and Oriental porcelain. The gardens are also superb, with many rare plants and trees and a fountain sculpted by the American artist Waldo Story.

Winslow

This small country town is full of charm and character, with houses, shops and inns grouped around the central market square. Though most of the buildings date from the 18th and 19th centuries, this is an ancient place and it is believed that Offa, the King of Mercia, stayed here in AD 752.

By far the most prominent building in Winslow is **Winslow Hall**, a delightful William and Mary house that was designed by Sir Christopher Wren. Unlike many houses, it has remained remarkably unchanged both inside and out, and it contains a fine collection of 18th century furniture and Chinese art. The gardens, too, are beautiful, with rare specimen plants that are of great interest to keen gardeners.

THE BLACK HORSE

AYLESBURY ROAD, GREAT MISSENDEN,
BUCKINGHAMSHIRE HP16 9AX
TEL: 01494 862537

> **Directions:** The inn is located 2 miles from Great Missenden on the A413 Amersham to Aylesbury road.

The Black Horse is a 250-year-old coaching inn whose entrance is a very distinctive porch made from wood gathered from the local forest. The exterior is very smart in black and white, with pretty lights along the front, while inside low beams assist the traditional atmosphere. Open throughout the day and

throughout the week, this is very much an inn for all the family and a delight to visit whatever the time and whatever the season, with the guarantee of a warm welcome from leaseholder Philip Walker and his staff. The bar serves a good choice of cask ales and a winter warmer of mulled wine, while the range of food served all day runs from sandwiches and baguettes to chilli con carne, tuna pasta bake, beef madras and a hearty helping of bubble & squeak with egg, bacon and beans that will fill the emptiest stomach. The Black Horse is a great place for socialising, whether it's joining in a game of darts, cribbage or dominoes or enjoying the live music sessions that take place every few weeks. In summer these take place in the large beer garden, which has a brilliant children's play area complete with a bouncy castle, swings and even a mini-assault course. And when the little ones have worked off their excess energy they can tuck into something from their very own menu; high chairs and baby changing facilities are available for the very young. The most unusual attraction of all is the sight of hot-air balloons taking off from the adjacent field and soaring majestically over the inn.

- 🕐 11-11
- 🍴 Snacks and full meals served all day
- £ All the major cards
- Ⓟ Car park, beer garden with children's play area
- 🎵 Hot air ballooning from adjacent field, regular themed evenings
- @ e-mail: phil@theblackhorse.net
- ❓ Great Missenden (Old Court House) 2 miles, Chesham 4 miles

Buckinghamshire

THE BLACK HORSE

MAIN ROAD, LACEY GREEN, BUCKINGHAMSHIRE HP27 0QU
TEL: 01844 345195

Directions: From J4 of the M40 take the A4010 towards Princes Risborough; turn right on minor road to Lacey Green.

The Black Horse is a splendid traditional village pub with a fine reputation for hospitality that stretches back more than 200 years. It looks delightful, with a smart white and red facade, attractive hanging baskets, a pretty little white fence and a well-trimmed hedge. A huge brick chimney dominates one end. A low beamed ceiling and a large open fireplace keep up the traditional look inside, creating a really delightful ambience in which to enjoy Lynne and Tony's hospitality, a fine selection of real ales (the inn is CAMRA-approved) and freshly prepared, generously served home cooking. The choice runs from toasties to salads, omelettes, burgers, steaks, mixed grill and an all-day breakfast. The

Sunday roasts are guaranteed to bring in the crowds. Food is served lunchtime and evening Tuesday to Saturday and lunchtime Sunday. The hosts can also provide outside bars and are happy to cater for functions. Darts, billiards and Aunt Sally are the time-honoured pub games, and there are regular quiz nights. Top sporting events are shown on a wide-screen TV.

The inn has ample parking space and a super beer garden with a children's play area and pets corner. The Black Horse stands on the main road in the village of Lacey Green, where a young Rupert Brooke was a regular weekend visitor. There's plenty to see in and around the village, including the oldest surviving smock mill in the country. Not far away is Speen Farm and the Home of Rest for Horses, whose most famous resident was the cavalry horse Sefton.

- 🕐 12-3 & 5-11 (Sat 12-11, Sun 12-10.30); closed Mon lunchtime
- 🍴 Home cooking every lunchtime, traditional Sunday lunch
- 💷 All the major cards
- 🅿 Car park, garden, children's play area, pets corner, function room
- 🎵 Darts, billiards, Aunt Sally, quiz nights, wide-screen TV
- ❓ Princes Risborough 3 miles, High Wycombe 6 miles

THE COCK & RABBIT

THE LEE, GREAT MISSENDEN, BUCKINGHAMSHIRE HP16 9LZ
TEL: 01494 837540 FAX: 01494 837512

> **Directions:** The Lee is a small village just east of the A413 Aylesbury to Amersham road, about 8 miles southeast of Aylesbury. The inn is the centre of the village.

Set amidst beech woods in an Area of Outstanding Natural Beauty, The Lee is a pretty, secluded village which has featured in television series including *Midsommer Murders*, *Treasure Hunt* and *Pie in the Sky*. The hamlet's most famous resident was Sir Arthur Liberty, founder of the Regent Street store, and his descendants still live here. Very few inns can fulfil the dual roles of quintessential country local and top-class Italian restaurant, but **The Cock & Rabbit** is one of them. Surrounded by a lovely garden, with a beautiful sun terrace, the place is an absolute delight, owned and run since 1986 by Gianfranco Parola.

He renovated the place from top to

bottom, creating the perfect spot for a drink and also somewhere to relax over a leisurely lunch or dinner. Many of the dishes on the menus in Café Graziemille take their inspiration from the owner's native Piedmont, but the choice is wide and among the typical delights on offer are salmon in a dill, cream and champagne sauce, and tiramisu made to Gianfranco's own special recipe. The food operation caters for all occasions and appetites, from bar snacks to lunch, dinner, barbecues and all kinds of functions – it's an ideal place to celebrate any special occasion, and a conference room is available for small business meetings. The village itself, tucked away in the heart of the Chilterns, is an ancient place with an Anglo-Saxon earthwork, Grim's Dyke, nearby.

- 🕐 12-2.30 (Sun to 3) & 6-11 (Sun 7-10.30)
- 🍴 Italian cuisine, snacks and full menu
- 💷 All the major cards
- 🅿 Car park, large grounds, sun terrace, conference/function room
- @ e-mail: info@gianfranco.demon.co.uk website: www.graziemille.co.uk
- ❓ Ridgeway Path 2 miles, Pulpit Hill 5 miles, Great Missenden (Old Court House) 5 miles

GATEHANGERS INN

ASHENDON, AYLESBURY, BUCKINGHAMSHIRE HP18 0HE
TEL: 01296 651296 FAX: 01296 655063

Directions: From the A41 turn left at Westcott from Aylesbury, right at Westcott from Bicester; Ashendon is about 3 miles on.

In a hilltop hamlet with views across the Vale of Aylesbury, the **Gatehangers Inn** is a wonderful 400-year-old redbrick building that was at one time a courthouse. As an inn, it was called The Red Lion for most of its life and its current name came about when some man from the village hung a gate on the allotments to keep animals from straying. After the gate had been hung they celebrated with a dinner and thereupon formed the Gatehangers Club, which still meets once a year for dinner. Today's visitors don't need to hang a gate to enjoy the excellent hospitality extended by Richard and Pat, the well-kept cask ales (with regularly changing guests) and the varied choice of home-cooked dishes featuring copious fresh vegetables and prime local meat. The hosts are happy to organise a set lunch for small parties or business meetings.

- 11-2.30 & 6-11, all day Sat & Sun; closed Mon & Wed lunch
- Bar snacks and full menu
- All the major cards
- 5 rooms, all en suite
- Car park
- Football, domino and quiz teams
- Local walks; Waddesdon Manor 3 miles, Bicester 10 miles, Aylesbury 10 miles

The inn is very much at the social heart of the community, with football, dominoes and quiz teams, and it also offers overnight Bed & Breakfast accommodation in three double rooms, a twin and a single, all with en suite facilities. It's a comfortable base for either business or leisure visitors, and its central location close to the A41 and M40 puts all the places of interest in the vicinity within quick and easy reach. One of the grandest buildings in the area is Waddesdon Manor, a magnificent country house built in the style of a French Renaissance chateau, set in glorious grounds and home to a superb collection of 18th century French decorative arts.

THE GREEN MAN

CHURCH END, EVERSHOLT, BEDFORDSHIRE MK1 7DU
TEL/FAX: 01525 280293

Buckinghamshire

> **Directions:** From the M1 J13 take the A4012 to Woburn then minor road signposted Eversholt. From J12 take the A5120 to Toddington (1 mile) then turn right on to minor roads to Tingfrith and Eversholt.

The year 1835 saw the completion of the handsome and substantial brick building that is now **The Green Man**. The outside is very smart in its coats of green and white paint, and inside all is bright and cosy, subtly updated by Russ and Alethea Long but still retaining many traditional features such as roaring log fires, country furniture, Regency-style striped wallpaper and attractive use of wood and fabrics. The carpeted bar and dining areas are very comfortable places to relax and unwind, and the beamed games room with pool table and dartboard displays trophies won by the locals. A function room with seats for up to 30 is an ideal choice for small parties

or get-togethers, while outside is a large covered courtyard area with overhead heating and pretty lights – a great place to enjoy a drink or a meal outside.

Food and drink are both serious subjects at The Green Man, with guest ales featuring among the liquid refreshment and anything from light snacks to full meals served lunchtime and evening. The Green Man, which overlooks the lovely old village church, is easily reached from the M1, leaving at either J12 or 13. It lies just down the road from one of the region's chief attractions, Woburn Abbey, a treasure house of wonderful paintings, furniture, porcelain and sculpture, and now also home to an important antiques centre. Here, too, are the Wild Animal Kingdom and Leisure Park, and there are miles of quiet walks in Aspley Woods, one of the largest area of woodland in the whole county.

- 🕐 Lunch and evening, all day in spring and summer
- 🍴 Snacks and full meals lunchtime and evening
- £ Not Diners
- Ⓟ Car park, covered courtyard area for barbecues, function room
- 🎵 Games room with pool and darts, occasional music evenings
- @ www.eversholt.net/greenman
- ❓ Woburn Abbey and Wild Animal Kingdom & Country Park 2 miles, Aspley Woods 2 miles

THE HORSE & JOCKEY

CHURCH ROAD, TYLERS GREEN, BUCKINGHAMSHIRE HP10 8EG

TEL/FAX: 01494 815963

Directions: Tylers Green lies close to Penn off the B474 Beaconsfield to Hazlemere road.

Two cottages dating from the middle of the 18th century came together to become a pub in 1821. **The Horse & Jockey** is a handsome stone hostelry with a tiled roof and an attractive tiled veranda, and the traditional look is continued inside with beams, country furniture, horse tackle, brasses and old patriotic posters. A social hub of the beautiful community of Tylers Green, the Horse & Jockey is run by Peter Darby, who came here as manager in 1982 and became the leaseholder 20 years later. He is one of the most enthusiastic and popular of hosts, and his inn is never empty; but finding a seat isn't the problem – it's deciding what to order from the

impressive selection of food and drink.

Up to five real ales are on tap to quench thirsts or to accompany anything from a light bite to a full meal. Sandwiches, jacket potatoes, ploughman's and platters make satisfying snacks, and one of the pub's specialities is baguettes with generous fillings – perhaps beef, tuna mayonnaise, Coronation chicken or sausage, bacon and egg. The main offerings run from familiar favourites such as scampi, haddock, steak & kidney pie and chilli con carne to daily specials like lemon paprika chicken, lamb bourguignonne, and grilled duck breast with mango salsa. Booking is advisable at the weekend. You can eat inside or out in the garden, and children are very welcome. One Thursday a month is steak night, with special meal deals, and another Thursday each month is quiz night.

- Lunchtime and evening (all day Fri, Sat & Sun)
- Home cooking
- £ Not Diners
- P Adjacent parking, garden
- Quiz first Thursday of the month
- @ email: pj.darby@btinternet.com
  website:
  www.the-horseandjockey.co.uk
- ? Penn 1 mile, Amersham 3 miles, Beaconsfield 3 miles, Chalfont St Giles 4 miles

THE LOWNDES ARMS

4 HIGH STREET, WHADDON, MILTON KEYNES,
BUCKINGHAMSHIRE MK17 0NB
TEL: 01908 501706 FAX: 01908 521815

> **Directions:** From J13 of the M1 take the A421 and turn right to Whaddon soon
> after Bletchley.

On the main street of a village on the southwestern edge of Milton Keynes, **The Lowndes Arms** has a history of hospitality that stretches back over 400 years. It's very much a family affair, with Tony and Ann at the helm, helped by their daughter Sarah, the dog JD and the resident cats, and the welcome is equally warm for first-time visitors and local 'regulars'. The half-timbered redbrick building, which for many years was called the Haunch of Venison, has a very traditional interior, just right for relaxing with something from the impressive range of drinks. These include six cask marque approved real ales, three lagers, two ciders, 31 spirits on optic, 14 malt whiskies and over 20 brandies and liqueurs, plus a comprehensive list of wines by bottle and glass. Food is a serious business here, too, and the choice runs from traditional country pub fayre to steaks (anything from an 8oz ribeye to an outrageous 64oz rump!), grills, vegetarian specials and superb fish dishes, many with a touch of the exotic. Lunch and bar food is served daily from noon to 3 and dinner in the restaurant from 6 to 9.30. Booking is advisable at the weekend, particularly for the Sunday roasts.

The attractions of the Lowndes Arms don't end with food and drink, as it also offers very comfortable overnight accommodation in 11 guest rooms with en suite bathrooms, television and tea/coffee making facilities. The courtyard and beer garden back on to excellent views over Whaddon Chase towards Milton Keynes in the distance. This is an ideal base for exploring the surrounding area.

- Lunchtime and evening (all day Sunday)
- Home cooking; steak and fish specialities
- All the major cards
- 11 en suite bedrooms
- Car park, beer garden
- Weekend barbecues
- email: info@lowndesarms.co.uk
  website: www.lowndesarms.co.uk
- Milton Keynes 2 miles, Bletchley 2 miles, Buckingham 6 miles

Buckinghamshire

THE OLD BEAMS

PAXTON CRESCENT, SHENLEY LODGE, MILTON KEYNES,
BUCKINGHAMSHIRE MK5 7AE
TEL: 01908 201054 FAX: 01908 201056

Directions: South of the Knowhill roundabout, turn on to Childs Way, first left on to Livesey Hill, first right on to Paxton Crescent; the inn is on the right round the first bend.

Tucked away in Shenley Lodge, **The Old Beams** is a former farmhouse that was developed and reconstructed as an inn in 1995. It is owned by McMullen Brewers of Hertford, and their AK and Country Best brews head the list of beers served in the bar. Steve and Shirley arrived as tenants in 2003, and the inn is open all day for food as well as drinks. Steve and head chef Lisa Partridge do a great job in the kitchen, producing a wide variety of dishes for the printed menu and the specials board. Sandwiches, baguettes, jacket potatoes and ploughman's lunches provide excellent quick snacks, while those wanting a full meal might start with stilton and garlic mushrooms or duck and apricot terrine and move on to battered cod, baked trout, lamb tagine or a splendid chicken, gammon and leek pie.

To finish, perhaps chocolate waffle cake or apple and blackberry flapjack crumble.

Diners can eat in the 70-cover non-smoking restaurant or anywhere else in the pub, and children are always welcome. The large lawned garden, with lots of picnic benches, a pond and an old farm wagon, is a real asset in the summer months. The area around the Old Beams still retains something of a village atmosphere though in the shadow of Milton Keynes. This modern town offers space, style and every amenity, and its 'suburbs' include the Shenleys, Whaddon and the one-time railway centre of Bletchley, where the great visitor attraction is Bletchley Park, the Victorian mansion that housed the wartime code-breakers. This major place of interest is just a short drive from the Old Beams.

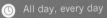

- 🕐 All day, every day
- 🍴 Home-cooked snacks and full menu
- £ Not Diners
- Ⓟ Car park, garden
- ❓ Milton Keynes 1 mile, Bletchley 2 miles

THE OLD BELL

TOWN LANE, WOOBURN GREEN, BUCKINGHAMSHIRE HP10 0PC
TEL: 01628 520406

Buckinghamshire

> **Directions:** From the A40, about 2½ miles west of Beaconsfield, turn left to Wooburn Green. The Old Bell is near the centre of the village, a short distance from the church.

Very few pubs can boast a top-notch, authentic Oriental restaurant, but **The Old Bell** has that rare distinction. A charming inn built about 200 years ago, it has the appearance and feel of an archetypal English country inn – ancient beams, wooden floors and many old bygones scattered around. There's also an interesting collection of fine ceramics on display, the work of the very talented Kim Lim, who runs this very splendid and very unusual hostelry with her husband Peter. Outside is a beer garden with picnic tables and lots of greenery.

A separate entrance leads into the jewel in the crown of The Old Bell, a restaurant serving almost exclusively Oriental cuisine. The extensive menu includes appetising dishes from Malaysia, Thailand, Singapore and Szechuan, and the mouthwatering choice offers a very good vegetarian selection. This fascinating combination of traditional village inn atmosphere and top-quality Eastern cuisine is not the end of The Old Bell's assets: six stylishly appointed en suite guest bedrooms provide an excellent base for visitors to the area. The proximity of the M4 and A40 make it an even more convenient port of call for travellers. Wooburn Green stands on the banks of the River Wye, which flows into the Thames a couple of miles downstream. Its chief attraction is Odds Farm Park which is great fun for the family, and children can try their hand at milking a goat or romp among the haybales in the playbarn.

- 🕐 Every lunchtime and evening
- 🍴 Mostly Oriental food, served every session
- 💷 All the major cards
- 🛏 6 en suite bedrooms
- 🅿 Car park, beer garden
- 🎵 Regular theme nights (meal + music)
- @ e-mail: peterlim@oldbell.co.uk website: www.oldbell.co.uk
- ❓ Odds Farm Park 1 mile, Cliveden 4 miles, Cookham (Stanley Spencer Gallery) 4 miles, Beaconsfield (Bekonscot model village) 2 miles

THE OLD QUEENS HEAD

HAMMERSLEY LANE, PENN, BUCKINGHAMSHIRE HP10 8EY
TEL: 01494 813371 FAX: 01494 816145

Directions: Take the B474 from Beaconsfield or Hazlemere to Penn. Turn by Penn Pond. The inn is about ½ a mile on the left opposite the church.

Leaseholder Patricia and General Manager Pip do a great job at **The Old Queens Head**, a charming Grade II listed building dating back to 1666. It overlooks the picturesque village church in one of the loveliest parts of Buckinghamshire. Inside, wonderful old beams and rafters are a striking feature, and the different areas are furnished in different styles, one with sturdy wooden chairs at little round tables, another with leather chairs at larger dining tables, a third with very comfortable and inviting leather sofas. A selection of real ales and keg ales is always available, along with an impressive choice of wines, and food is served in several non-smoking areas throughout the inn. The two main menus are supplemented by daily

specials, which might include Southern-style meat loaf, garlic and chilli crevettes, rare-grilled tuna and a classic steak & kidney pudding. The main menus are available every session except Sunday evening, when light snacks are served. The area around the inn provides plenty of interest and some excellent walks, and Penn itself is rich in history. It was a centre of the tiling industry for centuries, and Penn tiles provided the flooring for such places as Windsor Castle and the Palace of Westminster. Penn is perhaps best known as the ancestral home of the Quaker and founder of Pennsylvania William Penn, and there are several monuments to the Penn family in the church by the inn. In the churchyard is the grave of the spy Donald Maclean, who died in Moscow in 1983 and was brought back here for burial in the family grave.

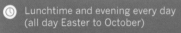

- 🕐 Lunchtime and evening every day (all day Easter to October)
- 🍴 Home cooking all sessions; light snacks only Sun eve
- £ Not Diners
- P Car park, beer garden
- 🎵 Jazz Wednesdays
- @ email: oqhpenn@aol.com website: www.oldqueenshead.co.uk
- ❓ Beaconsfield 2 miles, Amersham 3 miles, Chalfont St Giles 5 miles

THE OLD RED LION

IVY LANE, GREAT BRICKHILL, BUCKINGHAMSHIRE MK17 9AH
TEL: 01525 261715 FAX: 01525 261716

Directions: From Milton Keynes take the A5 south and turn off at Little Brickhill
on to minor road to Great Brickhill.

The Old Red Lion is a picturesque village pub dating back in part to the 17th century. The building is painted white, with a red-tiled roof, and at the back is a small car park offering great views over the countryside. Adam Tobin and Helen Maher came here as managers in January 2004, and have quickly made new friends with their excellent hospitality and accomplished home cooking. The pub is open all day, every day for drinks, among which are three real ales – Greene King IPA, Flowers Original and a rotating guest. Adam and Helen share the cooking, and the lunchtime list and evening à la carte provide plenty of variety; everything is well worth trying, and it needs a strong will to resist ending with one of the delectable desserts, perhaps a lemon tart, a chocolate mousse or a fruit crumble.

Evening meals are served in the 28-cover non-smoking restaurant, at one end of which is a handsome hearth stocked with mountains of logs to guarantee warmth on the coldest of days. Children are welcome in the restaurant. Great Brickhill is easily reached from the A5, and the M1 (J13) is only 5 miles away. Among the many places of interest in the vicinity are Woburn Abbey and Safari Park, and Bletchley Park, a Victorian mansion where 12,000 men and women worked round the clock to crack the secrets of the cryptic codes. At The Old Red Lion, Adam and Helen have certainly cracked the secret of how to keep their customers happy!

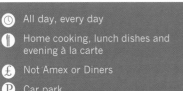

- 🕐 All day, every day
- 🍴 Home cooking, lunch dishes and evening à la carte
- £ Not Amex or Diners
- Ⓟ Car park
- @ email: fineales@oldredlion.co.uk
  website: www.oldredlion.co.uk
- ❓ Milton Keynes 4 miles, Leighton Buzzard 4 miles, Woburn 5 miles

THE OLD WHITE SWAN

LONDON END, BEACONSFIELD, BUCKINGHAMSHIRE HP9 2JD
TEL: 01494 673800

Directions: Beaconsfield lies on the A40 and is just off the M40 (J2).

It's just off the main street, but this immaculate old black-and-white inn could be in the heart of the countryside. **The Old White Swan** lies on the route once used by Dick Turpin, and it retains many original features from its days as a coaching inn. A wood burning fire, brass and copper ornaments, prints and pictures and mellow wood assist the traditional ambience, and long-time resident owners Michael and Rosemary contribute years of experience, a very friendly disposition and extensive local knowledge to the pleasure of a visit here. The Old White Swan is open all day for drinks, and food is served lunchtime seven days a week and every evening except Sunday.

The home-cooked dishes make extensive use of fresh local produce on menus that combine well-loved British classics with 'adopted' pub favourites such as chilli con carne or lasagne. Regulars know that they should leave room for one (or more!) of the delectable desserts, and the food is accompanied by a good selection of wines. There is a non-smoking area to enjoy a drink or meal. It can also be booked for small functions with seating for 18. The garden area, a veritable suntrap, is looking splendid after recent refurbishment. With the A40 and M40 so close at hand, the Old White Swan is a perfect place to take time out on a journey, and the vicinity provides excellent walking, a number of golf courses and a host of interesting places to visit.

- 🕐 12·11 Mon-Sat, 12·10.30 Sun
- 🍴 Home cooked meals and bar snacks
- £ Major cards except Amex & Diners
- Ⓟ Garden
- 🎵 Sky TV for big sporting events
- @ website: www.oldwhiteswan.co.uk
- ❓ In Beaconsfield: Church of St Mary & All Saints, Bekonscot Model Village; Chalfont St Giles (Milton's Cottage, Chilton Open Air Museum) 3 miles, Burnham Beeches National Nature Reserve 3 miles

THE PEACOCK

BOLTER END, HIGH WYCOMBE, BUCKINGHAMSHIRE HP14 3LU
TEL: 01494 881417

Directions: From High Wycombe or from the M40 (J5) take the A40 to
Stokenchurch then the B482 for about 1 mile to the village of Bolter End. From
Marlow take B482 through Lane End to the village of Bolter End.

The Peacock is a
delightful village pub in a
lovely leafy setting just
minutes from the M40
and A40 but a world away
in terms of character and
atmosphere. Built as a
private residence, it still
retains something of a
home from home feel,

and the comfortable traditional look is
assisted by lots of cosy corners, gnarled
old beams, a log-burning fire and a
wealth of pictures and prints. The inn
has recently been taken over by Andy
and Angela, whose aim is to provide an
agreeable place either to rest, relax or
unwind, or when the occasion is right to
party and have fun. Seeing that their
customers are 'well fed and watered' is

naturally an important part of the
business, and the usual range of drinks
including cask ales, a wide range of fine
wines and soft drinks is always available.
Fresh local produce features as much as
possible on an imaginative menu that
runs from delicious small snacks to full
meals; food is served every session and
all day on Sunday, and Andy and Angela
are happy to organise small parties or
celebratory get-togethers. When the sun
shines, the scene shifts outside, either to
the lawned area at the front or to the
lovely large garden behind the inn.

How much more pleasant and relaxing
would journeys along the busy motorways
and trunk roads be if drivers knew that
close to every turn off and every junction
an inn as delightful as The Peacock was
waiting with a welcome!

- Mon-Thurs 11.30-3, Fri/Sat 11.30-11, Sun 12-10.30; summer times may vary
- Snacks to full meals
- £ Not Diners
- Car park, large garden, function room
- @ e-mail: andy.callen@dine-on-line.com
- ? High Wycombe & Marlow 4 miles

THE ROTHSCHILD ARMS

82 WESTON ROAD, ASTON CLINTON, NR AYLESBURY,
BUCKINGHAMSHIRE HP22 5EJ
TEL: 01296 630320

Directions: Aston Clinton lies 3 miles east of Aylesbury off the A41.

The building that is now **The Rothschild Arms** dates from 1802 and was first recorded as a hostelry in 1847. It has borne its present name since 1877 and recognises the great influence that the Rothschild banking family had hereabouts (though the family mansion at Green Park was demolished in the 1950s). Caroline ('Cali') Birch, who was born across the road, long cherished the ambition to run this pub, and in May 2003 she became the tenant after working here for several years. She knows her customers well and they know her, and her popularity has made the Rothschild Arms one of the best-loved meeting places in the area. Behind the white-painted, bay-windowed frontage the atmosphere is warm and inviting, a convivial spot for enjoying a chat and a

glass of Adnams real ale or one of the keg ales. Good wholesome pub grub is served lunchtime and early evening from Monday to Friday. The local pool and darts teams meet in the bar five nights a week, and their success in the local leagues is shown by the many trophies proudly displayed. Cali also offers well-appointed overnight accommodation in four upstairs guest bedrooms – a single and a twin en suite and a single and a twin with shared facilities; the tariff includes a good English breakfast. The town of Aston Clinton gave its name to the Aston Martin car: the first was built in 1914 by Lionel Martin and was named because of its success in a hill-climb at Aston Clinton. In the 1920s, Evelyn Waugh wrote part of his first novel *Decline and Fall* while a schoolmaster in Aston Clinton.

- Lunchtime and evening (all day Fri, Sat & Sun)
- Pub dishes served Mon-Fri L and early evening
- 4 bedrooms (2 en suite)
- Car park opposite, garden, patio, children's play area, pets corner
- Pool, darts
- Aylesbury 3 miles, Wendover 2 miles, Stoke Mandeville 3 miles

THE SEVEN STARS

STAR LANE, DINTON, NR AYLESBURY, BUCKINGHAMSHIRE HP17 8UL
TEL: 01296 748241

Directions: The inn is quietly situated in the village of Dinton, off the A418 3 miles southwest of Aylesbury.

Situated in a quiet corner of the village of Dinton, **The Seven Stars** is a country pub with abundant charm and character. The oldest parts date from the 1640s, and the front section is made of witchert, a clay and straw construction unique to Buckinghamshire and Oxfordshire. The building is now Grade II listed, and the beautifully maintained exterior is complemented by an attractive, neatly planted beer garden set with picnic tables and parasols. In the cosy bar and dining room, the look is delightfully traditional, with original features such as exposed beams, a quarry-tiled floor and a stone inglenook fireplace, along with invitingly comfortable built-in settles in front of the fire. The Seven Stars is run by the husband-and-wife team of Claire and David Willett, who have built up a strong following, both local and further

flung, with their hospitality, their fine ales and their good food.

The well-stocked bar offers London Pride and Bombadier real ales, together with other popular beers, stouts, lagers and cider. At lunchtimes an excellent selection of snacks and traditional bar meals is supplemented by a daily specials board, while in the evening there is an à la carte menu. The delightful non-smoking dining room is elegantly furnished and appointed, with crisp tablecloths, polished cutlery and candlelight. The superb home-cooked food offers plenty of choice, and the fish and vegetarian dishes are particularly highly recommend: the pub is a National Sea Fish Industry award-winner, and with notice wheat- and gluten-free dishes can be prepared. Booking is advisable at weekends and for the regular themed food nights.

- 🕐 Lunchtime and evening
- 🍴 Home-cooked bar meals and evening à la carte
- 💷 Major cards accepted
- 🅿 Car park, beer garden
- 🎵 Monthly quiz
- @ email: secretpub.company@virgin.net
- ❓ Aylesbury 3 miles, Waddeson Manor 5 miles, Princes Risborough 6 miles

Buckinghamshire

THE WATTS ARMS

CASTLETHORPE ROAD, HANSLOPE, NR WOLVERTON,
BUCKINGHAMSHIRE MK19 7LG
TEL: 01908 510246

Directions: From J14 of the M1 take the B526; turn left at Gayhurst on minor
road marked Hanslope.

Open all day, every day for drinks, **The Watts Arms** is an attractive period building with bay windows at ground level and distinctive arched window surrounds on the first floor. Gary and Rebecca Jennings brought many years' experience in the licensed trade when they arrived as tenants in April 2004, and they have quickly made their mark at this lovely little pub.

Up to three real ales are always on tap, and food is served from 12 to 2 and from 7 to 9 every day; after food service stops in the evening, some dishes can be ordered to take away. Traditional home cooking is the speciality, and the choice on the blackboards changes frequently. The Sunday roasts are particularly popular, and booking is recommended.

This is a pub for all the family, and there's a children's play area in the spacious, secure beer garden. Entertainment includes a weekly quiz and occasional live music evenings. The village of Hanslope is an agreeable place for a stroll, and there are many attractions both rural and urban, within easy reach: they include the conurbations of Northampton and Milton Keynes, the Elizabethan mansion and baroque church at Gayhurst, the lakes and the stone circle at Great Linford, and the pretty village of Stony Stratford, often considered to be the jewel in the crown of the villages around Milton Keynes.

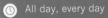

- 🕐 All day, every day
- 🍴 Home cooking; takeaway available
- 🅿 Off-road parking, beer garden, children's play area
- 🎵 Weekly quiz
- ❓ Gayhurst 2 miles, Newport Pagnell 5 miles, Northampton 10 miles

THE WHIP INN

PINK ROAD, LACEY GREEN, NR PRINCES RISBOROUGH,
BUCKINGHAMSHIRE HP27 0PG
TEL: 01844 344060 FAX: 01844 346044

Directions: From J4 of the M40 take the A4010 towards Princes Risborough; turn
right on minor road to Lacey Green.

'Make Our Pub Your Pub' is the invitation extended by Julie Davies and Nick Smith at **The Whip Inn**. That invitation holds good not just for the regular customers but also for the many visitors who pass by. From the outside the inn has a real picture postcard look, with black paint contrasting with white, and a fine slate roof. Inside, the scene is just as appealing, with its open fire, oak beams and friendly staff the Whip Inn has a relaxed and cosy atmosphere in the true tradition of an English country pub. Mine hosts keep the customers happy with a great selection of drinks, with an emphasis on cask conditioned ales. Apart from the regular ales there is an ever changing guest beer selected by the landlord to ensure his customers enjoy the great variety of beers brewed in Great Britain. They also offer a wide range of food, from light lunchtime bites to tasty temptations from the main menu, such as Thai king prawns, deep-fried goat's cheese, chargrilled steaks, minty lamb cutlets with redcurrant gravy or you can select from the specials of the day menu, where the emphasis is on Julies homemade food, or alternatively when the fresh fish has been delivered from Brixham try the jumbo cod in Nicks beer batter.

The Whip Inn is situated on the Chiltern Way and is a great area for walking with a number of circular walks starting and finishing at the pub. If you wander a few hundred yards up the road there is a point from which you can see five counties on a clear day. In the winter months warm yourself by the open fire and in the summer enjoy the garden overlooking the oldest smock windmill in the country. Local attractions include Hellfire Caves, Rest Home for Horses at Speen Farm and the Chiltern Steam Railway.

- 🕐 11-11
- 🍺 Full menu + lunchtime snacks
- 💷 All the major cards
- 🅿 Car park
- @ e-mail: info@whipinn.co.uk
  website: www.whipinn.co.uk
- ❓ Princes Risborough 3 miles, High Wycombe 6 miles

Please note all cross references refer to page numbers

OXFORDSHIRE

The southeastern corner of Oxfordshire is a place of ancient towns and villages which were well established settlements by the time of the Norman Conquest in 1066. Notable among these are the Roman town of Dorchester, the 7th-century abbey town of Abingdon, Henley-on-Thames - famous for its annual Regatta - and a mass of tiny villages and hamlets that are well worth exploring.

West Oxfordshire is a region of several different landscapes. The Berkshire Downs mark the southern border, with the Vale of the White Horse, the River Thames cuts the area in two, and to the north are the beginnings of the Cotswolds. The region's most famous feature, the White Horse, lies away to the west, to the south of Uffington. Here, the edge of the downlands are littered with Iron

Please note all cross references refer to page numbers

The Ridgeway

Age hill forts and other relics and it is also the line of the famous Ridgeway footpath, over 80 miles in length.

Oxford, the county town of Oxfordshire, has dominated the surrounding area for centuries. It was the influx of students and scholars in the 12th century that saw this walled Saxon town develop into the magnificent place it is today. Home to some of the finest buildings in the country, the city deserves leisurely exploration, and the wealth of beauty and historic interest is almost unsurpassed. The surrounding area is also full of interest. Many of the rural villages have been home to the city's best-known figures: in Elsfield to the north both John Buchan and RD Blackmore had homes, and during the 1920s at Garsington Manor, the socialite Lady Ottoline Morrell entertained the great artists, writers and thinkers of the day including DH Lawrence, Bertrand Russell, and Aldous Huxley.

The northwestern region of the county lies almost wholly in the Cotswold area, a place of honey-coloured stone buildings and quaint old market towns. Burford, the Gateway to the Cotswolds, and Chipping Norton are typical of the towns found further west, towards Gloucestershire, and they both owe their early prosperity to the wool gathered from Cotswold sheep.

To the east lies Woodstock, an ancient place which was once home to a medieval royal palace used as a hunting lodge for trips into Wychwood Forest, the royal hunting ground which stood to the west of the town and extended as far as Burford. Today, the town, a wealth of antique and tea shops, is best known for the magnificent Blenheim Palace, the thank you from a grateful Queen Anne to her loyal subject the Duke of Marlborough.

The vast Blenheim estate dominates the area around Woodstock and many of the villages have connections with the family and the house. One, in particular, is worthy of a visit: on a bleak November day in 1965, Sir Winston Churchill was laid to rest in a simple grave in Bladon church. The River Evenlode divides this region into two and along this stretch the

Magdelen College, Oxford

riverbanks are followed by the Oxfordshire Way. Some 65 miles long, this marked footpath passes through some of the most rural and scenic parts of the county from its start at Bourton-on-the-Water to its end at Henley-on-Thames.

North Oxfordshire, from Oxford to the Midlands, is an area of rich farmland on clay soil. The numerous rural villages, with ancient cottages and old stone farmhouses, give the impression of not having changed for centuries - only the farm machinery and the television aerials give away the march of time. By far the largest town in the area is Banbury, that ancient place of the nursery rhyme and the cross. A fine blend of the old and new, none of the town's rural heritage has been lost and today it is home to Europe's largest livestock market. Bicester is another ancient settlement - the Romans had a town nearby - and the settlement was first home to the Saxons. There are some fine houses to visit here, including Rousham, with one of the few complete William Kent gardens in the country. Lovers of rural architecture will delight in seeing Swalcliffe Barn, a magnificent 15th century structure that is also home to a range of agricultural vehicles.

Abingdon

This is an attractive town and it is also one of the region's oldest, growing up around a 7th century **Benedictine Abbey**. Twice sacked by the Danes for its gold and silver, the Abbey was all but derelict by the 10th century, but under the guidance of Abbot Ethwold, the architect of the great Benedictine reform, it once again prospered and was in its heyday larger than Westminster Abbey. Little remains today of this great religious house, but the **Gatehouse**, built in the late 15th century, is a splendid reminder. Built on to the abbey gateway is the **Church of St Nicholas**, much altered but still retaining some of its original Norman features.

The largest town in the Vale of the White Horse, Abingdon was also the county town of Berkshire between 1556 and 1869; at one time the Abbot here was the largest landowner in Berkshire after the Crown. This prosperity and importance has given the town an interesting history which can be discovered at the **Abingdon Museum** housed in the old County Hall.

Another of the town's pleasing buildings is the **Church of St Helen**, whose steeple dominates the view southwards along the street. Originally built in the 14th century, the church was remodelled in the 15th and 16th centuries, when the town prospered from a thriving wool trade, to provide an altogether larger and more elaborate building. However, the main glory of the church, the painted ceiling of the Lady Chapel, has been retained from the 14th century.

Beside the churchyard, which contains a curious small building that was the blowing chamber for the church organ, are three sets of almshouses. The oldest, Christ's Hospital, was founded in 1446, while the other two, Twitty's Almshouses and Brick Alley Almshouses, date from the early 18th century.

River Thames, Abingdon

Banbury

Famous for its cross, cakes, and the nursery rhyme, this historic market town has managed to hang on to many of its old buildings as well as become home to Europe's largest livestock market. The famous **Banbury Cross** in Horsefair dates only from 1859, replacing the previous one which had been demolished by the Parliamentarians during the Civil War. It was erected to commemorate the marriage of Queen Victoria's oldest daughter to the Prussian Crown Prince, and the figures around the base, of Queen Victoria, Edward VII, and George V, were added in 1914. This is obviously not the cross referred to in the old nursery rhyme.

The town's other legendary claim to fame is its spicy, fruity cakes, which are still made here. Banbury was also, at one time, famous for its cheeses, which were only about an inch thick. This gave rise to the expression 'thin as a Banbury cheese'.

On the east side of the Horsefair stands **St Mary's Church**, a classical building of warm-coloured stone and hefty pillars with some pleasingly eccentric touches. The original architect was SP Cockerell, though the tower and portico were completed between 1818 and 1822 by his son, CR Cockerell. The style reflects the strong influence on English architecture of Piranesi's Views of Rome, using massive shapes and giving stone the deliberately roughened appearance which comes from the technique known as rustication.

In **Banbury Museum** visitors can learn about the town's development, from the days when it came under the influence of the bishops of Lincoln, through the woollen trade of the 16th century, to the present day. The affects of the Civil War on the town were great: the Royalists

held Banbury Castle and were subjected to two sieges during the conflict. The completion of the Coventry to Oxford Canal in 1778, the coming of the railway in 1850, and the opening of the M40 in 1991, have all played their part in making Banbury a large and successful commercial town. To the southwest of Banbury, in an old courthouse, is the **Bloxham Village Museum**, where the displays showcase the lives of Oxfordshire's rural community down the centuries.

Bicester

Though the name (pronounced Bister) suggests that this was a Roman settlement, the town was not, in fact, established until Saxon times and the Roman name comes as a result of the nearby and long since vanished Roman town of **Alchester**. By the 12th century, the town was the home of both an Augustinian priory and a Benedictine nunnery. Growing up around these religious houses and its market, the town suffered a disastrous fire in the early 18th century and most of the buildings seen here today date from that time onwards. Hunting and horse-racing played as large a part in the prosperity of Bicester as agriculture, though industrialisation has been sporadic. The founding here of the Army's ordnance depot in 1941 brought much new development which continued until the 1960s.

The **Church of St Eadburg** still has traces of the original 12th-century building, though over the following centuries much work on enlarging the church was undertaken.

Bradwell Grove

The 120 acres of park and garden which make up the **Cotswold Wild Life Park** are home to a whole host of animals, many of whom roam free in the wooded estate. Rhinos, zebras, ostriches and tigers are just some of the animals in the spacious enclosures, while tropical birds, monkeys, reptiles and butterflies are all given the chance to enjoy the warmth of their natural habitat by staying indoors. With an adventure playground and a narrow-gauge railway, the park has something to offer every member of the family.

Broughton

The moated mansion **Broughton Castle** was built in 1300 by Sir John de Broughton on the site of an earlier family home. Extended and altered in the 16th century to turn it into a fine Tudor house, it has been owned by the

same family since 1451. Over the years, it has entertained several royal visitors including Queen Anne of Denmark, wife of James I. Both James I and Edward VII used the aptly named King's Chamber with its handpainted Chinese wall paper. The house played a part in the Civil War, when it was used by leaders of the Parliamentary forces to lay their plans.

Burford

Often referred to as The Gateway to the Cotswolds, Burford is an attractive old market town of honey-coloured Cotswold stone on the banks of the River Windrush. The site of a battle between the armies of Wessex and Mercia in 752, it was given after the Norman Conquest to William I's brother, Bishop Odo of Bayeux. Lying on important trade routes, both north-south and east-west, the town prospered, and from the 16th century was an important centre of the wool trade. After the decline of wool, Burford became an important stop on the coaching routes and many of the old inns still stand.

The grand **Church of St John the Baptist** was built on the wealth of the wool trade, developed from the Norman original. In the south wall of the tower stair is a carving, dated around AD 100, which shows the goddess Epona, with two male supporters; the monument erected to

Cotswold Wild Life Park

Edmund Harman, the barber-surgeon to Henry VIII, shows North American natives - possibly the first representation of native Americans in the country. In the south porch is a small plaque which commemorates three Levellers who were shot in the churchyard in 1649.

The Levellers were troops from Cromwell's army who mutinied against what they saw as the drift towards the authoritarian rule they had been fighting against. While they were encamped at Burford, the Levellers were taken by surprise by Cromwell's forces. After a brief fight, some 340 prisoners were taken and placed under guard in the church. The next day there was a court martial and three of the rebels were shot as an example to the rest, who were made to watch the executions, after which Cromwell relented.

The town's old court house, built in the 16th century with an open ground floor and a half-timbered first floor, is now home to the **Tolsey Museum**, an interesting building in its own right with collections covering the history of the town and the surrounding area. Other buildings worth seeking out also include the 16th century **Falkland Hall**, the home of Edmund Sylvester, a local wool and cloth merchant, and **Symon Wysdom's Cottages**, which were built in 1572 by another of the town's influential merchants.

Buscot

This small village in the valley of the upper Thames is home to two National Trust properties: **Buscot Old Parsonage** and **Buscot Park**. The parsonage is a lovely house, with a small riverside garden, built of Cotswold stone in 1703. Buscot Park is a much grander affair, a classic example of a late Georgian house. Home of the Faringdon Art Collection, which includes paintings by Rembrandt, Murillo, and Reynolds, is has a room decorated with a series of pictures by Edward Burne-Jones, the pre-Raphaelite artist who was a close friend of William Morris. Painted in 1890, they reflect Burne-Jones's interest in myths and legends and they tell the story of the Sleeping Beauty.

Anyone particularly interested in the work of Burne-Jones should also visit the village church, where a stained glass window showing the Good Shepherd was designed by him in 1891.

Charlbury

Now very much a dormitory town for Oxford, Charlbury was once famous for its glovemaking as well as being a centre of the Quaker Movement - the simple Friends' Meeting House dates from 1779 and there is also a Friends' cemetery. **Charlbury Museum**, close to the Meeting House, has displays on the traditional crafts and industries of the town, and the town's charters given by Henry III and King Stephen can also be seen. One of its best-loved buildings is the **Railway Station**, built by Isambard Kingdom Brunel, complete with its fishpond and hanging baskets.

On the far bank of the River Evenlode

from the main town lies **Cornbury Park**, a large estate that was given to Robert Dudley by Queen Elizabeth I. Although most of the house now dates from the 17th century, this was originally a hunting lodge in Wychwood Forest, and was in use since the days of Henry I. Glimpses of the house can be seen from the walk around the estate.

Lying just to the west of the town is **Ditchley Park**, a restrained and classical house built in the 1720s by James Gibbs. The splendid interiors were the work of William Kent and Henry Flitcroft, and Italian craftsmen worked on the stucco decorations of the great hall and the saloon; the first treated to give an impression of rich solemnity, the second with a rather more exuberant effect.

The house has associations with Sir Winston Churchill, who used it as a weekend headquarters during World War II when Chequers was thought to be unsafe.

Chastleton

Chastleton is home to one of the best examples of Jacobean architecture in the country. In 1602, Robert Catesby, one of the Gunpowder Plot conspirators, sold his estate here to a prosperous wool merchant from Witney, Walter Jones. A couple of years later, Jones pulled the house down and built **Chastleton House**, a splendid Jacobean manor house with a dramatic five-gabled front. The style suggests that the house could well have been designed by Robert Smythson, the most famous architect of his day.

The house contains a wonderful collection of original panelling, furniture, tapestries and embroidery, and of the rooms themselves, the Long Gallery, which runs the entire length of the top floor at the back of the house, is particularly impressive. It has a wonderful barrel-vaulted ceiling plastered in intricate patterns of interlacing ribbons and flowers.

Chipping Norton

The highest town in Oxfordshire, at 650 feet above sea level, Chipping Norton was once an important centre of the wool trade and King John granted the town a charter to hold a fair to sell wool. This later became a **Mop Fair**, a tradition that survives to this day.

The town's medieval prosperity can be seen in the fine and spacious **Church of St Mary**, which was built in 1485 with money given by John Ashfield, a wool merchant. The splendid east window came from the Abbey of Bruern, a few miles to the southwest, which was demolished in 1535 during the Dissolution. As with many buildings in the town, there was been substantial 19th century remodelling: the present church tower, for example, dates from 1823. In 1549, the minister here, the Rev Henry Joyce, was charged with high treason and hanged from the old tower because he refused to use the new prayer book introduced by Edward VI.

Still very much a market town today - the market is held on Wednesdays - Chipping Norton has been little affected by the influx of visitors who come to see this charming place. The **Chipping Norton Museum** is an excellent place to start any exploration and the permanent displays here cover local history from prehistoric and Roman times through to the present day.

Found just to the west of the town centre is the extraordinary **Bliss Tweed Mill**, designed by a Lancashire architect, George Woodhouse, in 1872 in the style of Versailles.

Compton Beauchamp

The pretty parish **Church of St Swithin** is built of chalk, presumably from the local downs, and its key features are the medieval glass and the Victorian wall paintings. St Swithin is an unusual dedication and it was perhaps made here as St Swithin was the Bishop of Winchester in the late 9th century and therefore something of a local lad.

Deddington

Surveyed in the Domesday Book with twice the value of Banbury, the town has never developed as Banbury and Bicester have, and it remains a prosperous agricultural centre with a still bustling market place.

Little can now be seen of the 12th century **Deddington Castle**. The castle itself had been destroyed by the 14th century, and the earthworks and surrounding moat are now largely covered by mature trees. Most of the building materials were put to good use

in other areas of the town, but excavations have revealed the remains of a curtain wall, a hall, and a small rectangular keep.

The **Church of St Peter and St Paul** is still very visible on the edge of the Market Place. In the 1630s, the church's steeple collapsed, taking part of the main building with it, and though rebuilding work begun soon afterwards, the intervention of the Civil War made it a long project. During this time, Charles I had the church bells melted down to provide his army with another cannon.

Close by is **Castle House**, where Piers Gaveston, Edward II's infamous favourite, was held before his execution in 1312. The house's two towers were added in the 1650s, when the house was in the ownership of one Thomas Appletree. A supporter of Cromwell, Appletree was ordered to destroy the property of Royalists and it was material from two local houses that he used in his building work.

Didcot

The giant cooling towers of Didcot's power station dominate the skyline for miles around and there is little left of old. One link with the past is the **Didcot Railway Centre**, a shrine to the days of the steam engine and the Great Western Railway. Isambard Kingdom Brunel designed the Great Western Railway and its route through Didcot, from London to Bristol, was completed in 1841. Until 1892 its trains ran on their unique broad gauge tracks and the GWR retained its

Didcot Railway Centre

The **Abbey Church of St Peter and St Paul** is all that remains of the Augustinian Abbey which was built on the site of the original Saxon Church in 1170. Its chief glory is the 14th century choir and the huge Jesse window, showing the family tree of Jesus, and still with its original glass. The story of the abbey, along with the history of settlement in the area going back to neolithic times, is told in the **Abbey Museum** housed in a former schoolroom built in 1652.

independence until the nationalisation of the railways in 1948. Based around the engine shed, where visitors can inspect the collection of steam locomotives, the centre also includes a beautiful recreation of a country station, complete with level crossing. Steam days are held through out the year when locomotives once again take to the track and visitors can also take in the Victorian signalling system and the centre's Relics Display.

Dorchester

This small town, situated on the River Thames and just a short walk from the River Thames, was once an important Roman station called Dorocina; later, it was here that Christianity was established in the southwest of England by St Birinus. Known as the Apostle of the West Saxons, Birinus was consecrated in Genoa, landed in Wessex in 634, and converted the King of Wessex the following year. In gratitude, the King gave Dorchester to Birinus and it became a centre of missionary activity.

Ewelme

At the centre of this pretty village is a magnificent group of medieval buildings, including the Church, almshouse, and school which were all founded in the 1430s by Alice Chaucer, grand-daughter of the poet Geoffrey, and her husband, the Duke of Suffolk; there is a wonderfully elegant alabaster carving of Alice inside the church. In the churchyard is the grave of Jerome Klapka Jerome, author of *Three Men in a Boat*, who moved to the village following the success of his book.

Founded in 1437, the **Almshouses** were built to house 13 poor men ,and two chaplains were provided to take care of them. They are one of the earliest examples of almshouses built around a quadrangle and they are also one of the earliest brick buildings in the county.

The **School** was founded in the same year and it too is of brick though it was extensively altered in Georgian times.

Filkins

This tiny Cotswold village is home to a flourishing community of craft workers and artists, many of whom work in restored 18th century barns. Wool has played a great part in the wealth of this area, and the **Cotswold Woollen Weavers** is a working weaving museum with an exhibition gallery and a mill shop.

Also found in this attractive village is the **Swinford Museum**, which concentrates on 19th century domestic and rural trade and craft tools.

Garsington

The main reason for visiting this village, which is surprisingly rural considering it's so close to Oxford, is the 16th century **Garsington Manor**. Between 1915 and 1927, this was the home of the socialite Lady Ottoline Morrell, who, along with her husband Philip, were unflaggingly hospitable to a whole generation of writers, artists, and intellectuals including Katherine Mansfield, Lytton Strachey, Clive Bell, Siegfried Sassoon, DH Lawrence, TS Eliot, Rupert Brooke, Bertrand Russell and Aldous Huxley. Huxley based an account of a country house party in one of his novels on his experiences at Garsington, thereby causing a rift with his hostess. She found his description all too apt, and felt

betrayed. Huxley insisted that he had not meant any harm, but she remained hurt and they were estranged for some time.

It seems that Lady Ottoline was not very lucky in the artists on whom she lavished her attention and hospitality. DH Lawrence also quarrelled with her after drawing a less than flattering, but clearly recognisable, portrait of life at her house in his *Women in Love*.

Garsington's other claim to literary fame is that Rider Haggard was sent to the school run by the Rev HJ Graham at the rectory in 1866. While there Haggard became friendly with a local farmer named Quartermain whom he must have remembered with affection as many years later he used the name for his hero in his novel *King Solomon's Mines*.

The village **Church of St Mary** is a pleasant building with fine views to the south over the Chilterns from its hilltop position, but it also looks over the industrial belt to the south of Oxford. Though the interior is chiefly Victorian, the church has retained its Norman tower; inside is an elegant memorial to Lady Ottoline.

Goring-on-Thames

This ancient town lies across the River Thames from its equally ancient neighbour, Streatly, and, whilst today they are in different counties, they were once in different kingdoms. This is a particularly peaceful stretch of the river, with the bustle of Pangbourne and Henley-on-Thames lying downstream and it is some distance to the towns of Abingdon and Oxford further upstream. But at one time the two settlements seem to have been often in conflict, and excavations in the area have unearthed numerous weapons which date back as far as the Bronze Age.

In the 19th century, after Isambard Kingdom Brunel had laid the tracks for the Great Western Railway through Goring Gap, the village began to grow as it became accessible to the Thames-loving Victorians. Though there are many Victorian and Edwardian villas and houses here, the original older buildings have survived, adding an air of antiquity to this attractive place.

Great Coxwell

This village is well known for its magnificent 13th century **Tithe Barn** and the contemporary **Church of St Giles**. A simple and elegant building, the church is often overlooked in favour of the barn which was originally built to serve the needs of the Cistercian Abbey at Beaulieu in Hampshire whose inmates were granted land here by King John. An impressive building some 152 feet long, with Cotswold stone walls of over four feet thick, this huge barn was used to store the tithe - or taxes - received from the tenants of the church land. At the Dissolution it passed into private ownership; today, it is owned by the National Trust.

Henley-on-Thames

Reputed to be the oldest settlement in Oxfordshire, this attractive riverside market town has over 300 listed buildings covering several periods. But it is the fine Georgian and Victorian houses and villas fronting on to the River Thames which epitomise the style of the place.

In 1829, the first boat race between Oxford and Cambridge took place here on the river and, within a decade, the event was enjoying royal patronage. Today, **Henley Regatta**, held every year in the first week of July, is a marvellous and colourful event, with rowers competing on the mile-long course from all over the world.

Beside the town's famous 18th century bridge are the headquarters of Leander Rowing Club, and here, too, is the **River and Rowing Museum**, a fascinating place that traces the rowing heritage

Henley Regatta

of Henley, the river's changing role in the town's history; a special display celebrates the almost superhuman achievements of the renowned oarsman, Steve (now Sir Steve) Redgrave, who rowed to Gold in five successive Olympic Games.

Apart from the boating, which is available throughout the summer, and the pleasant walks along the riverbanks, there are lots of interesting shops, inns, and teashops in the town. Most of the inns are old coaching houses with yards that were once the scene of bull and bear fights.

Just down river from the town centre lies **Fawley Court**, a wonderful private house that was designed by Christopher Wren and built in 1684 for Col W Freeman. Now owned by the Marian Fathers, the **Museum** it contains includes a library, documents relating to the Polish Kings, and memorabilia of the Polish army. The house, gardens, and museum are open to the public from March to October.

To the northwest of Henley lies another interesting house, **Greys Court**, which was rebuilt in the 16th century though it has been added to since. However, it does stand within the walls of the original 14th-century manor house and various of the old outbuildings can still be seen. The property of the National Trust, the gardens of the court contain the **Archbishop's Maze**, which was inspired, in 1980, by Archbishop Runcie's enthronement speech: he urged that people should help each other to unravel the secret of the maze of life.

Kelmscott

Located near the River Thames and dating from about 1570, **Kelmscott Manor House** was the country home of William Morris from 1871 to 1896. Morris loved the house dearly and it is the setting for the end of his utopian novel *News from Nowhere*, in which he writes of a world where work has become a sought after pleasure.

The house, which is open to visitors during the summer, has examples of Morris's work and memorabilia of Dante Gabriel Rosetti, who also stayed there. Rosetti is reputed to have found the village boring, so presumably the fact that he was in love with Morris's wife, Jane, drew him here. Morris himself is buried in the churchyard, under a ridge-shaped tombstone designed by his associate Philip Webb.

The church itself is interesting, the oldest parts dating from the late 12th century, and the village includes some fine farmhouses from around the end of the 17th and beginning of the 18th centuries.

Further along the river is the tiny hamlet of **Radcot**, which boasts the oldest bridge across the Thames - **Radcot Bridge** dates from 1154.

Kingston Lisle

Just to the southwest of Kingston Lisle's attractive Norman Church of St John lies the **Blowing Stone** (or **Sarsen**

Stone), a piece of glacial debris that is perforated with holes. When blown, the stone emits a sound like a foghorn.

Lower Heyford

Situated at a ford across the River Cherwell, which was replaced in the late 13th century by a stone bridge, the village lies on the opposite bank from its other half - Upper Heyford. To the south of the village lies **Rousham**, a fine house built in the mid-17th century for Sir Robert Dormer that is set in magnificent gardens. On the banks of the River Cherwell, the gardens were laid out by William Kent in 1738 and they represent the first phase of English landscape gardening. Fortunately little changed since it was first planted, Rousham is the only complete William Kent garden to have survived. The garden is open to the public all year round, while the house has limited opening times.

Mapledurham

Down a small lane leading to the River Thames, this tiny village is home to **Mapledurham House**, a watermill, and a church. The late-16th century home of the Blount family, Mapledurham House was built on the site of an older manor house and has remained in the same family ever since. As well as admiring the great oak

staircase and the fine collection of paintings, visitors will find the house's literary connections are equally interesting: Alexander Pope was a frequent visitor in the 18th century; the final chapters of John Galsworthy's *The Forsyte Saga* were set here; and it was Toad Hall in The *Wind in the Willows*. The house has also featured in films such as *The Eagle has Landed* and television series, including *Inspector Morse*.

Another attraction on the estate is the old riverside **Watermill**, a handsome late-15th century construction which stands on the site of an earlier building mentioned in the Domesday Book. The mill remained in operation until 1947 and it was then the longest surviving working mill on the river. Now fully restored, the traditional machinery can be seen in action grinding wholemeal flour which is then sold in the mill shop.

The village church is also worth a visit: during restoration work in 1863 the architect William Butterfield made extensive use of coloured brickwork and also refaced the tower with a bold

Mapledurham House

chequered pattern using flint and brick.

Minster Lovell

One of the prettiest villages along the banks of the River Windrush, Minster Lovell is home to the ruins of a once impressive 15th-century manor house. **Minster Lovell Hall** was built in about 1431 and was, in its day, one of the great aristocratic houses of Oxfordshire. One of the Lovell family was a prominent Yorkist during the Wars of the Roses, and after the defeat of Richard III at Bosworth Field he lost his lands to the Crown.

The house was bought by the Coke family in 1602, but around the middle of the 18th century the hall was dismantled by Thomas Coke, Earl of Leicester, and the ruins became lowly farm buildings. They were rescued from complete disintegration by the Ministry of Works in the 1930s and are now in the care of English Heritage. What is left of the house is extremely picturesque, and it is hard to imagine a better setting than here, beside the River Windrush.

One fascinating feature of the manor house which has survived is the medieval dovecote, complete with nesting boxes, which provided pigeons for the table, operating not very differently from a modern battery hen house.

Over Norton

To the northwest of the village lie the **Rollright Stones** - among the most fascinating Bronze Age monuments in the country. These great gnarled slabs of stone stand on a ridge which offers fine views of the surrounding countryside. They all have nicknames: the **King's Men** form a circle; the **King Stone** is to the north of the circle; and, a quarter of a mile to the west stand the **Whispering Knights**, remnants of a megalithic tomb. Naturally, there are many local legends connected with the stones: some say they are the petrified figures of a forgotten king and his men who were turned to stone by a witch - hence their names.

Oxford

The skyline of this wonderful city can be seen from many of the hilltops which surround it and the view is famously described by the 19th century poet, Matthew Arnold: "that sweet City with her dreaming spires". However, Oxford is not all beautiful, ancient buildings but also a place of commerce and industry, with factories and sprawling suburbs. The centre of the country's intellectual, political, and architectural life for over 800 years, it is still known throughout the world as a leading centre of learning.

It was a walled town in Saxon times, growing round a ford where the River Thames meets the River Cherwell, and the first students came here in the 12th century when they were forced out of Paris, at the time Europe's leading academic centre. Intellectual pursuits at the time were chiefly religious, and the town already had an Augustinian Abbey; in a short space of time, Oxford became the country's seat of theological thinking. However, there was much tension between the townsfolk and the intellectuals and, in the 14th century, in a bid to protect their students, the university began to build colleges - enclosed quadrangles with large, sturdy front doors. The first colleges, Merton, Balliol, and University, where soon joined by others, which o this day maintain their own individual style while also coming under the administration and jurisdiction of the University.

Merton College was founded in 1264 by Walter de Merton, Lord Chancellor of England, as a small community of scholars from the income of his Surrey estates. The present buildings mostly date from the 15th to 17th centuries, but Mob Quad is the university's oldest. The key feature of the college is its splendid medieval library, where the ancient books are chained to the desks. Once considered the poor relation to other, wealthier colleges, **Balliol College** was founded in 1263 as an act of penance by John Balliol, and for many years it was reserved for only the poor students. Most of the college buildings now date from the 19th century, when the college was instrumental in spearheading a move towards higher academic standards. Thought by some to have been founded by Alfred the Great, **University College** was endowed in 1249 although the present college buildings are mostly 17th century. The poet Shelley was the college's most famous scholar - but he was expelled in 1811 for writing a pamphlet on atheism. His memorial can be seen in the front quad.

One of the most beautiful colleges, **Christ Church**, was founded in 1525 as Cardinal College by Thomas Wolsey and then refounded as Christ Church in 1546 by Henry VIII after Wolsey had fallen from royal favour. The main gateway into the college leads through the bottom of Tom Tower (designed by Christopher Wren and home of the Great Tom bell) and into Tom Quad, the largest of the city's quadrangles. From here there is access to the rest of the college and also to the college's chapel. The only college chapel in the world to be designated a cathedral, Christ Church Cathedral is also England's smallest: it was founded in 1546 on the remains of a 12th-century building.

Another splendid college well worth a visit is **Magdalen**, whose extensive grounds include a riverside walk, a deer park, three quadrangles, and a series of glorious manicured lawns. The college's 15th century bell tower is one of the city's most famous landmarks. During the 17th century, the college was at the centre of a revolt against James II's pro-Catholic policies; a century later, academic standards had slipped so far that Edward Gibbon, author of The Decline and Fall of the Roman Empire, called his time at the college as "the most idle and unprofitable" of his whole life.

As well as the college buildings, Oxford has many interesting and magnificent places to explore. At the city's central crossroads, unusually named **Carfax** and probably derived from the Latin for four-forked, is a tower, **Carfax Tower**, which is all that remains of the 14th century Church of St Martin. A climb to the top of the tower offers magnificent views across the city. One of the most interesting buildings, the **Radcliffe Camera**, was built between 1737 and 1749 to a design by James Gibb. England's earliest example of a round reading room (camera is a medieval word for room), this splendid building still serves this purpose for the **Bodleian Library**. The library is named after Sir Thomas Bodley, a diplomat and a fellow of Merton College, who re-founded it in 1602 on the site of an earlier building. With over 5½ million books, it is one of the world's greatest libraries and one of only six entitled to a copy of every book published in Great Britain. The collection of early printed books and manuscripts is second only to the British Library in London and, though members of the University can request to see any book here, this is not a lending library and they must be read and studied on the premises.

Close by is the **Clarendon Building**, the former home of the Oxford University Press and now part of the Bodleian. Also in this part of the city is the **Bridge of Sighs**, part of Hertford College and a 19th century copy of the original in Venice - but here the bridge crosses a street rather than a canal.

The magnificent **Sheldonian Theatre** was designed and built in the style of a Roman theatre by Christopher Wren between 1664 and 1668 while he was Professor of Astronomy at the University. It is still used today as a place for University occasions including matriculation, degree ceremonies, and the annual Encaenia, when honorary degrees are conferred on distinguished people. As well as the superb wooden interior, the ceiling has 32 canvas panels depicting Truth descending on the Arts, the work of Robert Streeter, court painter to Charles II. The **Martyrs Memorial** in St Giles commemorates the Protestant martyrs Hugh Latimer, Bishop of Worcester; Nicholas Ridley, Bishop of London; and Thomas Cranmer, Archbishop of Canterbury. All were burnt alive at

Radcliffe Camera

a spot outside the city wall.

Naturally, the city has several museums, including the oldest in the country, the **Ashmolean**, opened in 1683 and originally established to house the collection of the John Tradescants, father and son. On display in this internationally renowned museum are archaeological collections from Britain, Europe, Egypt, and the Middle East; Italian, Dutch, Flemish, French, and English old masters; far eastern art, ceramics, and lacquer work; and Chinese bronzes. The Ashmolean's original building now houses the **Museum of the History of Science**, a remarkable collection of early scientific instruments including Einstein's blackboard and a large silver microscope made for George III.

In a splendid Victorian building near the University Science Area is the **University Museum** where the remains of a dodo, extinct since around 1680, and a mass of fossilised dinosaur remains are on display. Also here is the **Pitt Rivers Museum**, with its interesting collection taken from all over the world.

Musicians will enjoy the **Bate Collection of Historical Instruments**, whilst those captivated by old masters should take time to visit the **Christ Church Picture Gallery**, with its collection of works by Tintoretto, Van Dyck, Leonardo da Vinci, and Michelangelo.

Another place worthy of a visit and a particularly peaceful haven in the city are the **Botanic Gardens**, down by the river. Founded in 1621, when plants were the only source of medicines, this was a teaching garden where the plants grown here were studied for their medicinal and scientific use. The rose garden here commemorates the work of Oxford's scientists in the discovery and use of penicillin.

Shipton-under-Wychwood

The suffix 'under-Wychwood' derives from the ancient royal hunting forest, **Wychwood Forest**, the remains of which lie to the east of the village. The name has nothing to do with witches - wych refers to the Hwicce, a Celtic tribe of whose territory the forest originally formed a part in the 7th century. Though cleared during the Middle Ages, it was still used as a royal hunting forest until the mid-17th century. By the late 18th century there was little good wood left and the forest was rapidly cleared to provide arable land.

The forest was one of the alleged haunts of Matthew Arnold's scholar gypsy, and in the eponymous poem, published in 1853, Arnold tells the legend of the brilliant but poor Oxford scholar who, despairing of ever making his way in the world, went to live with the gypsies to learn from their way of life.

The village itself is centred around its large green, which is dominated by the tall spire of 11th century **St Mary's Church**. Here too can be found **The Shaven Crown**, now a hotel, which was built in the 15th century as a guest house for visitors to the nearby (and now demolished) Bruern Abbey. The superb **Shipton Court**, built around 1603, is one of the country's largest Jacobean houses.

South Newington

This small village, built almost entirely of ironstone, is home to the fine **Church of St Peter ad Vincula**. Inside can be found some of the county's best medieval wall paintings, dating from around 1330. What makes these paintings so special is the detail of the figures: Thomas à Becket, with blood spouting from his head; the martyrdom of Thomas of Lancaster, rebel against Edward II; a Virgin and Child; and St Margaret slaying a dragon.

Stanton Harcourt

This beautiful village is noted for its historic manor house, **Stanton Harcourt Manor**, which dates back to the 14th century. Famed for its well preserved medieval kitchen, one of the most complete to survive in England, the house is also visited for its fine collection of antiques and its tranquil gardens. It was while staying here, from 1717 to 1718, that Alexander Pope translated Homer's *Iliad*. He worked in a 15th century tower that is now called **Pope's Tower**.

The splendid Norman **Church of St Michael** is also worthy of a visit. The Harcourt chapel dominates, but there are other features of interest, including an intricate 14th century shrine to St Edburg.

Stonor

The village is the home of Lord and Lady Camoys and their house, **Stonor**, has been in the family for over 800 years. Set in the a wooded valley and surrounded by a deer park, this attractive house dates from the 12th century, though the beautiful, uniform facade is Tudor. The interior of the house contains many rare items, including a mass of family portraits, and there is also a medieval Catholic Chapel that was in continuous use right through the Reformation. In 1581, Edmund Campion sought refuge at the house and

Stonor House

there is an exhibition featuring his life and work. The gardens too are well worth a visit and they offer splendid views over the rolling parkland.

Sutton Courtenay

The village **Church of All Saints**, which dates back to Norman times, houses some fine stone carvings and woodwork but the real interest lies in the churchyard. Here can be found the grave of Herbert Asquith, the last Liberal Prime Minister (from 1908 to 1916) and also the grave of Eric Blair, better known as the writer George Orwell; several yew trees are planted here in his memory.

Swalcliffe

The village is dominated by the large **Church of St Peter and St Paul** which towers over all the other buildings here. Founded in Saxon times, the bulk of the building dates from the 12th, 13th, and 14th centuries and it is the tracery in the east window which makes the church noteworthy.

However, by far the most impressive building in Swalcliffe is the **Barn**, which has been acknowledged as one of the finest 15th century half-cruck barns in the country. Built as the manorial barn by New College, Oxford, it was used to store produce from the manor and never to store tithes. Today, it is home to a collection of agricultural and trade vehicles.

To the northeast of the village, on

Madmarston Hill, are the remains of an Iron Age hill fort.

Thame

Founded in 635 as an administrative centre for the Bishop of Dorchester, Thame first became a market town in the 13th century and its importance as a commercial centre is evident by the wide main street it still has today. Lined with old inns and houses, some of which go back to the 15th century, this is a delightful place to visit.

The imposing **Church of St Mary**, tucked away at one end of the High Street, was built in the 13th century, though the aisles were widened in the 14th century and the tower was heightened in the 15th century.

To the west of the church lies the **Prebendal House** which, in its oldest parts, dates from the 13th century. A prebend was an income granted to a priest by a Cathedral or Collegiate Church and, at Thame, the prebend was established in around 1140 by Lincoln Cathedral. A special residence for the holders of the office was first mentioned in 1234.

The town also has a famous **Grammar School**, housed in a Tudor building in Church Lane. The schoolmaster's house faces the road and over the doorway are the arms of Lord Williams, who founded the school in 1558. John Hampden, one of the Parliamentary leaders during the Civil War, was at school here and he also died at Thame. An MP from 1621, Hampden sat in Parliament whenever it had not been dissolved by the King. He denied the right of the King to raise taxes without the sanction of Parliament and in 1636 refused to pay the 'ship tax' the King was demanding. As a result he was successfully prosecuted and, at the same time, became a popular leader in the country. When the

Uffington

Civil War broke out he raised a regiment of infantry for the Parliamentary Army and fought with great bravery at Edgehill and Reading. However, he was wounded at the battle of Chalgrove Field in June 1643 and was carried back to Thame, where he died some days later in an inn which stood on the High Street.

A little to the south of the town is **Thame Park**, a house built on the site of a Cistercian Abbey founded in 1138 and which, after the Dissolution, became the home of Lord Williams. The present, privately owned house incorporates some of the former monastic buildings to which has been added a gracious Georgian house.

Uffington

This large village was the birthplace in 1822 of Thomas Hughes, the son of the vicar. The author of *Tom Brown's Schooldays*, Hughes incorporates many local landmarks, including the White Horse and Uffington Castle, in his much-loved work. The **Tom Brown's School Museum** tells the story of

Hughes' life and works.

The village is best known for the **Uffington White Horse**, a mysteriously abstract and very beautiful figure of a horse, some 400 feet long, created by removing the turf to expose the gleaming white chalk beneath. It is a startling sight visible for miles on the hillside, and many a tantalising glimpse of it has been caught through the window of a train travelling through the valley below. Popular tradition links it with the victory of King Alfred over the Danes at the battle of Ashdown, which was fought somewhere on these downs in 871, but modern thinking now considers that it dates from much earlier. Above the White Horse is the Iron Age camp known as **Uffington Castle**, and to one side is a knoll known as **Dragon's Hill** where legend has it that St George killed the dragon.

Wallingford

A strategic crossing point of the Thames since ancient times, Wallingford was first fortified, against the Danes, by Alfred the Great; the earth defences can be

Wallingford

seen to this day. Wallingford was also an important trading town: it received its charter in 1155 and for several centuries had its own mint. During the Civil War it was a Royalist stronghold and was besieged in 1646 by Parliamentary forces under Sir Thomas Fairfax. Its walls were breached after a 12-week siege. The Castle, built by William the Conqueror, was destroyed by Cromwell in 1652, but substantial earthworks can still be seen, and the Museum tells the story of the town from the earliest times.

Wantage

This thriving market town was the birthplace of Alfred the Great in 849 and remained a Royal Manor until end of the 12th century. In the central market place, around which there are some fine Georgian and Victorian buildings, is a huge statue of the King of the West Saxons, who spent much of his life (he died in 899) defending his kingdom from the Danes in the north before becoming the overlord of

England. An educated man for his time, Alfred had visited Rome as a boy, he not only codified the laws of his kingdom but also revived learning.

Unfortunately, only the **Church of St Peter and St Paul** has survived from medieval times and, though much restored in 1857 by GE Street, it retains some features from the original 13th century structure; visitors can also see a brass commemorating the life of Sir Ivo Fitzwarren, the father of Dick Whittington's wife, Alice.

Opposite the church is the **Vale and Downland Museum Centre**, which is found in another of the town's old buildings - a house dating from the 16th century - and a reconstructed barn. Dedicated to the geology, history, and archaeology of Wantage and the Vale of the White Horse, the displays cover the centuries from prehistoric times to the present day.

Built as the home of the Wantage Sisterhood, an Anglican Order, in the 19th century, **St Mary's Convent** was the work of three architects: GE Street; William Butterfield, architect of Keble College, Oxford; and John Pearson, architect of Truro Cathedral.

Just to the east of the town lies **Ardington House**, a beautifully symmetrical, early 18th century building that is the home of the Baring family. Its best feature is the Imperial Staircase -

where two flights come into one - of which this is a particularly fine example.

Witney

Situated at the bottom of the valley of the River Windrush, this old town was developed as a planned town in the early Middle Ages, under the guidance of the Bishop of Winchester; the site of the Bishop's Palace lies alongside **St Mary's Church**. By 1278, Witney had a weekly market and two annual fairs and in the centre of the market place still stands the **Buttercross**. Originally a shrine, the cross has a steep roof with rustic-looking stone columns; it was probably built in 1600.

Wool was the economic base of life here and Witney developed weaving and,

Cogges Manor Farm

in particular, the making of blankets. The Witney Blanket Company was incorporated in 1710 but before that there were over 150 looms working in the blanket trade employing over 3,000 people. The **Blanket Hall**, in the High Street, has on it the arms of the Witney Company of Weavers; it was built for the weighing and measuring of blankets in an age before rigid standardisation. The trade began in the 16th century and, even though there has been a great decline in the industry since World War I, there are still a couple of blanket factories here.

Just outside the town is the **Cogges Manor Farm Museum**, which stands on the site of a now deserted medieval village of which only the church, priory, and manor house remain.

Woodstock

To the north of the River Glyme is the old Saxon settlement, while on the opposite bank lies the newer town which was developed by Henry II in the 13th century to serve the Royal Park of Woodstock. There had been hunting lodges for the Kings of England here long before the Norman Invasion and it was Henry I who established the deer park around the manor of Woodstock.

The long gone medieval palace was the birthplace of the Black Prince in 1330 and Princess Elizabeth was held prisoner here in 1558 during the reign of her sister, Queen Mary. On ascending the throne, a grateful Elizabeth I granted the town a second weekly market and two fairs for its loyalty. The palace was damaged during the Civil War, when it served as a Royalist garrison, and the last remains were demolished in 1710.

The new town became an important coaching centre (many of the old inns surviving to this day), and prospered as a result of the construction of the Oxford Canal and later the railway. The old town's trade was glovemaking and traditionally a pair of new gloves are presented to a visiting monarch. Today's visitors can look round both the factory and showroom of **Woodstock Gloves**.

The town is also home to the **Oxfordshire County Museum**, which is housed in the wonderful and imposing 16th-century **Fletcher's House**. As well as the permanent displays on the life of the county through the centuries, the museum has a peaceful garden open to the public and, at the entrance, can be seen the town's old stocks.

The magnificent **Blenheim Palace**, one of only four sites in the country to be included on the World Heritage List, is what brings most people to Woodstock. The estate and cost of building the palace was a gift from a grateful Queen Anne to the heroic John Churchill, 1st Duke of Marlborough, for his victory at the Battle of Blenheim during the Spanish War of Succession. However, the Queen's gratitude ran out before the building work was complete and the duke had to pay the remainder of the costs himself.

As his architect, Marlborough chose Sir John Vanbrugh, whose life was even more colourful than that of his patron. He was at the same time both an architect (although at the time of his commission he was relatively unknown) and a playwright, and he also had the distinction of having been imprisoned in the Bastille, Paris. The result of his work was the Italianate palace (built between 1705 and 1722), which is now seen sitting in a very English park that was later landscaped by Capability Brown. Unfortunately, once completed, the new house did not meet with universal approval: it was ridiculed by Jonathan Swift and Alexander Pope whilst Marlborough's wife, Sarah, who seems to have held the family purse strings, delayed paying Vanbrugh as long as possible.

A marvellous, grand place with a mass of splendid paintings, furniture, porcelain, and silver on show, visitors will also be interested in the more intimate memorabilia of Sir Winston Churchill. Born here in 1874, Churchill was a cousin of the 9th Duke and the family name remains Churchill.

First grown by George Kempster, a tailor from Old Woodstock, the Blenheim Orange apple took its name from the palace. Though the exact date of the first apple is unknown, Kempster himself died in 1773 and the original tree blew down in 1853. On the southern edge of the Blenheim Estate is the village of **Bladon**, where in 1965 Sir Winston Churchill was buried in a simple grave in the churchyard after a state funeral. Also interred here are his parents, his brother John, his daughters and the ashes of his wife Clementine.

THE BELL AT CHARLBURY

CHURCH STREET, CHARLBURY, OXFORDSHIRE OX7 3PP
TEL: 01608 810278 FAX: 01608 811447

Directions: From London via the M40, follow signs for Blenheim Palace, then the A44 north. Charlbury is 3 miles off the A44 between Oxford and Chipping Norton. The Bell is in the centre of town.

Mellow Cotswold stone forms a backdrop and frame for **The Bell at Charlbury**, a handsome early-18th century building in the centre of town. The hotel offers comfortable accommodation, fine food and drink and excellent facilities for functions and meetings. It also has gardens set in an acre of its own grounds, providing seclusion in the heart of town. The 11 warm and distinctive bedrooms all have en suite facilities, TV, radio, direct-dial telephone, hairdryer, trouser press and hospitality tray. In the oak-beamed, stone-flagged bar and lounge, real ales and lagers are served, along with lunchtime bar meals, morning coffee and afternoon tea. The Bell appeals to lovers

of good food serving both bar and A La Carte cuisine, it is a romantic setting for enjoying a daily changing selection of the freshest ingredients. The food in the A La Carte restaurant is complemented by a wide-ranging, well-chosen wine list. The self-contained Cornbury Room provides a light, airy conference facility for up to 55 delegates, and the Bentley Room is ideal for smaller meetings or private parties. Horse riding, fishing, shooting, golf, car hire, air charters and tours can be arranged at the hotel, and there are facilities nearby for swimming, squash and tennis.

Once famous for glovemaking and as a centre of the Quaker movement, Charlbury has an interesting museum and a railway station built by Brunel. Close by are two grand houses that are well worth a visit - Cornbury Park and Ditchley Park.

- All day, every day
- Bar and A La carte restaurant
- All except Diners
- 11 en suite rooms
- Garden, function and conference rooms, car park
- email: reservationsatthebell@msn.com website: www.bellhotel-charlbury.co.uk
- Blenheim Palace 7 miles, Chipping Norton 5 miles, Witney 6 miles, Oxford 16 miles; shooting, fishing, golf, riding

THE CARPENTERS ARMS

132 NEWLAND, WITNEY, OXFORDSHIRE
TEL: 01993 702206 FAX: 01993 864879

> **Directions:** The inn is located on the B4022 at Newland, between the town centre and the A40.

A short walk from the centre of Witney or a short drive from the main A40 brings visitors to **The Carpenters Arms**, a fine building in local stone that started life as a coaching inn some 250 years ago. John Ferris brought many years experience in the trade when he took over the lease in November 2003; he has given the place a new lease of life and made it a firm favourite with all ages, both locals and visitors from outside the area.

He offers 2 real ales – Greene King IPA and a regularly changing guest ale and satisfies the inner man with a wide range of food served from 12 to 2.30 and from 6.30 to 9 every day. The printed menu and the specials board have something for everyone. Proof of the popularity of the Carpenters is the recent addition of a 35-cover non-smoking dining room at the back. The inn has a games room with pool, darts and fruit machines, and outside there's a car park and a small garden. Located at the foot of the valley of the River Windrush, Witney has plenty to interest the visitor, including St Mary's Church, the Buttercross, a wonderful Teddy Bear shop and the Blanket Hall, commemorating the most famous product of this one-time wool and weaving town.

- Lunch and evening, all day Fri, Sat & Sun; closed Tues lunch
- Home cooking
- Not Diners
- Car park, garden
- Pool, darts, fruit machines
- e-mail: sirrefltd@hotmail.com
- Minster Lovell 4 miles, Blenheim Palace 6 miles, Oxford 10 miles

THE COACH & HORSES

THE GREEN, ADDERBURY, NR BANBURY, OXFORDSHIRE OX17 3ND
TEL: 01295 810422

Directions: Adderbury lies about 4 miles south of Banbury off the A4260.

In the heart of a pleasant village a short drive south of Banbury, **The Coach & Horses** has a history that dates back over 400 years. Sally and John arrived here in February 2004 with ambitious plans for what is their first venture in the licensed trade, and they have quickly added their charm and friendliness to the attractions of the inn itself. The two connected brick buildings opposite the village green are very traditional in character both on the outside and within, and it's a pleasure to take time out to relax with a glass of real ale; there's a choice of three – Wadworth 6X, Henrys IPA and a frequently changing guest.

It's even more of a delight to stay to sample Sally's excellent cooking; her dishes are served every session except Sunday lunchtime or Monday (unless it's a Bank Holiday) and offer the best in tasty, satisfying pub fare: she is already making a name for her delicious soups! The non-smoking dining room has 16 covers, and children are always welcome. Each year, in April, Adderbury holds its Day of Dance on the green across the road from the Coach & Horses; morris dancing is just one of the jolly events at this annual fete. There are other attractions both rural and urban not far from the inn, including country walks, fishing on the Oxford Canal, the castle and the church at Deddington and the many places of interest in the historic market town of Banbury.

- Lunch and evening (all day Sat & Sun in summer)
- Traditional pub food
- Not Diners
- Car park
- Quiz Thursday
- Walking, fishing, Deddington 3 miles, Banbury 4 miles

THE CRICKETERS

Oxfordshire

THAME ROAD, WARBOROUGH, NR WALLINGTON,
OXFORDSHIRE OX10 7DD
TEL: 01865 858192

Directions: The village of Warborough lies on the A329 4 miles north of
Wallingford; leave the A4074 at Shillingford.

Maria and Leo took over **The Cricketers**
in 2002, since when they and their
excellent chef Peter have made it one of
the very best eating places for miles
around. Maria has also stamped her style
on the decor, and the rich red walls in
the bar create a warm, inviting ambience
for relaxing with a glass of the well-kept
real ales, including Greene King IPA
and Abbot. In the 30-cover non-smoking
restaurant, Peter, who trained with top
establishments in The UK, France and
America, sets the taste buds tingling
with his expert handling of daily source
fresh ingredients. Everything from the
stocks and sauces to the ice creams is
prepared in his kitchen, and his daily
changing blackboard menu takes its
inspiration from around the world. Some
dishes are familiar classics such as duck

confit or ribeye steaks, but even these
show Peter's distinctive touch: for
example, braised shoulder of lamb is
accompanied by fondant potatoes and
caramelised cauliflower purée.

Other dishes are more exotic and often
highly original, such as bang bang
chicken with peanut ice cream or
monkfish and scallops with a Chinese
broth and glass noodles. When the
weather is kind, the pretty, enclosed
garden at this classic Oxfordshire pub is
a delightful spot for a drink or a meal.
Inside or out, The Cricketers is definitely
a place for lovers of good food served in
relaxed, convivial surroundings. The area
around the pub and the village has some
very pleasant walks, the River Thames is
close by, and nearby places of interest
include the Abbey Church at Dorchester
and the unique Pendon Museum with its
amazing model village.

- 🕐 11-3 & 6-11
- 🍴 Home cooking with worldwide influences; summer barbecues
- 💷 Not Amex or Diners
- 🅿 Car park, enclosed garden
- ❓ Walking on the Thames Path; Dorchester 2 miles, Wittenham Clumps 3 miles, Pendon Museum 3 miles, Wallingford 4 miles, Oxford 11 miles

THE CROWN AT NUFFIELD

NUFFIELD, NR HENLEY-ON-THAMES, OXFORDSHIRE RG9 5ST
TEL: 01491 641335

Oxfordshire

Directions: The Crown is located at Nuffield, on the main A4130 Wallingford to
Henley road.

In the short time since they took over
The Crown at Nuffield, Simon and
Linda Till have transformed the old
place. Located on the main A4130 4
miles from Wallingford and 8 miles from
Henley, it has become a favourite both
as a social spot for local residents to meet
and as a country pub where the many
travellers and tourists can be sure of a
warm welcome and high standards of
hospitality, service, food and drink.
Behind the handsome brick and flint
frontage, the bar is stylish and
comfortable, and the patio garden at the
rear is a pleasant place in summer for an
alfresco drink or meal. Simon is a very
fine chef, and his wide-ranging menus
provide a pleasant dilemma: everything
sounds appetising, and results on the
plate do not disappoint. The main menu
offers delights such as tiny bubble &
squeak cakes with crispy ham and a
parmesan dressing, beer-battered fish,

pink-cooked duck breast, pasta with
halloumi cheese, and steak, kidney &
Brakspear ale pie. The pleasure level
stays high with desserts like creamy
vanilla, chocolate and biscuit mousse or
mango bavarois, rounded off by excellent
coffee – perhaps with a liqueur? At
lunchtime, sandwiches, jacket potatoes
and ploughman's platters are also
available; such is the popularity of The
Crown that booking is recommended for
all meals.

The pub enjoys a very agreeable rural
setting, with bluebell woods and the
Ridgeway Path nearby. Nuffield House,
the family home of the motorcar
magnate and philanthropist Lord
Nuffield, is occasionally open to the
public, and other local attractions
include golf at Huntercombe.
Wallingford is a short drive up the
A4130, while Henley is easily reached in
the other direction.

- 🕐 11.30-3 & 6.30-11, Sunday 12-4;
  closed Monday except Bank
  Holidays
- 🍴 Home cooking
- 💷 Not Amex
- 🅿 Off-road parking, patio garden
- ❓ Nuffield House 1 mile, Wallingford 4
  miles, Henley-on-Thames 8 miles

THE DUKE OF CUMBERLAND'S HEAD

MAIN STREET, CLIFTON, NR DEDDINGTON, OXFORDSHIRE OX15 OPE
TEL: 01869 338534 FAX: 01869 338643

Directions: The inn is located on the main street of Clifton, off the B4031 between Deddington and Aynho.

Close to the River Cherwell, the pretty village of Clifton has many interesting and attractive buildings. One of the most attractive is undoubtedly **The Duke of Cumberland's Head**, a 17th century Hornton stone building with a fine thatched roof and a large garden with lovely views. The interior is equally appealing, with a vast stone inglenook fireplace, black beams and rustic furniture. In the mid-19th century the licensee James Hall ran the inn not only as a place for refreshment but also as a grocery and a bakery - with a shop selling beaver hats for good measure.

The current owners Nick and Zara Huntington and their long-serving chef Kurt concentrate on the traditional offerings of a country pub, with locally

brewed real ales, a good selection of malts and a regularly changing variety of snacks, main meals and dishes of the day. The choice includes classics such as eggs benedict, scampi, haddock and steaks, European favourites like beef bourguignon or tuna niçoise, and 'Kurt specials' such as baked mussels with pesto, cherry tomato tatin, spinach & riccotta cannelloni, and wild boar with a leek and mustard sauce. The Sunday roasts and the monthly themed food evenings (Italian, seafood etc) are always great occasions, and Kurt's fine food is complemented by a long wine list with bottles from both Old and New Worlds. This outstanding inn also offers excellent overnight accommodation in five first-floor guest bedrooms - four doubles with private bathrooms and a single with shower en suite.

- Lunchtime and evening; closed Monday lunch except Bank Holidays
- Home cooking; themed evenings once a month
- Not Amex or Diners
- 5 rooms en suite
- Car park, garden
- Fishing on the Oxford Canal 1 mile; Deddington 2 miles, Aynho 2 miles, Banbury 7 miles

THE DUN COW

WEST END, HORNTON, NR BANBURY, OXFORDSHIRE OX15 6DA
TEL: 01295 670524 FAX: 01295 678516

> **Directions:** The village of Hornton lies off the A422 about 3 miles northwest of Banbury.

In the lovely village of Hornton, a short drive from Banbury, the **Dun Cow** is a fine old inn dating from the 17th century. One part of the roof is thatched, the other slate-tiled, and in the bars flagstone floors and a superb inglenook fireplace contribute to a delightfully traditionally look and feel. The inn is open every evening and weekend lunchtimes, and Martin Gelling and his family, owners since August 2002, have greatly enhanced its reputation as a place to seek out for its outstanding hospitality. Hook Norton Best and Charles Wells Bombardier head the list of real ales, and a chalkboard announces the dishes of the day, served from 12 to 3 at the weekend and each evening from 7 o'clock. Aberdeen Angus sirloin and T-bone steaks and steak & kidney pudding are popular choices but there are dishes to please everyone, including several vegetarian main courses.

A few minutes up the road from the inn is Upton House, renowned for its Old Masters, Brussels tapestries, Sèvres porcelain and 18th century furniture, as well as its superb gardens; also nearby are Wroxton Abbey and the historic town of Banbury. History is even closer to the Dun Cow, as the owners have made a name for themselves as suppliers of traditional ales and meads, as well as bars, lighting, staff etc, at the increasingly popular events staging re-enactments of historic events. Some of these re-enactors, from the Vikings to the Civil War have weekend trainiing sessions in the large field across the road from the Dun Cow. Across the road from the inn's garden there is a separate children's play area.

- 🕐 Every evening + Sat & Sun lunch
- 🍴 Home cooking, chalkboard menus
- 🅿 Car park
- @ e-mail: vitiswines@hotmail.com
  web: www.drunkenmonk.co.uk
- ❓ Upton House 2 miles, Banbury 3 miles

THE FOX & HOUNDS

HIGH STREET, UFFINGTON, OXFORDSHIRE SN7 7RP
TEL: 01367 820680

Directions: The inn is on the main street of Uffington, 5 miles west of Wantage off the B4507.

The **Fox & Hounds** is a very smart yellow-plastered building on the main street of a picture-postcard village five miles west of Wantage. Melanie and David came here as managers in July 2003 and in November of that year they became leaseholders. In their short time here they have achieved a lot, and they have many more plans for the future. A big brick hearth takes the eye in the bar, where Windsor-style stools are set at the wood-panelled bar counter; outside, there's a splendid garden and adjacent beer garden, and a further piece of land that can be used by campers.

Uffington Best Bitter is the favourite tipple, and there's always at least one other real ale and quality draught lagers.

⏰ 11-11

🍴 Home cooking, chalkboard menu

💷 Not Amex or Diners

🅿 Car park, garden, facilities for campers

🎵 Quiz 1 Wednesday a month

❓ Uffington White Horse 1 mile, Kingston Lisle (site of the Blowing Stone) 1 mile, Wantage 5 miles

Mel does the cooking, and the day's dishes are listed on a chalkboard – food is served every session except Sunday evening. Children are welcome, and there's a separate non-smoking section for diners. Uffington is famous as the site of one of country's best-known white horses; this one, carved into the chalk soil, is 400 feet long and can be seen for miles around. Above it is the Iron Age camp known as Uffington Castle, and nearby also is Dragon's Hill, where legend says St George slew the Dragon. Uffington was the birthplace of Thomas Hughes, author of *Tom Brown's Schooldays*, and his life and works are remembered in the Tom Brown's School Museum.

THE FOX & HOUNDS

15 SHIRBURN STREET, WATLINGTON,
OXFORDSHIRE OX49 5BU
TEL: 01491 613040 FAX: 01491 614031

Directions: Watlington is situated 3 miles from J6 of the M40.

In the heart of historic Watlington, **The Fox & Hounds** is a handsome and substantial brick building with parts dating back 700 years. Recently refurbished outside and in, it is one of the social hubs of the village, and the bar and lounge are delightful spots to relax with a glass of wine, one of Brakspears excellent brews, or a cup of coffee. In the restaurant, local produce is used as far as possible in dishes that typically range from chicken liver terrine and sesame beef satay for starters to steaks, sea bass and duck breast with a plum sauce and stir-fried vegetables. A quick and simple bar menu is also available, and a fine selection of wines from around the world to accompany the food.

- 11·11 (Sun 12·10.30)
- Bar & restaurant menus; hog roasts
- Not Amex
- 9 en suite bedrooms
- Car park, open-air cinema
- Quiz nights, music nights
- website: www.foxandhounds.net
- Ridgeway and Chiltern Way 1 mile, Stonor House 3 miles, High Wycombe 6 miles

With the M40 a short drive away, this is an excellent place to break a journey, whether for a drink or a meal, or for an overnight or longer stay. The inn has 9 en suite guest rooms in a stylishly converted barn, including a family room. Each room has its own distinctive character, and all are equipped with TV and tea/coffee making facilities. The Fox & Hounds has a thriving social side, with quiz nights, music nights, hog roasts and films shown on an open-air screen. This is great walking country – the Ridgeway and the Chiltern Way pass close by – and the rare red kite is often to be seen circling above the garden. The inn is managed by James Vernede, in the business for 20 years and a prominent figure in the Institute of British Innkeepers.

Oxfordshire

THE FOX INN

OXFORD ROAD, TIDDINGTON, OXFORDSHIRE OX9 2CH
TEL: 01844 339245

Directions: From J8a of the M40, take the A418 in the direction of Thame. Tiddington is about 3 miles along this road.

On the main road through the village of Tiddington, **The Fox Inn** is a charming old former coaching inn with flower tubs and hanging baskets adorning its smart

white-painted, roof-tiled facade. The tradition of hospitality extends back several centuries, and today's visitors can look forward to a warm welcome from the Bubbly Pub Partnership of Gavin and Lisa. It's very much at the heart of village life and an excellent place to enjoy a meal, to take a break from a journey or to pass a convivial hour or two among the gleaming brass and copper with the locals.

Traditional home-cooked English dishes are served lunchtime and evening,

and booking is recommended at the weekend, particularly for the Sunday roast with the option of 1, 2 or 3 courses. There's a discount for senior citizens Monday to Friday lunch, and children under 5 can tuck in free from their own menu when eating with their parents. The inn serves a wide variety of beers, with guest ales adding to the choice in summer. There are beer gardens to the front and rear, and the inn has ample off-road parking. Darts and Aunt Sally are the favourite games, and once a month there's an evening of music and other live entertainment. Just west of the village lies Rycote Chapel, notable for its ornate pews, one of them reputedly built for a visit by Charles I in 1625. Now looked after by English Heritage, this chapel is well worth a visit, and other attractions in the vicinity include the world-famous Waterperry Gardens just outside Wheatley.

- 🕐 Mon-Sat: 12-3 & 6-11; Sun 12-4 & 6-10.30
- 🍴 A la carte menu lunchtime and evening + snacks
- 💷 All major cards except Amex
- 🅿 Garden, off-road parking
- 🎵 Live music monthly
- ❓ Thame 5 miles, Rycote (Chapel of St Michael) 2 miles

THE GATE INN

UPPER BRAILES, NR BANBURY, OXFORDSHIRE OX15 5AX
TEL: 01608 685212

Directions: The village is located on the B4035 3 miles east of Shipston-on-Stour on the road to Banbury.

On the edge of the 'Warwickshire Cotswolds', **The Gate Inn** is a fine old hostelry built of local stone, with all the trappings that go to create a delightful old-world ambience. Inside, the scene is set by old beams, brass ornaments, a fire blazing in a stone hearth and a serving area decorated with hop bines. Outside, picnic tables are set out in the lawned garden. With more than 20 years' experience in the trade, Peter and Cathy took over The Gate in March 2000, and the welcome they extend is equally warm for newcomers as for familiar faces.

The well-kept real ales come from the nearby Hook Norton Brewery – Brewer of the Year 2004, and there's an excellent choice of other beverages.

- Lunchtime and evening; closed Mon L except Bank Holidays
- Home cooking – menus and daily specials
- Not Amex or Diners
- Car park, gardens, marquee for functions
- Shipston-on-Stour 3 miles, Boughton Castle 5 miles, Hook Norton 5 miles, Banbury 6 miles

Cathy is a superb cook and rightly proud of her skills in the kitchen, from where she produces great food for every session except Sunday evening, all Monday (except Bank Holidays) and Tuesday lunch. The choice on the printed menu and specials board runs from sandwiches and light snacks to home-baked ham, eggs and chips, super pies and casseroles, local trout, breast of duck and lamb with orange and rosemary, with delights such as treacle sponge to finish. There are special deals for senior citizens and a children's menu, and diners can eat either in the bar or in the non-smoking dining room. The Gate Inn is a popular venue for parties and other special occasions; hot and cold buffet menus are available, and marquees can be set up in the garden.

THE GEORGE & DRAGON

SILVER STREET, CHACOMBE, NR BANBURY, OXFORDSHIRE OX17 2JR
TEL/FAX: 01295 711500

Directions: The inn is located 1 mile north of J11 of the M40, off the A316

The **George & Dragon** is a stone-built inn of substance and quality standing by a small green in a picturesque village a couple of miles east of Banbury. Dating from the 17th century, it stands on what was once a drovers' road: cattle and sheep spent the night in the fields adjoining the inn while the drovers found refreshment and lodging in the inn, which once brewed its own beer. Inside, beams and inglenooks preserve much of the old-world appeal, and a great talking point for first-time visitors is an ancient well whose glassed over top has been incorporated into the bar counter. Another interesting feature is the collection of clocks put on display by tenants Jane and David, whose first venture in the licensed trade this is.

They have kept the inn's old customers and attracted new with their excellent hospitality, the well-kept ales (Everards Beacon and Tiger plus a guest) and the fine choice of dishes available every session except Sunday evening. Some of the dishes are tried and tested favourites such as scampi, steak or Cumberland sausage in a giant Yorkshire pudding, others a little more unusual – perhaps chicken fajita, tuna in an crushed peppercorn sauce or roasted vegetables with a honey and mustard sauce, served with rice. The George & Dragon also offers comfortable overnight accommodation in 2 upstairs letting Bed & Breakfast rooms with en suite facilities, each sleeping up to 4 guests. It is a very pleasant and convenient base both for business people (Banbury and the M40 are close by) and tourists exploring the many places of interest nearby.

- 🕐 11·11
- 🍴 Home cooking
- £ Not Amex or Diners
- 🛏 2 en suite rooms
- Ⓟ Car park, patio
- 🎵 Food theme and food quiz evenings
- @ e-mail: ganddchacombe@tiscali.co.uk
- ❓ Banbury 2 miles, Sulgrave Manor 3 miles

THE GOLDEN PHEASANT

91 HIGH STREET, BURFORD, OXFORDSHIRE OX18 4QA
TEL: 01993 823223 FAX: 01993 822621

Oxfordshire

Directions: From the A40 take the A361 into Burford High Street. The Golden Pheasant is on the right next to the Post Office.

In the heart of the tranquil town of Burford, **The Golden Pheasant** is a handsome 18th century building in Cotswold stone. A friendly welcome awaits both guests and local residents in the oak-beamed, stone-flagged bar and lounge, where a range of real ales, beers and lagers is available, along with morning coffee, afternoon tea and an all day brasserie menu prepared by Ryan Priddey and his team, complemented by a wide variety of wines. The arga room is available for hire. Accommodation is also a strong point at the Golden Pheasant with 10 rooms ranging from twins to characterful four-posters; all have private en suite bath or shower, TV, hospitality tray, direct-dial telephone and hairdryer. Rooms can be booked on a Bed & Breakfast or Dinner, Bed & Breakfast basis. Riding, fishing,

shooting, golf, car hire, air charters and tours can be arranged at the hotel, and there are facilities nearby for swimming, squash and tennis. The Golden Pheasant is in the same ownership as the Bell at Charlbury.

The hotel is a fine base for visiting the Cotswold villages and countryside and offers easy access to Oxford, Witney, Cirencester and Cheltenham.

Burford itself, often known as the 'Gateway to the Cotswolds', is an attractive old market town on the banks of the River Windrush. It has many interesting old buildings, many of them built on the prosperity of the wool trade, antique shops and a wildlife park (a mile outside Burford on the A361, but its crowning glory is the Church of St John the Baptist, a grand building with the atmosphere of a small cathedral.

- 🕐 All day, every day
- 🍴 All day brasserie
- 💷 All except Diners
- 🛏 10 rooms with en suite or private facilities
- 🅿 Car park
- ❓ Cotswold Wildlife Park 1 mile, Witney 6 miles

THE GRIFFIN INN

CULWORTH ROAD, CHIPPING WARDEN, OXFORDSHIRE OX17 1LB
TEL: 01295 660230

Directions: From the M40, J11, take the A361 towards Daventry. The village of Chipping Warden is about 5 miles along this road, and the Griffin Inn is in the middle of the village on the right.

Located in the heart of the ancient village of Chipping Warden and dedicated to 12 OTU Squadron, RAF, **The Griffin Inn** is a lovely unspoilt traditional country inn where Pauline has a warm welcome for regular customers and visitors to this attractive part of the world. The Cask Marque seal of approval attests to the range and quality of the real ales on offer, and the food is excellent, too. Flower tubs and climbing greenery make a pretty sight outside the mellow stone inn, while inside the old-world atmosphere is assisted by rough stone walls, real oak floors, a log burning stove and an open fire.

The Griffin is a very convivial spot, and the sense of fun that pervades the place is illustrated by the names and descriptions on the bar menu: Honey Hog (honey-roast gammon); Wings of Fire (hot, spicy chicken wings); Moby (a beautiful piece of cod served with chips and mushy peas). The A la Carte menu is superb and the Griffin boasts a chef of 2 rosette standard. Baguettes and speciality 'Chippy Steps' sandwiches come with a variety of generous fillings, and pizzas are a popular order too; any item on the menu can be ordered to take away. The inn organises regular entertainment which includes live music on the last Friday of the month and quiz evenings. There's a large garden to the rear of the inn, and ample off-road parking. The village is one of many Chippings – the name derives from the Saxon word for a market town where customers 'cheaped', or bargained, for goods.

Members of the British Institute of Innkeeping and Society of Licensed Victulers.

- 🕐 11-11
- 🍴 Home cooked bar meals
- 💷 Major cards except Amex and Diners
- 🅿 Garden, car park
- 🎵 Quiz nights; live music last Friday of the month
- @ website: www.thegriffininn.org
- ❓ Claydon Granary Museum 4 miles, Edgehill Country Park 6 miles

THE ISIS TAVERN

THE RIVERSIDE, IFFLEY LOCK, OXFORD OX4 4EL
TEL/FAX: 01865 247006

Directions: The Isis Tavern is situated at Iffley Lock. Motorists should park and walk across the bridge on to the riverside path.

Built as a farmhouse in about 1800, the **Isis Tavern** took on its current role as a riverside inn some 40 years later. At one time there was no direct access by road, and the beer had to be delivered by punt. A road now exists for deliveries only, and the customers who flock to this Greene King tavern do so from the other side of the river, crossing the bridge and walking along the riverside path. Open all day, every day, the Isis, its white-painted façade adorned with colourful window boxes and hanging baskets, is very popular with students from the nearby Oxford colleges and with tourists eager to watch a part of the history of university life. This is the point at which the springtime Torpids and the Summer Eights rowing races start, and when they are taking place the beer garden at the front of the tavern is a

keenly sought after spot from which to spectate.

Tenant Veronica Jardine has a cheery welcome for all, and the range of real ales, beers and lagers, cider, wines and spirits caters for thirsts generated by shouting on the rowers and dashing down the towpath. It's thirsty work, and it also build up an appetite, and the Isis comes to the rescue with a range of straightforward, satisfying bar snacks and meals served from noon right through to 9 o'clock in the evening. The first Iffley Lock was constructed in 1632, major rebuilding took place in 1774 and the present lock dates from 1924. The Isis is a very convivial place to visit whether or not it's the rowing season, a break from the bustle of the city proper and a chance to be close to some of the pageant and tradition of the University.

- 🕐 11-11 (Sun 12-10.30)
- 🍴 Bar food served 12 to 9
- 💷 All the major cards
- Ⓟ Beer garden
- 🎯 Darts
- ❓ All the attractions of Oxford are within easy reach

Oxfordshire

THE LAMB & FLAG

MIDDLETOWN, HAILEY, WITNEY, OXFORDSHIRE OX29 9UB
TEL: 01993 702849

Directions: Hailey is on the B4022 2 miles north of Witney.

When Julie English and Paul Doolan took over the **Lamb & Flag** in 2001, they brought with them many years' experience. This characterful old stone-built, slate-roofed inn, which dates back to the 17th century, is located a short drive north of Witney, and is easy to spot with its distinctive pub sign of a lamb in front of the flag of St George. Inside a real log fire makes it warm and inviting and two real ales head the list of drinks served in the bar. In the comfortable, well-furnished restaurant, Paul, a well-qualified and talented chef, has really put his stamp on the inn, offering a wide range of dishes to suit all tastes and appetites. The menus change regularly, with fresh local produce always to the fore, and among the dishes which have

won many friends are hearty meat dishes such as braised lamb shanks, mixed grill and steak cooked in Abbot Ale. Sunday lunch is guaranteed to be a popular occasion, and customers should always make sure that they leave room for one of the great home-made desserts. Children can choose from their own special menu, and everyone can take advantage of the discounts that are available throughout the year.

Pub games played at the Lamb & Flag include darts and bar billiards, and outside is a safe area for children to play.

The inn is an excellent place to seek out for its hospitality and good food, and a great place to pause for refreshment while touring the many nearby attractions; notable among these are the town of Witney, home of blankets and teddy bears; the picturesque remains of 15th century Minster Lovell Hall; and the wonderful Roman Villa at North Leigh.

- 🕐 12-2.30 & 7-11
- 🍴 Regularly changing full menu; children's menu
- 🅿 Garden with children's play area, Car Park
- 🎵 Bar billiards, darts, Aunt Sally in the summer
- @ website: www.lambandflagtablesir.com
- ❓ Witney (St Mary's Church, Buttercross, Blanket Hall, Cogges Manor Farm Museum) 2 miles, Minster Lovell Hall 4 miles, Blenheim 8 miles, Oxford 14 miles

THE MORNING STAR

98 PAPIST WAY, CHOLSEY, WALLINGFORD, OXFORDSHIRE OX10 9QL
TEL: 01491 651413 FAX: 01491 201731

Directions: Cholsey lies 2 miles south of Wallingford off the A329.

The Morning Star is a handsome redbrick building in the village of Cholsey, an easy drive from Wallingford to the north or Goring and Streatley to the south, off the A329. The pub sign is a classic of its kind, depicting not only the Morning Star but a farmer surveying the scene and a cockerel perched on a farm gate heralding the dawn. The pub is run by Lynda Sworn, whose parents and grandparents were in the licensed trade, and who herself had long experience of pubs when she took over. Lyn and Geoff generate a warm, friendly ambience in this Greene King pub, which serves a good range of beers, wines and spirits throughout the day, and a variety of favourite bar snacks and pub meals using local produce whenever possible.

The tenants and the regular customers are excellent company, and the pub is one of the most convivial in the area, with karaoke and quiz nights, darts, and live bands playing hits from the 60s, 70s and 80s; major sports events are shown on Sky TV. These things all happen in the locals bar, while the non-smoking lounge is a quiet, comfortable place to relax after a meal. Children are very welcome, and there's an area for them to play in the beer garden, where barbecues are a summer attraction. Visitors to the Morning Star and Cholsey should take time to have a look at the grave of the crime writer Agatha Christie in the churchyard of St Mary. A tall headstone marks her grave, and 25 trees were planted to commemorate the centenary of her birth in 1990. Cholsey is also close to a focal point for ramblers, with 3 favoured routes converging just across the Thames.

- 🕐 12-11
- 🍴 Bar snacks and meals
- 💷 All the major cards
- 🅿 Beer garden with children's play area; summer barbecue; car park
- 🎵 Live bands, karaoke, quiz nights
- ❓ Wallingford 2 miles, Didcot (Railway Centre) 6 miles

THE NEW INN

STRATFORD ROAD, WROXTON HEATH, NR BANBURY,
OXFORDSHIRE OX15 6HX
TEL: 01295 670376

Directions: The inn is on the A422 west of Banbury on the Stratford-on-Avon road.

Becky and Peter welcome visitors to the **New Inn**, a lovely old stone building standing by the A422 a short drive west of Banbury. The oldest parts of the inn date back several centuries, and it is thought that it was used for the stabling of horses at the time of the Battle of Edge Hill; later, it was for sometime used as a tollhouse. Today, it a very popular meeting place for the local community and a very pleasant place to pause on a journey or to use as a base both for both business and leisure visitors. In the bar, with its black beams, log fires and a wealth of copper and brass ornaments, draught keg ales and rotating guest ales are on tap to quench thirsts, and a wide range of home-cooked food (Peter is in charge in the kitchen) served every lunchtime and evening and all day

on Saturday and Sunday.

All tastes and appetites are catered for on the bar snack menu, the restaurant menu and the daily specials board; typical choices run from avocado prawns or grilled goat's cheese flavoured with honey and thyme for a starter to salmon, steaks, pot-roasted lamb shank and baked chicken breast wrapped in bacon with a creamy mushroom sauce. There are seats for 50 in the delightful non-smoking conservatory, and when the sun shines the picnic benches on the lawn come into their own. Children are welcome, and the New Inn is a popular venue for functions and special occasions. The overnight accommodation comprises a double room and a family room – both with en suite facilities – in a building adjoining the inn.

- 🕐 11-3 & 6.30-11, all day Sat & Sun
- 🍴 Bar snacks & restaurant menu
- £ Not Amex or Diners
- 🛏 2 en-suite rooms
- Ⓟ Car park, garden
- @ e-mail: phad65@aol.com
- ❓ Wroxton Abbey Gardens 1 mile, Banbury 2 miles, Upton House 3 miles

THE OLD ANCHOR INN

1 ST HELENS WHARF, ABINGDON, OXFORDSHIRE OX14 5EN
TEL: 01235 521726

Oxfordshire

Directions: Abingdon lies 3 miles south of Oxford on the A415.

The **Old Anchor Inn,** in one of Englands oldest towns, is situated on the river Thames. The regular ales include Morlands Original, Greene King Abbot Ale and Speckled Hen with seasonal and guest ales, also draught Hoegaarden and Budvaar etc with a

selection of wines by the bottle or by the glass. Candlelight and wood panelling contribute to an atmospheric setting in which to enjoy a drink or casual meal. Specialising in seafood, The Old Anchor has a mouthwatering selection of dishes, Paella, Bantry Bay Mussels and Pan Fried Tiger Prawns to name but a few. There is also an interesting selection of meat and vegetarian dishes which could include Lamb Pan Fried in Red Wine with Aubergines, Pork with Apple, Bay and Cinnamon, Moussaka, Stilton and Walnut Potato Bake or a Carrot, Cream Cheese and Coriander Wrap.

Live music is an important part of The Old Anchors programme with Blues on a Sunday at 4pm and Thursday night is Music Night at 8.30pm.

The Old Anchor has a patio, and visitors arriving by boat can tie up at the pub's own moorings. Abingdon's many attractions include the nearby Church of St Helen with its wonderful Lady Chapel.

- Winter 12-3 & 6-11, Sun 12-10.30 Summer 12-3 & 5-11 Sat 12-11.00 Sun 12-10.30 Over 21's
- Daily changing menu and seafood menu, bookings recommended.
- All the major cards
- On street parking and moorings
- Live music, blues Sunday at 4pm, music night Thursday at 8.30pm
- In Abingdon: riverside walks, Benedictine Abbey, Church of St Helen, Museum, almshouses;

Oxfordshire

THE PACKHORSE INN

MILTON HILL, ABINGDON, OXFORDSHIRE OX13 6AG
TEL: 01235 832323 FAX: 01235 832425

Directions: Milton Hill is on the A4130 5 miles south of Abingdon, 3 miles west of Didcot.

Situated on a prominent corner site on the A4130 south of Abingdon, **The Packhorse Inn** is an attractive white-painted brick building topped by an immaculate tiled roof. Hanging baskets adorn the exterior, which looks particularly beautiful when lit at night. The promise of the outside is more than fulfilled within, where the ambience in the spacious bars is very warm and inviting. Sandy and Richard acquired the inn in 2001, since when they have refurbished the whole place to a very high decorative standard.

They take their food and drink very seriously here, with five real ales heading the liquid list and a wide range of home cooking that is winning new friends all the time and keeps the 100+ covers in demand. After choosing from a dozen or more starters, many of the clients go for one of specialities, perhaps a seafood platter, spaghetti carbonara or a super steak - pepper, Diane or tournedos Rossini. On Sunday, traditional roasts are served from 12 right through to 8 o'clock. The Packhorse has ample off-road parking and a large beer garden with picnic tables and an enclosure with goats, chickens and other farm creatures that will keep the children interested for hours. Inside entertainment includes a pool table, juke box, occasional karaoke nights and a DJ at the New Year's Eve party. Among the many places of interest in the vicinity are Milton Manor, an Inigo Jones-designed gentleman's residence set in glorious parkland; the pretty village of East Hendred; and the towns of Abingdon and Didcot.

- 12-3 & 6-11, Sun all day
- Snacks and full menu
- All major cards except Amex
- Beer garden with farm animal enclosure, ample car parking
- Pool table, jukebox, occasional karaoke nights
- email: packhorseinn@btconnect.com
- Abingdon 5 miles, Didcot (Railway Centre), Wantage 5 miles

THE PLOUGH INN

ORCHARD LANE, EAST HENDRED, OXFORDSHIRE OX12 8JW
TEL: 01235 833213 FAX: 01235 835074

> **Directions:** East Hendred lies on the A417 between Wantage and Rowstock Corner.

The **Plough Inn** is a 16th century building in the village of East Hendred, one of the prettiest villages in Oxfordshire, with lots of old half-timbered cottages and thatched cob walls. Fred and Suzanne Trigg and their staff provide a warm welcome, traditional hospitality and a range of food and drink to satisfy all tastes and appetites and to cater for all thirsts. Bar snacks include jacket potatoes, baguettes and grilled panini with a wide choice of tasty fillings, along with favourites such as gammon, egg and chips and a selection of chef's daily specials. Dishes on the main à la carte menu may be ordered at the bar or in the restaurant which has a non-smoking area and run from crispy-coated camembert and Thai fish cakes to lemon butter salmon supreme, smoked haddock and prawn pasta and lamb shank with red

wine and rosemary or a hint of mint. This menu is also supplemented by chef's specials such as a 16oz buffalo steak with mustard sauce, and a wide selection of delicious desserts is on offer to round off a meal in style. Food is served from noon to 2.30 and from 7 to 9.30 each day except for Monday evening. Visitors who are pressed for time can order their lunch in advance by telephone or e-mail, and other options at the Plough include a children's menu and menus tailored to events such as Valentine's Day, Hallowe'en and Christmas parties. Corporate parties are welcome, and the whole restaurant can be booked for special occasions.

Drinks include a range of fine beers such as IPA and Abbot Ale, fine wines by glass or bottle, soft drinks and alcohol-free beer, teas and speciality coffees. The Plough has ample off-road parking and a large, mature garden with seating areas and an enclosed area where children can romp in safety.

- 🕐 12-2.30 & 6-11
- 🍴 Bar snacks & à la carte menu, Sunday roasts, children's menu
- 💷 All the major cards
- 🅿 Garden, children's play area, car park
- @ email: theplough@fsinns.co.uk website: www.theplough.fsinns.co.uk
- ❓ Wantage (Vale & Downland Museum Centre, Ardington House, St Mary's Convent) 4 miles, Didcot 6 miles

THE RED COW

THE GREEN, CHESTERTON, OXFORDSHIRE
TEL/FAX: 01869 241337

Directions: From J9 of the M40 take the A41 towards Bicester and turn off left to Chesterton.

Steve and Sue are the hospitable landlords at **The Red Cow**, a splendid old inn built of local stone. It stands in a prominent position on the main road through the village of Chesterton, a short drive south of Bicester. The outside of the inn is distinguished by a splendid slate-roofed porch supported by ancient wooden pillars. Inside, open log fires add to the warm, welcoming ambience created by Steve and Sue, who have greatly added to the inn's appeal since arriving here in June 2003. Built in the 17th century and called simply The Cow for its first few years, this Greene King inn serves all the expected drinks including cask ales, and it is also a great place to pause for a snack or tuck into something more substantial from the menu: the chef uses local produce as much as possible for the dishes, among

which steak & ale pie is a great favourite. When the sun shines, the beer garden comes into its own, offering plenty of space for children to burn off surplus energy.

The Red Cow is not the only reason to pause awhile in Chesterton; the area surrounding the inn is rich in remains of past centuries, including traces of the Roman occupation, and walking around the village itself reveals various distinct stages of development, from Norman to medieval, Victorian and post-World War II. The neighbouring substantial town of Bicester is of Saxon origin and has at various times been an ecclesiastical town, a centre of hunting and horseracing and the site of an important Army ordnance depot. One of the few really old buildings is the Church of St Eadburg, which still shows some traces of its 13th century origins.

- 12-3 & 6-11 (Fri/Sat 12-11, Sun 12-10.30); closed Mon lunchtime
- Traditional home-cooked food
- Not Amex or Diners
- Beer garden with space for children to romp
- Karaoke nights
- Ancient remains in village and at Bicester (1 mile

THE RED LION

HIGH STREET, ISLIP, OXFORDSHIRE OX5 2RX
TEL: 01865 375367 FAX: 01865 842555

> **Directions:** From the A34. about 7 miles north of Oxford, turn right on the B4027 to Islip (1 mile). The Red Lion is on the main street of the village.

Islip is a pleasant little village standing beside the River Ray. It was the birthplace of Edward the Confessor, Saxon king and founder of Westminster Abbey. He was born in 1004 in the royal palace at Islip, but sadly no trace of that building survives. Luckily, the same is certainly not true of **The Red Lion**, a fine old coaching inn with many original features. Hosts Darren and Kate Ward and chef Perry Wheeler have turned The Red Lion into one of the most sought after destination restaurants in the area, as well as maintaining its role as a popular village inn. Dishes on the mouthwatering menu, served either in the bar or in the non-smoking restaurant, feature the best and freshest seasonal ingredients prepared to order and served by friendly staff who are

rightly proud of the reputation the inn has built up. Skill and imagination combine in dishes such as goat's cheese and pesto mushrooms, roasted belly of pork with a cider sauce and chicken sauced with the local Blue Oxford cheese.

The Red Lion's attractions do not end with the hospitality, the fine food and the excellent range of beers and wines, as it also has three guest bedrooms, making it a quiet, comfortable base from which to explore the many places of interest in the area, whether it's walking the Oxfordshire Way (it skirts the village) or discovering the almost endless list of things to see and do in Oxford.

- 🕐 12-2.30 & 6-11, all day Sat & Sun
- 🍴 A la carte menu
- 💷 All the major cards
- 🛏 3 guest rooms (2 doubles, 1 single)
- 🅿 Car park, garden
- 🎵 Pool, darts, Aunt Sally, skittles
- @ e-mail: kateward@work·1971.fsbusiness.co.uk
- ❓ Oxfordshire Way skirts the village; Oxford 7 miles, Blenheim Palace 9 miles

THE RED LION

GORING ROAD, WOODCOTE, OXFORDSHIRE RG8 0SD
TEL: 01491 680483

Directions: The inn lies opposite the green and cricket pitch in a village on the B471 4 miles north of Pangbourne. From Reading take the A4074 Wallingford road for about 8 miles; Woodcote is signposted on the left.

In the heart of the picturesque village of Woodcote, opposite the green and cricket pitch, **The Red Lion** is a handsome building dating from 1845. Its facade is adorned in spring and summer with colourful hanging baskets and flower tubs, and inside there's a roomy L-shaped bar with old beams and an open fire. The warm, inviting feel is reinforced by the welcome from the new landlords Sally and Maurice Cook, son Sam and daughter Louisa, who took over the reins in March 2004 and are enhancing the inn's reputation for hospitality. Sally cooks when it's the chef's day off, and they both do an excellent job in the kitchen, producing a wide range of dishes from the printed menu and the specials board to be enjoyed in the 40-cover non-smoking restaurant. Some of the dishes are pub stalwarts such as homemade steak & kidney pie and cod in freshly made batter with chips, others just that little bit different, like chilli con carne served in a crisp tortilla basket, vegetable stack or teriyaki steak stir-fry. There is also an excellent choice of steaks from the grill including rump, sirloin and T-bone.

Visitors at both ends of the age span are encouraged, with children always welcome and special deals offered Monday to Saturday lunchtime for senior citizens. The inn is open lunchtime and evening and all day Saturday and Sunday. It is also handy for anyone with business in Goring, Pangbourne or Reading, all of which are an easy drive away.

- Lunchtime and evening (all day Sat and Sun)
- Home cooking
- Car park, patio garden
- Pool, darts
- email: sally-and-maurice@hotmail.com
- Pangbourne 4 miles, Goring 3 miles, Reading 8 miles

THE RED LION INN

115 HIGH STREET, CHALGROVE, OXFORDSHIRE OX44 7SS
TEL: 01865 890625

Directions: From the M40 (J6) take the B4009 through Watlington. At the T junction turn right on to the B480; after 400 yards take the right fork towards Stadhampton (B480); Chalgrove is about 4 miles along this road.

Opposite the War Memorial in the centre of Chalgrove, **The Red Lion** offers a traditional village pub atmosphere and a fine selection of food and drink. In a village with many picturesque houses, this strikingly pretty inn boasts one garden overlooking the village street and another to the rear, where families are welcome. Since before the first known written record of 1637, The Red Lion has been and still is owned by Chalgrove Parish Church. A few centuries ago the inn provided dining and carousing facilities for the 'naughty' church wardens; the tradition of hospitality is now carried on in more conventional style by Annie and James Shepherd, who have a warm welcome for all their customers. The food at The Red Lion is quite outstanding. The lunch and evening bar menu runs from sandwiches and jacket potatoes to classics such as chilli (con carne or vegetarian with quorn), beer-battered fish with chips and mushy peas, and chicken, bacon and mushroom pie. Children have their own special menu. The dinner menu tempts at every turn with dishes both familiar (garlic prawns, pepper steak, mixed grill, brandy snap baskets) and more unusual, such as duo of duck legs or fillets of mackerel with curry spices. A well-chosen wine lists offers bottles from both Europe and the New World, and beer-lovers can enjoy real ales from family brewers. This delightful inn makes a wonderful venue for business meetings and special occasions, with space for conferences up to 16 and dinners up to 26.

- 🕐 12-3 & 5.30-11 (Sat from 6, Sun 7-10.30); open all day summer weekends
- 🍴 Lunch and evening bar menu, full dinner menu (no food Sunday evening)
- 🅿 Gardens front and rear
- 🎵 Folk club second Monday of the month; darts, cribbage
- @ email: annie@redlionchalgrove.co.uk
- ❓ Medieval wall painting Chalgrove church; Battle of Chalgrove field 1 mile, Thames Path 5 miles, Henley 10 miles, Oxford 12 miles

Oxfordshire

THE RED LION INN

**8 RED LION STREET, CROPREDY, BANBURY, OXFORDSHIRE OX17 1PB
TEL: 01295 750224**

Directions: From the M40 (J11) take the A361 towards Daventry. After just over a mile take the minor road to the left signposted Cropredy (1 mile). Go over the canal bridge, turn sharp right and follow the road around the church.

There can be few more picturesque hostelries than **The Red Lion Inn**, with its walls of mellow honey-coloured local stone and its roof of immaculate grey thatch. Beams, log fires and rustic furnishings make an equally attractive sight inside, and owners Adam and Karen have worked very hard to create the ambience that makes this such a delightful place to visit. Four real ales, always including one from a local brewery, head the list of liquid refreshments, and the menu caters admirably with all tastes and appetites. Fresh local produce is used whenever possible in a range of well-prepared dishes

that take their inspiration from all parts of the globe: deep-fried brie with cranberry sauce, cod in beer batter, sirloin steak with all the traditional trimmings, devilled lamb shank, Hungarian goulash, hot Thai trout served with sticky rice and salad. There are always several vegetarian main courses and a kids menu, and the Sunday roast menu is served lunchtime and evening. A set menu is also available, along with sandwiches and baguettes for lighter bites. Besides the bar and restaurant, the inn has a non-smoking lounge, a children's/family room and a beer garden. Special occasions such as Hallowe'en and Valentine's Day are always celebrated at this convivial inn, which also hosts occasional live music nights and a quiz every Thursday at 9.30; pool and darts are the favourite games with the regulars.

The Red Lion stands next to Cropredy Lock on the Oxford Canal, and is adjacent to the 13th century church, which contains relics from the Civil War Battle of Cropredy Bridge.

- ⏰ Mon-Fri 12-2.30 & 6-11 (Tues & Fri from 5.30); Sat 12-3.30 & 6-11; Sun 12-3.30 & 6.30-10.30. Summer hours are flexible
- 🍴 Meals and bar snacks every session; Sunday roasts; Tues & Fri fish & chip nights
- 💷 All except Amex and Diners
- 🅿 Patio, car park
- 🎵 Quiz nights (Thursday at 9.30), occasional live music nights; pool, darts
- @ email: adam@welbro.co.uk website: www.pubsite.co.uk
- ❓ Canalside walks, Banbury 4 miles, Broughton Castle 7 miles, Upton House 8 miles

THE ROMANY INN

BRIDGE STREET, BAMPTON, OXFORDSHIRE OX18 2HA
TEL: 01993 850237 FAX: 01993 852113

> **Directions:** The inn lies on the A4095 between Witney and Faringdon.

'There is nothing which has been contrived by man, by which so much happiness is produced, as by a good tavern or inn.' When Dr Johnson penned these words, he must have had in mind something very like **The Romany Inn**, a fine old hostelry standing at the heart of a historic Oxfordshire village. Behind sturdy weathered walls in mellow Cotswold stone, the convivial bar features exposed brick, heavy oak beams and a log fire set into a pillared alcove. The inn also has a restful lounge and a choice of place to settle down to a meal – the bar-restaurant or the intimate dining room with a copper-canopied fireplace.

Trevor, who owns and runs the inn with Jane and Barbara, does the cooking, and his printed menus and the daily specials board provide an across-the-board choice. The Sunday lunch of 1, 2 or 3 courses is always very popular, while among the liquid refreshment on offer Archers Village is the regular real ale. There's a good wine list to complement the food, and coffees and teas are also available. Dr Johnson would be impressed by the welcome, the food and the drink, but The Romany has even more to offer: 11 single and double letting bedrooms, all en suite, all with TV and tea/coffee makers. That makes the inn an excellent choice for an overnight stay, or a break for a weekend or longer. There's plenty to see in Bampton, including the medieval grammar school, the parish church, the 14th century gatehouse of the castle and the charming little town hall in the market place.

- 🕐 11-11
- 🍴 Home cooking
- 💷 Not Amex or Diners
- 🛏 11 en suite rooms
- 🅿 Off-road parking, beer garden, children's play area
- @ e-mail: romany@barbox.net
- ❓ Witney 4 miles, Faringdon 5 miles, Pusey House 5 miles

THE SAYE & SELE ARMS

MAIN ROAD, BROUGHTON, NR BANBURY, OXFORDSHIRE OX15 5ED
TEL: 01295 263348 FAX: 01295 272012

Directions: The inn is on the main road in Broughton, 3 miles southwest of Banbury on the B4035.

Paul and Carol have enjoyed over 20 successful years in the licensing trade, most recently taking over the **Saye & Sele Arms** in 2002. After a top to toe refurbishment it now looks even smarter than it did when new, some 300 years ago. The original stone walls, sturdy wooden beams and an open fire create a splendidly warm and welcoming ambience in the public rooms. Four cask ales are always available on an extensive, Cask Marque approved guest beer program, and the choice of food also changes regularly. All appetites are catered for with a selection that runs from bar snacks and light bites to a full restaurant menu; the Sunday lunchtime roasts always attract a full house, so it's best to book in advance to be sure of a table. Food is served every session except Sunday evening. The sheltered beer garden and terrace are popular spots when the weather is kind. The moated mansion Broughton Castle, just a few steps from the inn, is the grandest building in the area, but visitors who pause for refreshment at the Saye & Sele Arms will find plenty more to see nearby, including Bloxham Village Museum and the various attractions in Banbury. This is also a good walking area, and there are several golf courses in the vicinity.

The inn has been called either the Twistleton Arms or the Saye and Sele Arms at different times in its life. Both names refer to the owners of nearby Broughton Castle, still a family home and now also a popular location for film producers.

- 11.30-2.30 (Sat to 3, Sun 12-3) & 7-11 (Sun to 10.30)
- Bar snacks and full meals; Sunday roast
- All except Diners
- Car park, beer garden and terrace
- Aunt Sally
- email: mail@sayeandselearms.co.uk website: www.sayeandselearms.co.uk
- Golf, walking; Broughton Castle 100 yards, Banbury 3 miles

THE SEVEN STARS

THE GREEN, MARSH BALDON, OXFORDSHIRE OX44 9LP
TEL: 01865 343255

> **Directions:** From Oxford take the A4074 Reading road. After about 3 miles turn left on to minor road at Nuneham Courtenay. Marsh Baldon is a short drive along this road.

A short drive south of Oxford, on the green in the village of Marsh Baldon, **The Seven Stars** is a Grade II listed tile-roofed redbrick building whose facade is attractively adorned with window boxes and greenery in pots. The interior is equally appealing, and tenants Allan and Kate have worked very hard in the short time since their arrival to make it the warm, comfortable and inviting place it is. Open log fires keep the cold weather at bay, and visitors can take their pick from a wide variety of seats, from bar stools through darkwood country furniture to cushioned sofas. Real ales, including a frequently changed guest, are popular for quenching thirsts, and in the non-smoking restaurant area the printed menu and blackboard specials present an impressive choice of home-cooked food. Typical dishes of the day run from breaded brie and tempura prawns to lasagne, cod & pancetta fishcakes, lamb chops with mash & onion gravy, salads, and vegetarian options; seafood specials add still further to the choice in the evening.

The Seven Stars is a very convivial spot, very much the hub of village life, and the quiz nights, race nights and occasional live music events are always well attended, so too annual celebrations such as Valentine's Day and Hallowe'en. Families are welcome, and there are areas for children to play in the huge beer garden. Just along the road at Nuneham Courtenay is Nuneham Park, a Palladian mansion set in parkland laid out by Capability Brown. This parkland is now the Arboretum of Oxford University and is well worth a visit; the site contains superb mature pines, bamboos, camellias and a bluebell wood.

- Winter Mon-Fri 12-2.30 & 6-11, Sat & Sun all day; summer all day every day
- Home-cooked food available every day
- All except Amex
- Beer garden, children's play area
- Occasional live music, quiz & race nights
- Oxford 5 miles

Oxfordshire

SIX BELLS ON THE GREEN

WARBOROUGH, NR WALLINGFORD, OXFORDSHIRE
TEL: 858265 FAX: 01865 858464

Directions: From Wallingford, take the A4074 then turn on to the A329 at a major roundabout. From the M40, leave at J7 and take the A329 southbound.

Ben Salter, who spent 22 years with the RAF, including a spell with the Queen's Flight, is now flying high at the controls of the **Six Bells on the Green**. This lovely old country inn, built as two cottages in about 1550, makes a picturesque contribution to a very

picturesque scene; its beautiful, steeply raked thatched roof extends past the first-floor windows, and the village boasts one of the prettiest cricket greens in the whole country, famously featuring in such productions as *Midsomer Murders* and *Two Fat Ladies*. The promise of the outside is more than fulfilled within, where exposed stone walls, log fires and traditional decor and furnishings paint a very attractive scene.

The home-cooked food is traditional, too, and can be accompanied by real ales from Brakspear's nearby Henley brewery or a full range of wines. In summer, the beer garden is the place to be, with plenty of picnic-style tables and lovely views over the countryside. All these assets make the Six Bells a great place to seek out in its own right, and it's also a good place to stop on a journey, to take a break from business in the nearby towns or to pause for refreshment while touring the region. Among the many places of interest hereabouts are the pretty village of Ewelme, home and final resting place of Jerome K Jerome; Shillingford, where the Irish poet W B Yeats lived; and the little Thameside town of Dorchester with its Abbey Church and Museum.

- 11.30-2.30 & 6-11; Sun 12-3
- Traditional English food on a changing menu
- All except Amex & Diners
- Beer garden, cricket pitch
- Occasional live music
- Wallingford 4 miles

THE STAR INN

WATERY LANE, SPARSHOLT, OXFORDSHIRE OX12 9PL
TEL: 01235 751539 (& FAX · PHONE FIRST)

Directions: Sparsholt lies just north of the B4507 4 miles west of Wantage.

A hostelry since the 17th century, the **Star Inn** is a handsome building in red brick layered with stone, topped by a slate roof. Inside, a log fire warms the bar, and twinkling ceiling lights add to the inviting feel. This really appealing free house is run in the most friendly and enthusiastic style by Lee Morgan and Carina Lewis, and in the year since they took over they have made a great impression with both their growing band of regulars and visitors finding the inn for the first time. Four real ales are always on tap, along with a range of other beers both bottled and draught, lagers, cider, wines and spirits - even champagne for special occasions. And special occasions

are a way of life here. Burns Night, Valentine's Day, St Patrick's Day, St George's Day......they all get celebrated, along with regular Casino Nights and almost any excuse for a party!

Food is a great attraction here, and talented chef Lee covers the whole range of pub favourites and a whole lot more besides. There are sandwiches plain and toasted, baguettes, ploughman's platters, jacket potatoes, steaks, daily changing fish specials, Sunday lunches with a choice of roasts, fresh vegetables and all the trimmings. The adventurous can tuck into more unusual options such as kangaroo, ostrich, wild boar or alligator, and the home-made sweets are definitely not to be missed. The Star is also a great base for walking in the open countryside or touring the many sights, both scenic and historic, in the area. The 8 comfortable en suite rooms range from singles to a family room and one with facilities for disabled guests.

- 12-3 Mon-Fri, 6-11 Mon-Fri, 12-11 Sat, 12-10.30 Sun
- Full menu snacks and full meals, daily specials
- All the major cards
- 8 en suite rooms
- Car parking on & off road
- Burns Night, Valentines, St Patrick's Day, St George's Day, casino nights
- email: lee-carina@btconnect.com website: www.starinnsparsholt.tk
- The Ridgeway Walk 2 miles, Kingston Lisle 2 miles, Uffington (White Horse, Dragon's Hill, Castle) 3 miles, Wantage 4 miles

STURDY'S CASTLE

BANBURY ROAD, TACKLEY, OXFORDSHIRE OX5 3EP
TEL: 01869 331328 FAX: 01869 331686

Directions: Sturdy's Castle is situated on the main A4260 Oxford to Banbury road approximately 2 miles from Woodstock.

In a prominent position on the main Oxford-Banbury road, **Sturdy's Castle** provides the perfect base for the business traveller or for touring the sights of Oxfordshire. Refurbished to a high standard, Sturdy's has a traditional bar, an 80-cover restaurant and a separate accommodation block. Lunchtime and à la carte, supplemented by daily specials, offer plenty of excellent eating throughout the day, and in summer the large beer garden is a delightful spot for drinking and dining while enjoying the Oxfordshire air. The separate accommodation block close to the restaurant has 20 smart, practical bedrooms, all with en suite facilities, tea/coffee-makers, TV and telephone. Two of the twin rooms are suitable for

disabled guests and 4 of the doubles can sleep families of up to four. Interconnecting rooms are available. A traditional full English breakfast is served for B&B guests.

The inn has a separate function room that is available for private hire. Any type of function can be catered for, and the room has its own skittle alley. With this facility and the ample on-site parking, Sturdy's Castle is the perfect venue for a business meeting or conference, and anything from buffets to full meals can be arranged. For leisure visitors, there's easy access to the many places of interest that bring visitors from all over the world; Woodstock and the magnificent Blenheim Palace are only 2 miles from the inn, and it's an easy drive south to the almost endless sights to be seen in Oxford, less than 10 miles away.

- 🕐 11-11
- 🍺 Bar and Restaurant menus
- £ All except Amex and Diners
- 🛏 20 en suite rooms
- Ⓟ Function/conference room, car park, beer garden
- @ email: vanessa.porch@sturdyscastle.com website: www.sturdyscastle.com
- ❓ Blenheim Palace 2 miles, Oxford 9 miles

THE VINES RESTAURANT & COUNTRY HOUSE HOTEL

BURFORD ROAD, BLACK BOURTON, OXFORDSHIRE OX18 2PF
TEL: 01993 843559 FAX: 01993 840080

Directions: The Vines can be reached from the A4095 Faringdon-Witney road, the A420 Swindon-Oxford road and the A40 Cheltenham-Witney road.

Long renowned as a venue for fine dining in elegant surroundings, **The Vines** now offers excellent overnight accommodation in six superbly equipped, spacious and comfortable en suite bedrooms. The handsome Cotswold stone frontage is adorned with tubs of flowers, and the interior has been renovated with style and taste. John Clegg, of the BBC Real Rooms Team, designed the restaurant, where the à la carte evening menu (Monday to Saturday) tempts with superb dishes such as Thai style chicken salad, roasted sea bass with a thyme butter sauce, and pork tenderloin with sage mash and a red wine sauce.

Sandwiches and light bites are served at lunchtime Tuesday to Saturday, with a traditional roast on Sunday. An extensive choice of wines (including wine from the local vineyard) complements the fine food, but the wine list is not the only evidence that wine is taken very seriously at The Vines. Each of the bedrooms is named after a grape variety: Rosetto, the largest room, features a Victorian brass bedstead and a seating area for two, while Trebbiano, a family room with a double and a single bed, shows an Egyptian influence in its decor.

Rooms can be booked on a room only or Dinner, Bed & Breakfast basis; a full English breakfast is served in the restaurant, with the alternative option of a continental breakfast. The Vines has a very large, secure car park, a front lawn and a delightful side garden.

- 12-2.30 & 6-11; closed Monday lunchtime
- Light lunchtime menu; evening full à la carte
- All major cards except Amex
- 6 rooms with en suite showers
- Gardens, car park
- Regular food & live entertainment events
- email: vinesrestaurant@aol.com website: www.vinesblackbourton.co.uk
- Local vineyard and churches, Burford 4 miles, Kelmscott (home of William Morris) 4 miles

Oxfordshire

THE WHITE HART

NEWLAND STREET, EYNSHAM, OXFORDSHIRE OX29 4LB
TEL: 01865 880711 FAX: 01865 880169

Directions: Eynsham lies just off the A40 midway between Oxford and Witney.

The White Hart is a fine old stone building in the attractive Thameside village of Eynsham, midway between Oxford and Witney, with the main A40 running close by. The premises have been a public house since the mid-18th century, but they date back much further, and much remains of the original 1366 building – first a courthouse, then a coaching inn when stables were added. Potted plants adorn the outside, while in the bar several interesting features take the eye, including beams, rustic furniture, paintings on various themes, a huge stone inglenook with wine racks and a model sailing ship, and another with a hooded wood-burning grid.

Locals, business people, travellers and tourists can all look forward to a warm welcome and traditional hospitality

- Lunch and evening, all day Sat & Sun
- Home cooking
- £ Not Amex or Diners
- 3 en suite rooms
- P Garden, terrace, function room
- @ e-mail: whiteharteynsham@aol.com&
  website:www.whiteharteynsham.co.uk
- ? Thames Path; Witney 4 miles, Bladon 4 miles, Blenheim Palace 6 miles, Oxford 6 miles

dispensed by Russell and Jacky, first-time leaseholders who came here in the spring of 2003. Four real ales – Greene King IPA and Abbot Ale, Morlands Original and a guest – are waiting to quench thirsts, and good home-cooked food is served every session except Sunday and Monday evening. The lunchtime choice could be anything from sandwiches, paninis and jacket potatoes to daily hot and cold specials, and for those in a hurry dishes can be ordered in advance. Favourites on the evening menu include local trout and a steak & Guinness pie full of goodness and flavour. A stone-walled function room can be booked for meetings and conferences, social evenings or special occasions, and a buffet service is available. The stable block has recently been converted into three tastefully appointed en suite guest bedrooms, let throughout the year on a Bed & Breakfast basis. The inn has a garden and a terrace.

THE WHITE HART

12 ST ANDREW'S ROAD, OLD HEADINGTON, OXFORDSHIRE OX3 9DL
TEL: 01865 761737

Directions: The White Hart is situated opposite St Andrew's parish church in Old Headington on the eastern outskirts of Oxford.

Linda Vinall and Dick Underwood know how to turn a good pub into an outstanding pub, and they have certainly worked the oracle at **The White Hart**, which stands opposite the Church of St Andrew in Old Headington, on the eastern edge of Oxford. Behind the stone facade with its smart green sign and shuttered windows, they have completely refurbished the 17th century premises

while retaining all the period charm in the spacious, comfortable bar and dining areas.

They have also transformed the beer

- 🕐 12-11 (Sun to 10.30)
- 🍴 Home-cooked bar snacks and meals
- £ All the major cards
- 🅿 Beer garden
- 🎵 Quiz nights and live music evenings
- @ email: dick@whitehart.eclipse.co.uk
- ❓ The many attractions of Oxford are all within easy reach

garden, where picnic tables are set out on the lawn, with trees and greenery all around and a high stone wall to provide shelter and seclusion. Four real ales – two fixed, two regularly changing guests – are always on tap, and there's a broad selection of other beers and lagers, wines and spirits. Linda is an excellent cook, and the dishes that she prepares make the best use of fresh local produce. The tenants and their regular customers ensure a happy, relaxed atmosphere at The White Hart, and the quiz and live entertainment evenings planned for 2004 will make it an even more convivial spot.

THE WHITE HOUSE

**1 GROVE ROAD, BLADON, NR WOODSTOCK, OXFORDSHIRE OX20 1RQ
TEL/FAX: 01993 8115823**

Directions: The inn lies by the A4095 in Bladon, just off the A44 Oxford to Woodstock road.

Nestling on the edge of the Blenheim Estate, **The White House** has been dispensing hospitality since 1661. It carries its years very well, and was recently voted Best Village Pub 2004 in the London & Home Counties region in the Morning Advertiser Pub Industry Awards. This accolade was earned by the efforts of tenants Eddie and Maeve Bradbury, who work hard to maintain the highest standards of innkeeping and have made this one of *the* places to visit in the region.

Wood is used to great effect in the bar, where brass and copper ornaments take the eye and a log-burning stove keeps the chill away. Mulled wine by the fire in winter makes way for Pimms in the garden in summer, and throughout the year thirsts are quenched by real ales and appetites satisfied by some really outstanding food.

The choice covers classics such as steaks, fish & chips, home-made burgers and the Sunday roast as well as the unfailingly popular house speciality – eight varieties of locally produced sausages (including three vegetarian versions) served with creamy mash (plain, mustard, cheesy, or with the kick of horseradish) and a choice of onion gravy or a spicy tomato sauce. The pleasure level stays high to the end with treats like chocolate chip sponge or spotted dick. Monday night is charity quiz night, mellow light music is played on the last Friday of the month, and there are regular singalong nights, meat draws and the Snowball Club prize draws. Bladon is known far and wide as the place where Sir Winston Churchill is buried; he lies with several of his family in the churchyard opposite the inn.

- 🕐 11·11 (Sun 12·10.30)
- 🍴 Home cooking
- 💷 Not Diners
- 🅿 Car park
- 🎵 Quiz Monday
- @ e-mail: info@whitehousepub.com
  website: www.whitehousepub.com
- ❓ Grave of Sir Winston Churchill opposite the inn; Blenheim Palace and Woodstock 2 miles, Long Hanborough (bus museum) 1 mile, Oxford 5 miles

WOODSTOCK ARMS

8 MARKET STREET, WOODSTOCK, OXFORDSHIRE OX20 1SX
TEL/FAX: 01993 811251

Directions: The Woodstock Arms is located in the centre of Woodstock, 10 miles north of Oxford on the A44.

Thousands of tourists flock each year to the town of Woodstock, mostly to visit the grand and magnificent Blenheim Palace, one of only four sites in the country to be accorded World Heritage status. But Woodstock has many other attractions, and one of them is definitely the **Woodstock Arms**, a handsome 17th century stone building in the centre of town. Customer care comes first with Sylvia and Alan, who in their two years here have seen its business thrive and its clientele grow. Original beams and walls and open log fires set a splendidly traditional scene in the bar, where a wide range of ales, beers, lagers, ciders, wines and spirits is always on hand to provide refreshment and to reinvigorate tired tourists. The locals love the place, too, and everyone is united in praise of the food served here: it's always fresh and wholesome,

and the main menu, which changes fortnightly, is supplemented by daily specials that include very popular fish dishes. Food is served from noon right through to about 9 o'clock in the evening.

The site on which the Woodstock Arms stands has an interesting history, parts of it being a tailor's shop and the town's wool barn as well as inns called the Three Tuns, the Duke of Wellington and the Royal Oak. One part of the building was named the Woodstock Arms in about 1748, a name that was extended to all parts when they were amalgamated in 1879. The appearance of the exterior dates from that time, while the interior has seen constant development to suit changing tastes, but always in keeping with the building's age and status.

- 11-11 (Sun 12-10.30)
- Bar snacks and full meals
- All the major cards
- Courtyard garden
- email: sylvia.lodge@btinternet.com
- Blenheim Palace 1 mile

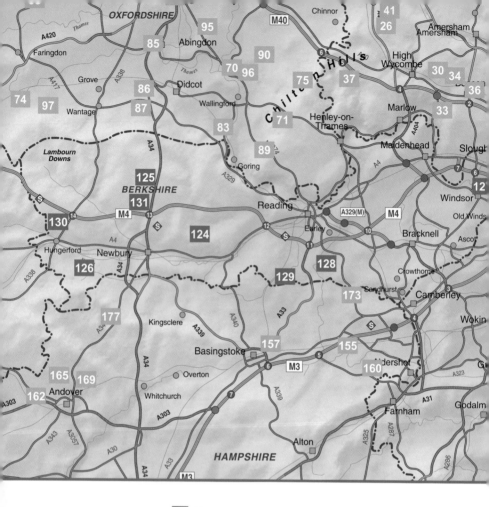

Please note all cross references refer to page numbers

BERKSHIRE

The western area of Berkshire is dominated by the old cloth town of
Newbury, which today is better known for its racecourse. The training of
racehorses is also a serious pursuit in the region, and the villages of Lambourn
and East Ilsley are famous for the horses trained on the undulating downlands
which run along the northern county border. Major communication routes -
notably the M4 - cross this region, and the ancient Ridgeway path, England's
oldest road, follows the county border with Oxfordshire. Thought to have
become a route in the Bronze Age, it has been used by generations over the
centuries as a thoroughfare for trade with the remoter parts of southwest
England. Now the **Ridgeway National Trail**, it runs from Ivinghoe Beacon in
Buckinghamshire to Avebury in Wiltshire. Completed in 1810, the Kennet
and Avon Canal crosses southern England from Bristol to join the River
Thames at Reading. Entering the county at Hungerford, this major waterway
passes through a charming rural landscape as it winds through villages and
market towns. The canal prospered
until the arrival of the Great Western
Railway in 1841, but by the 1950s it
was largely unnavigable. Fortunately,
after a full clearing and restoration
programme, the canal can once again
be travelled its full length, providing a
wide variety of leisure activities for all.

Reading dominates the central
region of Berkshire: a thriving
commuter town with excellent links
both to London and the West.
Although at first glance the town may
seem to be very much a product of the
19th and 20th centuries, there has

Kennet Horse

been a settlement here for many years; the town grew up around the Abbey, the remains of which can be seen in Forbury Gardens.

Water dominates this area of Berkshire as the two main waterways, the River Thames and the Kennet and Avon Canal, join together at Reading. The Thames, forming the northern county border with Oxfordshire, has, along its southern banks, many delightful riverside villages where boating has been a key feature for many years. The Victorian and Edwardian passion for the river led to the growth of many of the villages as fashionable places for a day trip or short holiday, and they remain pleasant places to visit today.

The eastern region of the Royal County of Berkshire is dominated by the 900-year presence of the Crown at Windsor. The building of the great castle was begun by William the Conqueror and, today, after the many additions and alterations over the centuries, it remains a magnificent sight that provides a

River Thames, Sonning

unique landmark for miles around. A major tourist attraction and still a royal residence, the Castle is just one of the many places of interest which the small town of Windsor has to offer.

Across Windsor Great Park, the remains of the royal hunting forest, lies Ascot Racecourse. Racing takes place throughout the year (though the course will be closed for extensive rebuilding after mid-2004), but for one meeting each summer this is *the* place to see and be seen, as racegoers flock from all over the world to attend the June Royal Ascot meeting.

The Thames also plays a great part in this area of Berkshire. There are numerous picturesque riverside towns and villages, several of which developed into fashionable riverside resorts during the Victorian era. Cookham, with its time-honoured Swan Upping ceremony; Maidenhead, with the massive Boulter's Lock and Brunel's famous railway bridge; and Wraysbury, where King John signed the Magna Carta to appease the rebellious barons, are all places that not only exude history but provide pleasant walks along the river's banks.

Aldermaston

It was in this tranquil village, in 1840, that the William Pear was first propagated by John Staid, the village schoolmaster. First known as the Aldermaston pear, a cutting of the plant is believed to have been taken to Australia where is it now called the Bartlett pear. Still retaining much of its original 12th-century structure and with a splendid Norman door, the lovely **St**

Aldermaston Wharf

Mary's Church provides the setting for the **York Mystery Cycle**, nativity plays dating from the 14th century which are performed here each year. Using beautiful period costumes and contemporary music, including a piece written by William Byrd, the cycle lasts a week and the plays attract visitors from far and wide.

Close to the village there is a delightful walk along the Kennet and Avon Canal to **Aldermaston Wharf**. A Grade II listed structure of beautifully restored 18th-century scalloped brickwork, the wharf is home to the **Kennet and Avon Canal Visitor Centre**, where the canalman's cottage houses an exhibition on the canal with information on its leisure facilities.

More recent history has seen the famous protest marches of the 1950s outside the Atomic Research Establishment.

Aldworth

The parish **Church of St Mary** is famous for housing the **Aldworth Giants** - the larger than life effigies of the de la Beche family which date back to the 14th century. The head of the family, Sir Philip, who lies here with eight other members of his family, was the Sheriff of Berkshire and valet to Edward II. Though now somewhat defaced, the effigies were so legendary that the church was visited by Elizabeth I. Outside, in the churchyard, are the remains of a once magnificent 1,000-year-old yew tree that was sadly damaged in a storm.

Nearby, at **Little Aldworth**, the grave of the poet Laurence Binyon, who wrote the famous lines "At the going down of the sun and in the morning, we shall remember them," can be seen in the churchyard and, opposite the Bell Inn, there is one of the deepest wells in the country. Topped by great beams, heavy cogs, and wheels, it is some 327 feet deep.

offers a wide range of habitats from open water to marsh, for the many species of plants, birds, and animals, and insects found here.

Ascot

A small village until 1711 when Queen Anne moved the Windsor race meeting to here and founded the world famous **Ascot Racecourse**. Its future secured when the Duke of Cumberland established a stud at Windsor in the 1750s, by the end of the century the meetings were being attended by Royalty on a regular basis. Today, Royal Ascot, held every June, is an international occasion of fashion and style with pageantry and tradition that is followed by racing enthusiasts from far and wide.

To the west lies **Englemere Pond**, a Site of Special Scientific Interest and also a local nature reserve. Once part of the royal hunting ground which surrounded Windsor Castle and still owned by the Crown Estate, the main feature is the shallow acidic lake which

Basildon

This small village is the last resting place of the inventor and agricultural engineer, Jethro Tull, and his grave can be seen in the churchyard. Outside the churchyard is another memorial, a classic pavilion built in memory of his parents by the late Mr Childe-Beale which is today the focal point of **Beale Park**. Covering some 300 acres of ancient water meadow, the park is home to a wide range of birds and animals. There are carefully tended small herds of unusual farm animals, including rare breeds of sheep and goats, Highland cattle, deer, and South American llama, over 120 species of birds living in their natural habitat, and a pets' corner. However, the park's work is not confined to the keeping of animals and, as well as planting a **Community Woodland**, an ancient reed bed has been restored. The park's other main attraction housed in the pavilion is the **Model Boat Collection**, which is one of the finest of its kind.

However, the village's main feature is the National Trust owned **Basildon Park**, an elegant, classical house designed in the 18th century by Carr of York. Built between 1776 and 1783 for Francis Sykes, an official of

Ascot Races

the East India Company, the house is almost text book in style, though it does have the unusual addition of an Anglo-Indian room. The interior, finished by JB Papworth and restored to its original splendour after World War II, is rich in fine plaster work, pictures and furniture, and the rooms open to the public include the Octagon Room and a decorative Shell Room. The name Basildon may be familiar to users of writing paper: the head of the papermaking firm of Dickinson visited the house, liked the name and decided to use it for his Basildon Bond paper.

Binfield

Binfield is famous as the childhood home of Alexander Pope, and to the south of the village is **Pope's Wood**, where he is said to have sought inspiration. Other connections include John Constable, who sketched the parish church while here on honeymoon, and the doughty racehorse trainer Norah Wilmot, one of the first lady trainers to hold a licence in her own right - until 1966, lady trainers were forced to train in the name of their head lads.

Bracknell

Designated a new town in 1948, Bracknell has developed quickly from a small place in poor sandy heathland into a large modern town with one of the first purpose-built shopping centres in the country, opened in the 1960s. As well as being home to a number of high tech companies, Bracknell is also the home of the Meteorological Office.

Seen from many parts of the town, and a very prominent landmark, is the centrally located **Bill Hill**. At the top of the hill can be found a circular mound of earth, hollowed out at the centre, which is all that remains of a Bronze Age round barrow. Used throughout that period, these burial mounds, which may cover either individuals or groups, are the most common prehistoric monuments in the country.

What remains of the great royal hunting ground, **Windsor Forest** (also called **Bracknell Forest**) lies to the south of the town, a vast area with over 30 parks and nature reserves and some 45 miles of footpaths and bridleways. Of particular interest in the area is The **Lookout Discovery Park**, an interactive science centre that brings to life the mysteries of science and nature. Throughout the woodland surrounding the centre there are nature trails and walks to points of interest as well as the inappropriately named **Caesar's Camp** - not a Roman fort but an Iron Age hill fort built over 2000 years ago, though close by lies the Roman link road between London and Silchester. Locally known as the **Devil's Highway**, it is said to have acquired the name as the local inhabitants, after the Romans had left, thought that only the Devil could undertake such a feat of engineering.

Combe

This isolated hamlet is overlooked by **Walbury Hill**, which, at 974 feet, is the highest point in Berkshire. A popular place with walkers, it has an Iron Age hill fort on the summit, from there are superb panoramic views. Close to the hill lies **Combe Gibbet**, one of the last public hanging places in the country. The gibbet was first used in 1676 to hang a pair of adulterous murderers and has a crossbar with a 'his' side and a 'hers' side. To the north is **Inkpen Common**, a Site of Special Scientific Interest where, along with the heath and woodland, a wet valley bog and pond have been created in an old clay pit.

Donnington Castle

Cookham

This pretty, small town, on the banks of the River Thames, was made famous by the artists Sir Stanley Spencer, who used Cookham as the setting for many of his paintings. Born here towards the end of the 19th century, the town's tribute to its most renowned resident is the **Stanley Spencer Gallery**, a permanent exhibition of his work which is housed in the converted Victorian chapel Stanley visited as a child.

Donnington

Despite being so close to the town of Newbury, Donnington has managed to retain its village identity and atmosphere. To the west of the village, and visible from the road, is **Donnington**

Grove House. Built in 1759 and designed by the architect John Chute, this was the home in the late 18th century of the Brummell family; Beau Brummell, the instigator of the Bath Society, lived here as a child.

However, most visitors to the village come to see the **Donnington Castle**, a late 14th century defence that was built by Sir Richard Abberbury. Once a magnificent structure, only the twin towered gatehouse survives amidst the impressive earthworks. Now owned by English Heritage, the castle had its most eventful period during the Civil War when it was the scene of one of the longest sieges of the conflict. Charles I's troops were held here for 20 months and this was the time when most of the castle was destroyed.

Dorney

One of the finest Tudor manor houses in England, **Dorney Court**, just a short walk from the River Thames, has been the home of the Palmer family since 1530. Built in around 1440, it is an enchanting building which houses some real treasures, including early 15th and 16th century oak furniture, beautiful 17th century lacquer furniture, and 400 years of family portraits. It is also here that the first pineapple in England was grown in 1665.

On **Dorney Common** is the traditional English village of **Boveney**, which served as a wharf in the 13th century for timber transported from Windsor Forest. The flint and clapboard church of St Mary Magdalene, down by the riverside, was the setting for several scenes from Kevin Costner's film *Robin Hood Prince of Thieves*.

East Ilsley

This attractive downland village has managed to retain several interesting features and, in particular, by the village pond can be seen the winding mechanism of the now long disused village well. However, it is on sheep that the village prospered and from the beginning of the 17th century East Ilsley

Eton College

held fortnightly sheep fairs that were second only in size to Smithfield, London. At their peak in the 19th century, permanent pens were erected in the main street to contain the animals and on one single day it was recorded that 80,000 sheep were penned.

There is an old jingle about the village which goes: "Far famed for sheep and wool, though not for spinners, for sportsmen, doctors, publicans, and sinners." Naturally, whilst the sheep fairs were flourishing, the publicans were also making good money, but after the last fair, in 1934, the number of inns fell from as many as 26 to just three.

Today, along with its neighbour, West Ilsley, the village is associated with the training of racehorses.

Eton

Just across the River Thames from Windsor, this town has grown up around **Eton College**, the public school founded in 1440 by Henry VI. Originally intended for 70 poor and worthy scholars and to educate students for the newly created King's College, Cambridge, the college has been added to greatly over the years. Of the original school buildings, only the College Hall and the kitchen have survived; the great gatehouse and Lupton's Tower were added in the 16th century and the Upper School dates from around

1690. However, the school has kept many ancient traditions over the years including the black tail coats that were originally worn on the death of George III in 1820.

For centuries the college has educated the great and the good, including 19 prime ministers, artists, poets, and authors including William Pitt the Elder, Harold Macmillan, Thomas Gray (author of *Elegy Written in a Country Churchyard*), Henry Fielding, Shelley, George Orwell, and Ian Fleming. Eton has also been famous in the past for its strict discipline, personified in 1832 by a master who told the pupils when they rebelled: "Boys, you must be pure of heart, for if not, I will thrash you until you are."

Fawley

This small downlands village is known to many avid Thomas Hardy readers as the village of Marygreen in one of his most tragic novels, *Jude the Obscure*. The writer's grandmother, Mary Hardy, is known to have lived here with her aunt for the first 13 years of her life following the death of both her parents. Though Mary never spoke of her painful memories, her sad early life was known to Hardy and they certainly coloured his view of the village. The ill-fated hero of the book, Jude Fawley, is said to have been based on Hardy himself, and when the writer visited the village to trace his relatives he wrote in his journal "I entered a ploughed field which might have been called the Valley of Brown

Melancholy, where the silence was remarkable."

Greenham

Greenham Common and the adjacent **Crookham Common** make up the largest area of lowland heathland in Berkshire. In 1941, land was taken over by the Air Ministry and became an important military base, first for British squadrons and then for the American Air Force. In 1981, nuclear-armed Cruise missiles arrive at Greenham, and with them a group of anti-nuclear protesters. The weapons and the protesters are long gone, and the site is being returned to nature. Designated a Site of Special Scientific Interest (SSSI), it is home to many rare and endangered plants and animals.

Hampstead Norreys

Just to the north of the village lies **Wyld Court Rainforest**, a fascinating conservation centre that is owned by the World Land Trust. The Trust, a charitable organisation founded in 1989, not only purchases and protects areas of tropical forests all over the world but also concerns itself with education. Here, at the indoor rainforest, visitors have the opportunity to walk through the humid and shadowy jungles of the Lowland Tropical Forests, the cool, orchid-festooned and ferny Cloudforests, and the Amazon with its amazing flowers and wonderful bromeliads. There is also a unique collection of spectacular and

Kennet and Avon Canal, Hungerford

rare plants, along with tranquil pools, the sounds of the tropics, and rainforest animals including marmosets, tree frogs, iguanas and dwarf crocodiles.

Hungerford

Although not mentioned in the Domesday Book, by the Middle Ages this old market town was well established, and the manor of Hungerford had some distinguished lords including Simon de Montford and John of Gaunt. A quiet and peaceful place, Hungerford's heyday came in the 18th century when the turnpike road from London to Bath, which passes through the town, was built. By 1840, the town had eight coaching inns serving the needs of travellers, and the prosperity continued with the opening of the **Kennet and Avon Canal** but the building of the railway took much of the trade away and the town reverted back, once more, to its early, gentle lifestyle. However, several of the old coaching inns have survived

and, in particular, The Bear Hotel. Although it has an impressive Georgian frontage, the building actually dates back to 1494, making it one of the oldest in the town. It was here in 1688 that a meeting took place between William of Orange and representatives of James II which culminated in the end of the House of Stuart and the flight of James II to France.

As well as still holding a weekly market, the town also continues the ancient tradition known as the Hocktide Festival or Tutti Day (tutti meaning a bunch of flowers). Held every year on the second Tuesday after Easter, the festival was originally used as a means of collecting an early form of council tax. During the colourful event, two men carrying a six foot pole decorated with ribbons and flowers go around each household collecting the tax. To ease the burden of their visit, the men share a drink with the man of the house, give him an orange, and kiss his wife before collecting their penny payment. Today, however, though the visits are made no money is collected.

Hurst

This attractive, scattered village is home to a Norman church, well endowed with monuments, and a row of 17th century almshouses.

Just to the south lies **Dinton Pastures**

Country Park, a large area of lakes, rivers, hedgerows, and meadows rich in wildlife. Until the 1970s, this area was excavated for sand and gravel, but the former pits are now attractive lakes and ponds: one of which has been stocked for coarse fishing and the largest is set aside for canoeing and windsurfing.

Lambourn

Lying up on the Berkshire Downs, in the extreme west of the county, this village, which has the feel of a small town, is a well known centre for the training of racehorses.

Apart for the horses, Lambourn has plenty to amuse and occupy the visitor. Its medieval **Church of St Michael** is one of the finest parish churches in Berkshire. Originally Norman, and constructed on the cruciform plan, over the years the church has been greatly altered and extended, though the west end still has its Norman doorway, complete with zigzag ornamentation. Close to the church can be found the pleasing **Isbury Almshouses**, built around a quadrangle, founded in 1502 though the present houses date from 1852.

The **Lambourn Trainers' Association** organise guided tours of the village's famous stables and also the trips up to the gallops to view the horses going through their paces.

To the north of the village are **Lambourn Seven Barrows**, one of the most impressive Bronze Age burial sites in the country. However, the name is

somewhat misleading as there are no fewer than 32 barrows up here but arguably the best group consists of six bowl barrows, two double bowl barrows, two saucer barrows, and a single disc barrow.

Maidenhead

Transport has long played an important role in the development of Maidenhead, first with the traffic on the Thames, then as a stop on the London to Bath coaching route, and finally with the coming of the railway. The **Maidenhead Rail Bridge** was built by Isambard Kingdom Brunel in 1839 to carry his Great Western Railway over the Thames. The bridge, which comprises the widest, flattest brick arches in the world, was hailed at the time as the pinnacle of engineering achievement and has been immortalised in Turner's painting *Rain, Steam and Speed*.

Newbury

This crossroads town has, for many years, dominated the rural area of West Berkshire. Prospering during the Middle Ages, and afterwards, on the importance of the woollen industry, the town became famous as **The Cloth Town**. Among the various characters who made their money out of the weaving of the wool the best known is Jack o' Newbury (John Smallwood or Winchcombe), who died in 1519. Asked to raise two horsemen and two footmen for Henry VIII's campaign against the Scots, Jack

The Kennet, Newbury

nave. Unfortunately, the church has seen much restoration work, particularly during the Victorian age, but the fine pupil and elaborately decorated nave roof have survived.

During the Civil War there were two battles fought nearby, in 1643 and 1644, and following the war, the town's clothing industry declined. However, the 18th century saw the construction of turnpike roads and Newbury became a busy coaching stop on the road from London to Bath. The town further opened up to travellers and the needs of carriers with the completion of the **Kennet and Avon Canal** in 1810. **Newbury Lock**, built in 1796, was the first lock to be built along the canal and it is also the only one to have lever-operated ground paddles (the sluices that let in the water) which are known as 'Jack Cloughs'.

Back in the centre of the town, in the Market Square is the **Newbury Museum**, housed in the 17th-century cloth hall and the adjacent 18th-century granary, a store used by traders travelling the canal. As well as the archaeological section, the history of the town is fully explained, including the two Civil War battles.

Just to the north of the town lies **Shaw House**, a splendid example of Elizabethan architecture and one of the finest in Berkshire. It was built in 1581

raised 50 of each and led them himself. However, they only got as far as Stony Stratford in Buckinghamshire before news of the victory of Flodden reached them and they turned for home. In fact, Jack o' Newbury was rather more than just a local merchant and his life story has become a local legend. He was apprenticed to a rich Newbury clothmaker, and when his master died, Jack married the widow; upon her death, he inherited the wealthy business. Over the years he became one of the town's leading merchants employing as many as a thousand people. After displaying his loyalty to the king, Jack was offered a knighthood which he turned down on the grounds that he wanted to remain equal with his workers.

Evidence of the town's wealth can be seen in the splendid 'Wool' **Church of St Nicholas** which was constructed between 1500 and 1532. Built on the site of a Norman church, no expense was spared and Jack of Newbury gave the money for the magnificent five bayed by a wealthy clothing merchant, Thomas Dolman, who chose to put his money into this elaborate house rather than his business, much to the displeasure of his workers.

To the south lies the Victorian **Falkland Memorial**, dedicated to Lord Falkland who was killed at the first battle of Newbury in 1643. To the east of the town, alongside the railway line, **Newbury Racecourse** stages both flat and National Hunt racing.

Pangbourne

Situated at the confluence of the River Pang and the River Thames, the town grew up in the late 19th and early 20th centuries as a fashionable place to live. As a result there are several attractive Victorian and Edwardian villas to be seen including a row of ornate Victorian houses known as the Seven Deadly Sins. It was to here that the author Kenneth Graham retired, living at **Church Cottage** beside the church. Graham married late in life and it was while living here that he wrote *The Wind in the Willows*, based on the original bedtime stories that he invented for his son; they were set along the banks of the river between Pangbourne and Marlow.

An elegant iron bridge links the town with **Whitchurch**. It was at **Whitchurch Lock** that

the characters in Jerome K Jerome's *Three Men in a Boat* abandoned their craft, after a series of mishaps, and returned to London.

Reading

This thriving commuter town is a delightful combination of over a thousand years of history and a vibrant and modern city. There are Victorian brick buildings nestling beside beautiful medieval churches, famous coaching inns opposite high tech offices and some of the best shopping in the area. However, Reading began as a Saxon settlement between the Rivers Thames and Kennet. A defensible site, it was used by the Danes as a base for their attack on Wessex in the 9th century.

The town grew up around its **Abbey**, which was founded in 1121 by Henry I, the youngest son of William the Conqueror, and it was consecrated by Thomas à Becket in 1164. The abbey went on to become one of the most

Pangbourne

important religious houses - its relics include a piece of Jesus' shoe, the tooth of St Luke, and a slice of Moses' rod - and parliament was known to meet here on occasions. As Henry I is also buried here, Reading is one of only a handful of towns where Kings of England have been laid to rest. Today, the abbey ruins can be found in **Forbury Gardens** on the banks of the River Kennet. Fortunately, some of the abbey's wonderful architecture can still be seen, in particular St Laurence's Church and the abbey Gatehouse. The Gatehouse was, after the Reformation, turned into a school and, in 1785, Jane Austen was a pupil here. The gardens are also home to the **Maiwand Lion**, which commemorates the men of the Berkshire Regiment who died in the Afghan Campaign of 1879.

Another originally Norman building in the town is **St Mary's Church**, the south arcade of which dates from around 1200. The most attractive feature here is the church tower: erected in 1550 it has a highly distinctive chequerboard pattern which uses stone blocks and flint panels.

Adjacent to the abbey ruins is another of Reading's famous buildings - **Reading Prison**. Hardly a tourist attraction, it

was here that Oscar Wilde was imprisoned and where he wrote *De Profundis*. His confinement here also inspired the writer to compose the epic *Ballad of Reading Gaol* whilst staying in Paris in 1898.

Though the town developed during the Middle Ages as a result of a flourishing woollen industry, it was during the 18th century with the coming of both the turnpike roads and the opening of the **Kennet and Avon Canal** which saw the town boom. By the 19th century, Reading was known for its three Bs: beer, bulbs, and biscuits. As the trade of the canal and River Thames increased, the movement of corn and malt explains the growth of the brewing trade here whilst bulbs is a reference to Sutton Seeds who were founded here in 1806. The world renowned biscuit-making firm of Huntley and Palmer began life here in 1826, when Joseph Huntley founded the firm, to be joined, in 1841, by George Palmer, inventor of

Blake's Lock Museum

the stamping machine.

The Story of Reading, a permanent exhibition at the **Reading Museum**, is the ideal place to gain a full understanding of the history of the town, from the earliest times to the present day. Here, too, can be seen the world's only full size replica of the Bayeux Tapestry, made in the 19th century and which features Edward the Confessor, once Lord of the Royal Manor in Reading, as a central figure. As a contrast to the museum's displays depicting the life of the town in the 20th century, The Silchester Gallery is devoted to the describing day to day life at Calleva Atrebatum, the Roman town of Silchester, using Roman artefacts unearthed there during early excavations.

Situated on the banks of the River Kennet and housed in a range of canal buildings, **Blake's Lock Museum** describes the life of the town in the 19th and early 20th centuries. Originally part of a pumping station built at Blake's Weir in the 1870s, the buildings themselves are also of interest and are superb examples of Victorian industrial architecture combined with decorative Reading brickwork. As well as covering the town's close links with its waterways and the part they played in Reading's prosperity, visitors can wander around the reconstructed shops and workshops.

Lying to the south of the town centre, the university campus is home to the **Museum of English Rural Life**, where not only is there a splendid wagon collection but also displays covering farm tools, machinery, and equipment, as well as rural crafts.

Sandhurst

The town is famous as being the home of the **Royal Military Academy**, the training place for army officers since it was established in 1907. The academy's **Staff College Museum** tells the history of officer training from its inception to the present day. Long before the academy was founded, in Saxon times, this settlement, in the valley of the River Blackwater, was part of the Parish of Sonning. Although there are no written records of a church having been here, in 1220, William de Wanda, Dean of Salisbury, visited a new and beautiful chapel at Sandhurst. The present Church of St Michael and All Angels, situated high above the River Blackwater, was built in 1853 to the design of GE Street. However, it takes several old features from the previous church, including the Norman-style doorway and an old beam supporting the wooden roof that is inscribed to Charles I and dated 1647.

Close by is **Trilakes**, a picturesque country park set in 18 acres.

Sonning

A pretty little village leading down to the Thames, very popular for summer outings. On Grove Street stands **Turpin's**, a house that belonged to Dick Turpin's aunt and provided the highwayman with occasional refuge. Behind the wall of the old bishop's palace is Deanery Gardens, a house built in 1901 to a design of Sir Edwin Lutyens.

Swallowfield

This ancient settlement has been inhabited since prehistoric times and, by 1071, the manor was held by Roger de Breteuil, the originator of the Domesday Survey. Since then, the manor house, **Swallowfield Park**, has been associated with both royalty and notable personalities. The present house (unfortunately now all but a shell) was built in 1678 by Wren's assistant William Talman, for the 2nd Earl of Clarendon who acquired the estate upon marrying the heiress. In 1719, the park was purchased by Thomas Pitt, a former Governor of Madras, who used the proceeds of the sale of a large diamond he bought in India. The diamond can now be seen in the Louvre in Paris, and Pitt's story was the basis of the novel, *The Moonstone*, by Wilkie Collins, who visited the house in 1860. The Italian Doorway, by Talman, is probably the house's most outstanding remaining feature, marking the entrance to the walled garden containing a dogs' graveyard.

Thatcham

Believed to be the oldest village in Britain, it is hard to imagine that this now large suburb of Newbury was once a small place. **Thatcham Moor** is one of

the largest areas of inland freshwater reed beds in the country and, as well as the reeds which can grow up to six feet in height, the area supports numerous species of marshland and aquatic plants. Birds also abound here - it is an important breeding ground for reed and sedge warblers.

Wargrave

This charming village developed as a settlement in the 10th century at the confluence of the Rivers Thames and Loddon on an area of flat land in a wooded valley. Mentioned in the Domesday Book, when it was referred to as Weregrave, in 1218, the Bishop of Winchester was granted the rights to hold a market here by Henry III. However, this was obviously not a great success as there is no record of a market taking place after the 13th century.

Now an attractive riverside village, the peace was disturbed here in 1914 when suffragettes burnt down the church in protest at the vicar's refusal to remove the word 'obey' from the marriage service. In the churchyard however, undisturbed by the riot, lies the **Hannen Mausoleum**, a splendid monument that was designed for the family by Sir Edwin Lutyens in 1906.

Another interesting sight here can be found on the outskirts of the village, at Park Place. In 1788, the estate was owned by General Henry Conway, Governor of Jersey and, in recognition of his services, the people of the island gave the general a complete **Druids' Temple**.

The massive stones were transported from St Helier to the estate and erected in a 25 foot circle in the gardens of his mansion. In 1870, Park Place was destroyed by fire and the estate broken up but today the temple stands in the garden of **Temple Combe**, close to a house designed by the American architect Frank Lloyd Wright. The only house of his in this country, it was built in 1958 on an elaborate U-shaped design and has suede panelled walls inside.

Windsor

This old town grew up beneath the walls of the Castle in a compact group of streets leading from the main entrance. Charming and full of character, this is a place of delightful timber-framed and Georgian houses and shop fronts, with riverside walks beside the Thames, and a wonderful racecourse. The elegant **Guildhall**, partly built by Wren in the 17th century, has an open ground floor for market stalls, with the council

chambers on the first floor.

The grand central station, in the heart of the town, was built in 1897 to commemorate Queen Victoria's Diamond Jubilee and it is now home to a fascinating exhibition, **Royalty and Empire**, which charts the life and times of the country's longest reigning monarch. Close by, in the High Street, is another exhibition well worth visiting, the **Town and Crown Exhibition**.

A trip to the **Dungeons of Windsor** provides a step back in time and an investigation of the town's history with a special regard for stories of crime and punishment from the early days of 13th-century lawlessness through to the harsh Victorian era. The Household Cavalry have their home in Windsor, at Combermere Barracks, where the superb **Household Cavalry Museum** displays collections of their uniforms, weapons, and armour from 1600 through to the present day.

In a perfect setting beside the River Thames, **Royal Windsor Racecourse** is one of the most attractive in the country. Though much less grand than neighbouring Ascot, the Monday summer evening meetings are particularly enjoyable.

However, it is **Windsor Castle**, situated on Castle Hill, which draws thousands of tourists annually to

Windsor Castle

this small town. The largest castle in the country and a royal residence for over 900 years, the castle was begun in the late 11th century by William the Conqueror as one in a chain of such defences which stood on the approaches to London. Over the years various monarchs have added to the original typical Norman castle , the most notable additions being made by Henry VIII, Charles II, and George IV.

Various aspects of the castle are open to the public, in particular the sixteen state apartments which hold a remarkable collection of furniture, porcelain, and armour. Carvings by Grinling Gibbons are to be seen everywhere and the walls are adorned with a plethora of masterpieces, including paintings by Van Dyck and Rembrandt. On a somewhat smaller scale, but nonetheless impressive, is **Queen Mary's Dolls' House** Designed by Sir Edwin Lutyens for Queen Mary, this is a perfect miniature palace, complete with working lifts and lights and also running water. Taking over three years to build, 1500 tradesmen were employed to ensure that every last detail was correct and the house was presented to the queen in 1924. In November 1992, a massive fire swept through the northeast corner of the castle and no-one in the country at the time will forget the

incredible pictures of the great tower alight. After much restoration, the affected rooms, including the massive St George's Hall, the scene of many state banquets, have all been completed and are once again open to the public.

Windsor Castle is not just a defensive structure but it was also an ecclesiastical centre and, within its walls, is the magnificent **St George's Chapel** Started by Edward IV in 1478, and taking some 50 years to finish, the chapel is not only one of the country's greatest religious buildings but also a wonderful example of the Perpendicular Gothic style. It is the last resting place of ten monarchs, from Edward IV himself to Henry VIII with his favourite wife Jane Seymour, Charles I, George V with Queen Mary, and George VI, beside whom the ashes of his beloved daughter Princess Margaret were laid in February 2001. It is also the Chapel of the Most Noble Order of the Garter, Britain's highest order of chivalry.

Frogmore House, a modest manor

Legoland Windsor

house from the early 18th century, stands in Home Park, and over the years it has acted as a second, more relaxed royal residence than nearby Windsor Castle. During Queen Victoria's reign it was the home of her mother, the Duchess of Kent and now, famously, it is also home to the magnificent **Royal Mausoleum** dedicated to Prince Albert and also where Queen Victoria herself is buried beside her husband.

To the south of the town lies **Windsor Great Park**, a remnant of the once extensive Royal Hunting Forest, and a unique area of open parkland, woodland, and impressive views. The **Long Walk** stretches from the castle to Snow Hill, some three miles away, on top of which stands a huge bronze of George III on horseback put there in 1831. Queen Anne added the three mile ride to nearby Ascot race course. On the park's southern side lies **Smith's Lawn**, where polo matches are played most summer weekends. Windsor Great Park is also the setting for the Cartier International competition, polo's highlight event held every July, and the National Driving Championships.

First laid in 1931, **The Savill Garden**, created by Sir Eric Savill, is one of the best and finest woodland gardens to be seen anywhere. A garden for all seasons, there are colourful flower gardens, secret glades, and alpine meadows.

Finally, to the southwest and in 150 acres of parkland, is **Legoland Windsor**, where there are a whole range of amazing lego models on display which have been made from over 20 million bricks, together with educational and fun rides and amusements for all ages.

Winterbourne

Just south of the village lies **Snelsmore Common Country Park**, one of the most important natural history sites in the county. The common comprises several different habitats, including woodland, heathland and bog, and it supports a correspondingly wide variety of plant and animal life.

THE BLADEBONE INN

CHAPEL ROW, BUCKLEBURY, BERKSHIRE RG7 6PD
TEL/FAX: 0118 971 2326

Directions: From the A4 at Thatcham take the minor road to Upper Bucklebury and Bucklebury.

The Bladebone Inn takes its name from a prehistoric mammoth bone that was unearthed nearby and is now the pub sign. The inn is a handsome period building in a picturesque setting, and behind the redbrick frontage the bars and dining area feature beams, brick hearths and bar counter and a variety of furniture, including wicker chairs, sofas and classic upright dining chairs. This is a pub restaurant with an ever growing clientele, who come here to socialise and to enjoy the excellent food and drink. The inn is owned and run by Jean Claude and Tracey Rawady; Jean Claude is Lebanese by birth and a chef by training, and the house speciality of Lebanese mezze is becoming the talking point among the region's foodies.

Mezze comprise many dishes brought to the table at the same time to be shared by the party: starters and dips, the classics of Lebanese cuisine, include pickles and olives; hommos (chick pea paste), baba ghanouj made with aubergines and sesame seeds; tabbouleh, based on crushed wheat; patties filled with minced lamb or spinach, and marinated chicken wings; then comes the substantial mixed grill of succulent chicken and lamb, with Lebanese coffee and baklava to finish. The excellent Chateau Musar red wine is the perfect accompaniment to this healthy, wholesome cuisine. The menu also ranges far and wide elsewhere, with dishes ranging from garlic prawns and moules marinière to Cajun chicken, Thai-style duck breast and penne pasta. Flying the British flag are the real ales, usually London Pride and a guest ale from the West Berkshire Brewery.

- Lunchtime and evening (closed Sun eve and all Mon except for private functions)
- A la carte lunch and dinner including Lebanese specialities
- £ Not Amex or Diners
- Gardens, adjacent car park
- @ email: jeanclaude2@btinternet.com
- ? Thatcham 3 miles, Aldermaston 3 miles

THE COACH & HORSES

WORLDS END, BEEDON, NR NEWBURY, BERKSHIRE RG20 8SD
TEL/FAX: 01635 248743

Directions: From the M4 (J13) take the A34 for 2½ miles.

Originally a private residence, this handsome old stone cream-painted stone building is now a very pleasant country inn to pause for refreshment on a journey, to seek out for a meal or to stay overnight while travelling or touring the area. The licensee of **The Coach & Horses**, Adrian Pearce, is a countryman at heart, and a lover of country pursuits, which means that the likes of partridge and pheasant make seasonal appearances on the regularly changing bar menus. The two bars – lounge and public – provide a choice in which to enjoy a glass of well-kept real ale (three and a guest are always on tap), and the separate dining area is non-smoking. The inn fields a darts team in the local league, and the quiz nights are very popular occasions.

As well as serving lunch and dinner, the Coach & Horses is also open for morning coffee. It has plenty of parking space and a garden with a section where children can play in safety. The area around Beedon is excellent walking and sporting country, and there are many pleasant little villages to explore. Among the nearest are East and West Ilsley, well-known centres for the training of racehorses. The A34 offers easy access north and south, and the M4 is only a few minutes away by car. This makes the inn a very pleasant and convenient base, and a comfortable night's rest is assured in the two bedrooms, which have TVs, tea trays and a shared bathroom facility.

- 🕐 12-3 & 6-11
- 🍴 Bar and Restaurant meals
- 💷 All the major cards
- 🛏 2 rooms with shared facilities
- 🅿 Car park, garden, play area
- 🎵 Darts, quiz nights
- ❓ Walking, golf; East Ilsley 3 miles

THE CROWN & GARTER

Berkshire

GREAT COMMON, INKPEN, NR HUNGERFORD, BERKSHIRE RG17 9QR
TEL: 01488 668325

> **Directions:** From the A4 2 miles east of Hungerford, or the A338 on the southern edge of Hungerford, take minor road signposted Inkpen.

The Crown & Garter is a fine redbrick country inn with a history of hospitality that dates back more than 300 years – an early visitor was King James I, who dropped in on his way to visit his mistress, who lived nearby. The inn is run very professionally by Gill Hern, her father James and her son Matthew, who have made this one of the very best places in the area for a drink, a meal or an overnight or extended stay. It is also a most sociable inn, with quiz nights, charity nights, ladies nights and other events making almost every night a special night. Three real ales from the West Berkshire Brewery head the list of liquid refreshment, and there are some interesting and unusual bottle beers, but

it's the food that sets this inn apart.

Choosing from the wide and varied menu is a pleasant problem, but everything on the plate is as good as it reads, from a chargrilled chicken club sandwich, wild mushroom risotto, Szechuan prawn salad, confit of duck and leek terrine to braised lamb's kidneys, cod and pancetta fishcakes and honey-roasted pork with fondant potato, baked onion and a whisky sauce. One section of the menu is devoted to Thai curries, based on chicken, prawn or beef and ranging from mild to very hot. The delicious problem continues to the end, when the choice might include lemon posset with shortbread or pear crumble with cinnamon custard. This is not just a great place for a meal, it's a perfect base for exploring the area, and the eight bedrooms in a modern purpose-built extension, all with en suite bath and power shower, open on to a lovely private garden; one room is adapted for disabled guests.

- 🕐 Lunchtime and evening
- 🍴 Wide variety of food served; special food night Thursday
- £ All the major cards
- 🛏 8 en suite rooms
- Ⓟ Car park, garden, patio
- 🎵 Quiz nights, charity nights; ladies nights Mon-Wed
- @ email: gill.hern@btopenworld.com website: www.crownandgarter.com
- ❓ Kennet & Avon Canal short walk, Kintbury 2 miles, Hungerford 4 miles, Newbury 6 miles

ARTHUR ROAD, WINDSOR, BERKSHIRE SL14 1RZ
TEL: 01753 840748

Directions: On a corner site in the town of Windsor.

Proudly occupying a prominent corner site in the centre of town, **The Duke of Connaught** is equally popular with the local community and with the tourists who come to Windsor in their thousands throughout the year. Inside, owners Jan and Mel Collinge have created a very spacious and comfortable ambience in which to relax with a glass or two of the excellent Greene King ales or to enjoy something from the bar menu, which is available lunchtime and evening Monday to Friday, from 12.30 to 5 on Saturday and from 1 o'clock to 4 on Sunday. Filled baguettes make satisfying snacks, while main meals run from traditional bangers & mash, breaded haddock or steak & kidney pudding to

three-cheese and broccoli pasta bake, chilli con carne or chicken tikka masala. Sunday roasts always have a loyal following, and all the meats and sausages on the menu are supplied by Salways of Windsor.

Parking is available a short walk away, and many of the area's leading visitor attractions are very close by. Closest of all is Windsor Castle, while also easily reached are Thorpe Park, Legoland Windsor - where the Lego models were built with over 20 million bricks. This is an excellent area for walking, either in Windsor Great Park or along the banks of the Thames. To enjoy all these amenities at leisure The Duke of Connaught is an ideal place to choose as a base. It has four recently refurbished guest bedrooms - 3 en suite doubles and a single with its own private bathroom.

- ⏰ 11-11
- 🍴 Home cooking, Sunday roasts
- £ All the major cards
- 🛏 4 bedrooms (3 en suite)
- Ⓟ Free on street parking, courtyard garden.
- ♪ Darts, live music evenings
- @ website: www.dukeofconnaught.fsnet.co.uk
- ❓ Windsor Castle ½ mile, river and country walks nearby, Legoland 2 miles, Thorpe Park 2 miles

THE FOX & HOUNDS

CHURCH ROAD, FARLEY HILL, NR READING, BERKSHIRE RG7 1UB
TEL: 0118 973 3266

Berkshire

> **Directions:** The inn lies 4 miles south of Reading off the A327

The **Fox & Hounds** is a substantial and attractive inn located a short drive south of Reading just off the A327. Hanging baskets and flower troughs adorn the well-maintained black-and-white exterior, and there's a lovely traditional look to the bars, with beams, flagstones, small-paned windows and an open log fire that never goes out. With Amanda Hawkins in the kitchen and partner David behind the bar, no one ever goes hungry or thirsty at this delightful country inn. Amanda's honest home-cooked food caters a wide range of tastes and appetites: plain or toasted sandwiches served with a salad garnish and potato salad make satisfying quick meals, while those with more time could tuck into a tasty daily special such as steak & mushroom pie (made with locally reared beef and Farley Hill mushrooms), chicken à la King, steak

served with all the trimmings or a vegetarian dish of green peppers stuffed with rice, vegetables and pine nuts. Three real ales are on tap to quench thirsts, and there's a good selection of wines and other drinks.

The excellent food and hospitality make the 40-cover function room a popular choice for corporate events, weddings, birthdays or other special occasions. The Fox & Hounds has ample off-road parking, and at the rear is a garden that has magnificent views down a deep valley and across 3 counties. There are picnic tables and plenty of room for children to romp. The open spaces around the inn provide excellent walking, and places of interest in the vicinity include the village of Arborfield, home base of REME and site of their museum, nearby California Country Park and the charming grounds of Swallowfield Park. And it's just a short drive to Reading with its churches, museums and excellent shopping.

- 🕐 12-2.30 (Sat to 3) & 5-11; all day Sunday
- 🍴 Home-cooked snacks and meals
- 💷 All the major cards
- 🅿 Off-road parking, garden, function room
- @ email: fox-and-hounds@btconect.com
- ❓ Walking, cycling, golf; Reading 4 miles

THE NEW INN

FAIR OAK LANE, STRATFIELD SAYE, NR READING,
BERKSHIRE RG7 2EH
TEL: 0118 9332 255 FAX: 0118 9333 814

Directions: Turn off the A33 at the Wellington Hotel (right from Reading, left from Basingstoke). The inn is just over ½ a mile on, signposted on the left.

The New Inn is a very fine redbrick building a short distance from the main A33 about halfway between Basingstoke and Reading and equally convenient for both. The inn, whose sign is a painting of the building itself, was taken over at the end of 2003 by Neil and Rose Lyons, a couple of many interests Neil was formerly a lecturer and Rose a hairdresser. Inside are several intimate bar areas with lots of snug corners and a particularly welcoming ambience – just right for relaxing with a glass of one of the real ales available. Each section has its own appeal, some with simple country furniture, one with comfortably upholstered church pews and chairs; flowers and plants are arranged to very pleasing effect, and pictures and prints of days gone by add extra interest.

But what really takes the eye is a vast blackboard covered with the day's dishes…. and there are dozens of them, some familiar pub classics, others more unusual: pork ribs, jumbo cod in batter, pepper steak & brie baguette, lamb & mint pie or vegetables with a sweet & sour dip. The inn has ample car parking space and a large garden with lots of picnic tables and a children's play area with swings and slides. A 'must-see' attraction along the road is Stratfield Saye House, one of many rewards bestowed by a grateful nation on the Duke of Wellington after his defeat of Napoleon at Waterloo. This grand house is filled with fine paintings and furniture and many of the Duke's personal belongings.

- 🕐 12-11
- 🍴 Home cooking; Sunday roast; summer barbecues
- 💷 All the major cards
- 🅿 Car park, garden
- 🎵 Pool competitions, quiz nights, karaoke sessions
- @ e-mail: rose@lyons2251fsnet.co.uk website: www.thenewinn-stratfieldsaye.co.uk
- ❓ Walking, cycling, golf; Silchester Roman site 5 miles

TALLY HO

HUNGERFORD NEWTOWN, BERKSHIRE RG17 0PP
TEL/FAX: 01488 682312

Directions: From J14 of the M4 take the A338 towards Hungerford. Hungerford Newtown is about a mile along this road.

Easily found on the A338 between the M4 (J14) and Hungerford, the **Tally Ho Inn** is a handsome and substantial redbrick building with a very warm and friendly licensee in Ann Stroud. Flower baskets make a pretty scene in spring and summer, and inside is spick and span after recent refurbishment by the owning brewery. The large open-plan bar area, with its beamed oak ceiling, open fire, comfortable seats and well-chosen pictures, is a delightful place to relax with a pint of one of the three real ales always on tap.

The food is a great attraction at this fine old inn, with Ann at the helm in the kitchen and her family and staff providing excellent personal service. Ann sources as many of her raw materials as possible from local producers and suppliers, and the blackboard menus offer a particularly wide choice of wholesome, appetising dishes. Her pies and the puddings (steak & kidney, bacon & onion, chicken and leek) are always among the most popular orders, and other choices range from curries and steaks to seafood casserole, a classic trout with almonds and several vegetarian main courses. Very much at the heart of village life, the Tally Ho provides regular entertainment with live music evenings and monthly quiz nights, and once a year it stages a rounders match. The ancient market town of Hungerford is literally just down the road, and the nearby M4 provides quick and easy access to points east and west.

- 🕐 12-3 & 6-11.30 weekdays, 12-4 & 6-11.30 weekends
- 🍴 Home cooking, meals served 12.2.30 & 7-9 everyday
- £ All the major cards
- Ⓟ Car park
- 🎵 Monthly quiz, music evenings, annual rounders match
- @ email: duvalstroud@aol.com
- ❓ Walking, golf; shopping in Hungerford 2 mls, Newbury 10 mls

YE OLDE RED LION

GREEN LANE, CHIEVELEY, NEWBURY, BERKSHIRE RG20 8XB
TEL: 01635 248379

Directions: From the M4, Exit 13, take the A34 north towards Oxford and after 500 yards turn left to Chieveley. As you enter the village, Ye Olde Red Lion is on the left.

With its cream-painted walls, latticed windows and attractive front patio, **Ye Olde Red Lion** has a very inviting appearance. It was built in the 1700s as a coaching inn and the old beams, brasses and many collectables scattered around the walls evoke a more leisurely age. Just moments from the M4 and the A34, Chieveley is a pleasant little village set on the edge of the Berkshire Downs. The Royal County of Berkshire Agricultural Showground is just a couple of miles away and the prosperous town of Newbury with its racecourse and extensive shopping opportunities lies a few miles to the south.

Your host at Ye Olde Red Lion is Paul Clarke who took over here in 2002 and has quickly established a reputation for providing excellent cuisine, fine ales and wines, and a warm welcome. He offers a surprisingly extensive menu, with lots of variety. You'll always find a good old traditional home made pie, but also Steak Fajitas, served with Tortilla Pancakes, along with succulent steaks that range from an 8oz Rump, Sirloin or Fillet to amighty 16oz Rump or T-Bone. Amongst the poultry dishes there's a Chicken Envortino (breast of chicken stuffed with asparagas and Parma ham), or, if you enjoy spicy dishes, you should definitely try one of the home made Madras curries. In addition ther are delicious seafood or pasta dishes as well as vegetarian options.

- ⏲ Mon-Sat 11.00-15.00, 18.00-23.00; Sun 12.00-15.00, 19.00-22.30
- 🍽 Restaurant and bar meals
- 💷 All major credit and debit cards
- 🅿 Two large car parks
- 🎵 Darts, pool, occasional live entertainment
- @ email: paul-redlion@tiscali.co.uk
- ❓ Newbury town and racecourse 4 miles, good walking country.

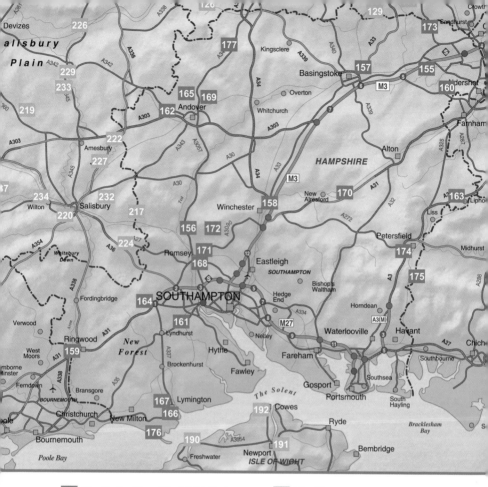

155	The Barley Mow, Winchfield, Hook	166	The Kings Arms, Lymington
156	The Bear & Ragged Staff, Michelmersh, Romsey	167	The Kings Head, Lymington
		168	The Luzborough House, Romsey
157	The Crown, Old Basing	169	The Oak, Smannell, Andover
158	The Eclipse Inn, Winchester	170	The Ship Inn, Bishops Sutton, Alresford
159	The Fish Inn, Ringwood	171	The Star Inn, Romsey
160	The Foresters, Church crookham, Fleet	172	The Wheatsheaf at Braishfield, Braishfield, Romsey
161	The Forest Inn, Ashurst		
162	The George Inn, Thruxton, Andover	173	The White Hart, Eversley
163	The Green Dragon, Liphook	174	The White Hart, Petersfield
164	The Green Dragon at Brook, Brook, Lyndhurst	175	The White Hart, South Harting, Petersfield
		176	The White Horse, Milford-on-Sea
165	The Hare & Hounds, Charlton Down, Andover	177	The Yew Tree, Highclere, Newbury

Please note all cross references refer to page numbers

HAMPSHIRE

North Hampshire is quite heavily populated, dotted with prosperous, sprawling towns such as Aldershot and Basingstoke. What is surprising is that, once you turn off the busy main roads, you can find yourself driving along narrow country lanes where, if you meet an approaching vehicle, a diploma in Advanced Driving Skills could be very helpful.

This area forms part of the North Downs. Honouring the perverse tradition of English place-names, the Downs are actually uplands, softly-rolling, wooded hills in whose folds lie scores of picturesque villages. As the crow flies, central London is little more than 30 miles away; for many of the northeastern Hampshire villages, even today, the metropolis might just as well be 300 miles distant.

There are few grand houses in the area, though The Vyne near Basingstoke and the Duke of Wellington's home, Stratfield Saye House, are both very imposing. Two smaller dwellings also attract visitors in their thousands to this corner of the county: Jane Austen's House at Chawton, near Alton, and a few miles to the south in the village of Selborne, The Wakes, home of the celebrated naturalist, Gilbert White. Lovers of steam railways can combine a visit to these two houses with a ride on the Watercress Line, which runs between Alton and Alresford.

Some of Hampshire's grandest

Fishing on the River Test

scenery lies in the northwestern part of the county as the North Downs roll westwards towards Salisbury Plain. There's just one sizeable town, Andover, and one major city, Winchester: the rest of the region is quite sparsely populated (for southern England) with scattered villages bearing evocative names such as Nether Wallop. Winchester is of course in a class of its own with its dazzling Cathedral, but there are many other attractions in this area, ranging in time from the Iron Age Danebury Ring, through the Victorian extravaganza of Highclere Castle, to Stanley Spencer's extraordinary murals in the Sandham Memorial Chapel at Burghclere.

A goodly proportion of Hampshire's 1.2 million inhabitants live along the coastal crescent that stretches from Southampton through Portsmouth to Havant. Inland, though, there are parts of the South Downs as peaceful and scenic as anywhere in the county. Southampton boasts one of the finest natural harbours in the world and has been the leading British deep-sea port since the days of the Norman Conquest. Portsmouth did not develop as a port until the 16th century but makes up for its shorter history by its romantic associations with such legendary ships as *HMS Victory*, the *Mary Rose*, and *HMS Warrior*.

Thatched Cottage, Wherwell

Portsmouth is also a popular seaside resort providing, together with its neighbour, Hayling Island, some seven miles of sandy beaches. Southsea Castle and the massive Portchester Castle have interesting historical associations, and the ruins of Netley Abbey and the Bishop's Palace at Bishop's Waltham are both outstandingly picturesque.

The New Forest

The New Forest, as is the way with English place-names, is neither New nor a Forest, although much of it is attractively wooded. The term New Forest came into use after William the Conqueror proclaimed the area a royal hunting ground, seized some 15,000 acres that Saxon farmers had laboriously reclaimed from the heathland, and began a programme of planting thousands of trees. To preserve wildlife for his sport (the deer especially), William adopted all the rigorous venery laws of his Saxon royal predecessors and added some harsh measures of his own. Anyone who killed a deer would himself be killed. If he shot at the beast and missed, his hands were cut off. And, perhaps most ruthless of all, anyone who disturbed a deer during the breeding season had his eyes put out.

There are still plenty of wild deer roaming the 145 square miles of the Forest Park, confined within its boundaries by cattle grids (known to Americans as Texas Gates). You are much more likely though to see the famous New Forest ponies, free-wandering creatures which nevertheless are all privately owned.

The largest wild area in lowland Britain, the Forest is ideal walking country with vast tracts virtually unpopulated but criss-crossed by a cat's cradle of footpaths and bridleways. The Forestry Commission has also established a network of waymarked cycle routes which make the most of the scenic attractions and are also designed to help protect the special nature of the Forest.

Aldershot

Back in 1854, Aldershot was a village of some 800 inhabitants. Then the Army decided to build a major camp here and the population has grown steadily ever since to its present tally of around 55,000. The story of how Aldershot became the home of the British Army is vividly recounted at the **Aldershot Military Museum**, which stands in the middle of the camp and is a must for anyone with an interest in military history. The last two surviving Victorian barrack blocks contain a wealth of fascinating information: for example, there's a detailed cutaway model of a cavalry barracks showing how the soldiers' rooms were placed above the stables, an economic form of central heating described as "warm, but aromatic".

It was the army at Aldershot who became the first aviators in Britain, using Farnborough Common for their flying, and building their aircraft sheds where the Royal Aircraft Establishment stands today. The **Airborne Forces Museum** has many interesting exhibits illustrating the part these pioneers played during the early days of the 20th century and during two World Wars. In memory of those who lost their lives in these conflicts, **The Heroes Shrine** in Manor Park commemorates the dead of World War I, while the nearby walled and sunken garden, shaded by a huge deodar tree, honours the fallen of World War II.

Another celebrated military figure, the Duke of Wellington, is celebrated by an imposing bronze statue on Round Hill. It originally stood in London on top of the Triumphal Arch at Hyde Park Corner and was removed to Aldershot in 1885.

Alresford

Pronounced Allsford, Alresford was created around 1200 by a Bishop of Winchester, Geoffrey de Lucy, as part of his grand plan to build a waterway from Winchester to Southampton. Where the river Arle flows into the Itchen, he constructed a huge reservoir covering 200 acres, its waters controlled to keep the Itchen navigable at all seasons. The **Bishop's Reservoir** is now reduced to some 60 acres but it's still home to countless wildfowl and many otters. Known today as Old Alresford Pond, it's one of the most charming features of this dignified Georgian town. Alresford can also boast one of the county's most beautiful streets, historic **Broad Street**, lined with elegant, colour-washed Georgian houses interspersed with specialist shops and inviting hostelries.

Alresford's most famous son was Admiral Lord Rodney, a contemporary of Lord Nelson, who built the grand Manor House near the parish church, but the town can also boast two famous daughters. One was Mary Sumner, wife of the Rector of Alresford, who founded the Mother's Union here in 1876. The other was Mary Russell Mitford, author of the fascinating collection of sketches of 18th century life, *Our Village,*

The Watercress Line

setting for a dramatic episode during the Civil War. A large force of Roundheads drove some 80 Royalists into the church where 60 of them were killed. The Royalist commander, Colonel Boles, made a last stand from the splendid Jacobean pulpit, firing repeatedly at his attackers before succumbing to their bullets. The church door and several of the Norman pillars are still pock-marked with bullet holes fired off during this close-combat conflict. More cheerful are the comical carvings on these pillars of animals and birds, among them a wolf gnawing a bone and two donkeys kicking their heels in the air.

Nearby is the old cemetery and the well-tended Grave of Fanny Adams. The expression 'Sweet Fanny Adams' arose from the revolting murder in 1867 of a young girl in the town who was hacked into pieces by her assassin. With macabre humour, sailors used the phrase 'Sweet Fanny Adams' to describe the recently-issued tinned mutton for which they had a certain mistrust. Over the years, the saying became accepted as a contemptuous description for anything considered valueless (and eventually for nothing at all). A poor memorial for an innocent girl.

There's a different sort of monument in Amery Street, a narrow lane leading off the market place. On a small brick

published in 5 volumes between 1824-1832.

One of Alresford's attractions that should not be missed is the **Watercress Line**, Hampshire's only preserved steam railway, so named because it was once used to transport watercress from the beds around Alresford to London and beyond. The line runs through 10 miles of beautiful countryside to Alton where it links up with main line services to London. Vintage steam locomotives make the 35-minute journey up to 8 times a day, and there are regular dining trains as well as frequent special events throughout the year.

Alton

Surrounded by hop-fields and some of Hampshire's loveliest countryside, Alton is an appealing market town with a history stretching back far beyond Roman times. Alton boasts a large number of old coaching inns, and the impressive, partly-Norman **St Lawrence's Church**, which was the house is a plaque commemorating the Elizabethan poet Edmund Spenser who came to Alton around 1590 to enjoy its "sweet delicate air".

Well worth a visit while you are in Alton is the **Allen Gallery** in Church Street, home to an outstanding collection of English, Continental and Far Eastern pottery, porcelain and tiles. The Gallery's other attractions include the unique Elizabethan Tichborne Spoons, delightful watercolours and oil paintings by local artist William Herbert Allen and a comfortable Coffee Lounge. Across the road, the **Curtis Museum** concentrates on exploring 100 million years of local history with displays devoted to local industries and celebrities; the Roman Selborne Cup and the imposing Anglo-Saxon Alton Buckle; and a colourful Gallery of Childhood with exhibits thoughtfully displayed in miniature cases at an ideal height for children.

A good time to visit the town is mid-July when the **Alton Show** takes place. Established in 1840, this is one of

southern England's most important agricultural gatherings with a wide range of events featuring such attractions as Heavy Horses, llamas, beagles, gun dogs and birds of prey.

Andover

Andover has expanded greatly since the 1960s when it was selected as a 'spillover' town to relieve the pressure on London's crowded population, but the core of this ancient town retains much of interest. One outstanding landmark is **St Mary's Church**, completely rebuilt in the 1840s at the expense of a former headmaster of Winchester College. The interior is said to have been modelled on Salisbury Cathedral and if it doesn't quite match up to that sublime building, St Mary's is still well worth a visit.

Equally striking is the **Guildhall** of 1825, built in classical style, which stands alone in the Market Place where markets are still held every Tuesday and Saturday. Andover has also managed to retain half a dozen of the 16 coaching inns that serviced 18th century travellers at a time when the fastest stage coaches took a mere 9 hours to travel here from London. As many as 50 coaches a day stopped at these inns to change horses and allow the passengers to take refreshments.

The town's story is told in the **Andover Museum & the Museum of the**

Flood Meadows, Alton

Iron Age in Church Close.

Another good way of getting to know the town is to join one of the guided tours along the **Andover Heritage Trail** starting at the Tourist Information Centre. Also starting here are two trails which lead to collections of poems in praise of the lovely Test Valley.

Two miles east of Andover, **Finkley Down Farm Park** provides a pleasant day out for families with young children. Youngsters can feed and handle the animals, groom a pony, ride on a mini-tractor, and expend any excess energy in the well-equipped playground. Romany caravans and farming bygones are on display and other attractions include a tea room, gift shop and picnic area.

Another good family day out can be enjoyed at **The Hawk Conservancy**, 4 miles west of the town. With more than 200 birds to see in 22 acres of grounds, the Hawk Conservancy is one of the largest collections of raptors in the world. Flying demonstrations take place three times daily and include species such as owls, eagles, vultures and condors, falcons, kites, hawks and secretary birds.

Basingstoke

It comes as something of a surprise to discover that this busy, prosperous town with its soaring multi-storey buildings can boast no fewer than 25 parks and open spaces. They include the 16-hectare **War Memorial Park**, an 18th century park complete with bandstand, aviary and sports facilities, and

Southview Cemetery, a site with a fascinating history. Some 800 years ago, during the reign of King John, England languished under an Interdict pronounced by the Pope. Throughout the six years from 1208 to 1214, any baby christened, or dead person buried, lacked the official blessing of Mother Church. At Basingstoke during those years, the deceased were interred in the graveyard known as **The Liten** and when the Interdict was finally lifted, the ground was consecrated and a chapel built, the **Chapel of the Holy Ghost**. Today, the chapel is a striking ruin surrounded by a well-managed site which provides a peaceful refuge from the bustling town.

As befits such a thriving place, Basingstoke offers visitors a wide choice of attractions: theatre, cinema, a vast Leisure Park, and an "Old Town" area which is a lively cosmopolitan mix of bars, theme pubs and restaurants. Here too is the excellent **Willis Museum**, which charts the town's history with a variety of lively displays.

Just to the east of Basingstoke, **Basing House** was once one of the grandest residences in the realm. Built during the reign of Henry VIII, it rivalled even the king's extravagant mansions. Less than a hundred years later, during the Civil War, Cromwell's troops besieged the house for an incredible three years, one of them reporting that the mansion was 'as large as the Tower of London'. When Basing House was finally captured, the victorious New Army burnt it to the ground, but a magnificent 16th century barn survived, its timber roof a marvel of the carpenter's craft.

The Vyne, 4 miles north of Basingstoke, was built in the early 1500s for Lord Sandys, Lord Chamberlain to Henry VIII. This splendid house enjoys an idyllic setting with lawns sweeping down to a shimmering lake. A classical portico was added in 1654, the first of its kind in England. The Vyne's treasures include a fascinating Tudor chapel with Renaissance glass, a Palladian staircase, and a wealth of old panelling and fine furniture.

Beaulieu

The ruins of a 13th century Cistercian Abbey, a stately home which grew up around the Abbey's imposing gatehouse, and the **National Motor Museum** sited in its grounds are three good reasons why the village of Beaulieu has become one

Beaulieu Abbey

of the county's major visitor attractions. When Lord Montagu of Beaulieu first opened his family home to the public in the 1950s, he organised a display of a few vintage motor vehicles in homage to his father who had been a pioneer of motoring in Britain. That modest clutch of cars has now expanded to include some 250 of the oldest, newest, slowest and fastest motor cars and motor bikes in British motoring history, plus some rare oddities. The motoring theme is continued in fun features such as Go Karts, Miniature Motors, and 'Fast Trax', described as the 'best in virtual racing simulators'.

It was an ancestor of Lord Montagu, the 2nd Duke of Montagu, who created the picturesque riverside village of **Buckler's Hard** in the early 1700s. It was designed as an inland port to receive and refine sugar from the Duke's West Indian estates and His Grace planned his model village on a grand scale: the streets, for example, were to be 80 feet wide. Unfortunately, the enterprise failed and only a single street was built. That 18th century street remains intact and unspoiled, and one of its buildings has been converted into a **Maritime Museum** reflecting the subsequent history of the village when it became a ship-building centre. More than 50 naval ships were built at Buckler's Hard, amongst them one of Nelson's favourite ships, the *Agamemnon*.

Just across the Beaulieu River

from Buckler's Hard, as the crow flies, is **Exbury Gardens**. By road, that's about a 10-mile detour but one which is definitely worth making. One visitor described the Exbury Gardens as "Heaven with the gates open". Created by Lionel de Rothschild in the 1920s, Exbury is still run by his descendants

Bishop's Waltham

Bishop's Waltham is a charming and historic small town. It was the country residence of the Bishops of Winchester for centuries and through the portals of their sumptuous **Palace**, built in 1136 by Henri de Blois, have passed at least 12 reigning monarchs. Among them were Richard the Lionheart returning from the Crusades, Henry V mustering his army before setting off for Agincourt, and Henry VIII entertaining Charles V of Spain (then the most powerful monarch in Europe) to a lavish banquet. The Palace's days of glory came to a violent end during the Civil War when Cromwell's troops battered most of it to the ground. The last resident Bishop was forced to flee, concealing himself beneath a load of manure. The ruins remain impressive, especially the Great Hall with its three-storey tower and soaring windows. The Palace is now in the care of English Heritage and entrance is free. The town itself offers visitors a good choice of traditional and specialist shops, amongst them a renowned fishmonger, butcher, baker - even a candle-maker. And just north of the town you can visit one of the

country's leading vineyards.

South of Bishop's Waltham, at **Waltham Chase**, **Jhansi Farm Rare Breed Centre** is dedicated to the conservation of rare breed farm animals, some of them critically endangered. The Farm has a pets' corner housing a large variety of pure-bred rabbits, guinea pigs, chipmunks and birds, a souvenir and pet shop, tea room, picnic and play area, nursery and water gardens, with events such as sheep shearing and hand spinning taking place throughout the season.

Burghclere

The village is home to the **Sandham Memorial Chapel**, which was built in the 1920s to remember the dead of World War I. What, however, makes this chapel so interesting are the internal murals which entirely cover the walls that are considered by many to be Stanley Spencer's greatest achievement. An extraordinary project, the murals illustrate the artist's experiences as a medical orderly during the war and he celebrates the everyday routine of a soldier's life The pictures reach a climax with the huge Resurrection of the Soldiers which completely fills the east wall. This modern chapel is found amidst beautiful and tranquil scenery with views across Watership Down.

Chawton

From the outside, the home in which Jane Austen spent the last eight years of her life, **Chawton House**, and where she wrote three of her most popular novels (*Mansfield Park*, *Emma* and *Persuasion*), is a disappointingly dull, blank-faced building. Sadly, once you step inside, the interior is equally dispiriting. You can see the sitting-room in which she penned those cleverly-crafted novels, the bedroom to which she retired, but the house is curiously empty, as elusive as the author herself.

The Wakes, the home of Gilbert White in **Selborne**, about 3 miles south of Chawton, is quite different. A humble curate of the parish from 1784 until his death in 1793, Gilbert spent his spare hours meticulously recording observations on the weather, wildlife and geology of the area. *The Natural History and Antiquities of Selborne* was first published in 1788, has never been out of print, and still provides what is perhaps the most entertaining and direct access to late-18th century life, seen through the eyes of an intelligent, sceptical mind. The Wakes also contains the **Oates**

Museum dedicated to Francis Oates, the Victorian explorer, and his nephew Captain Lawrence Oates, a member of Captain Scott's ill-fated South Pole expedition.

Crawley

Crawley is a possibly unique example of an early-20th century model village. The estate was bought in 1900 by the Philippi family, who set about adding to the village's store of genuine traditional cottages with faithful fakes built in the same style. (They also provided their tenants with a state-of-the-art bath house and a roller skating rink.) Sensitive to tradition and history, they did nothing to blemish the partly Norman church, leaving its unusual interior intact. Instead of stone pillars, St Mary's has mighty wooden columns supporting its roof, still effective more than 500 years after they were first hoisted into place.

East Meon

Tucked away in the lovely valley of the River Meon and surrounded by high downs East Meon has been described as "the most unspoilt of Hampshire villages and the nicest". As if that weren't enough, the village also boasts one of the finest and most venerable churches in the county. The central tower,

Thatched Cottage, East Meon

with walls 4 feet thick, dates back to the 12th century, and is a stunning example of Norman architecture at its best. Inside, the church's greatest treasure is its remarkable 12th century Tournai font of black marble, exquisitely carved with scenes depicting the fall of Adam and Eve. Only four of these wonderful fonts are known to exist in England and East Meon's is generally regarded as the most magnificent of them.

Just across the road is the 15th century **Courthouse**, which also has walls 4 feet thick. It's a lovely medieval manor house where for generations the Bishops of Winchester, as Lords of the Manor, held their courts. It would have been a familiar

Fareham

Many aspects of this charming old town are exhibited in **Westbury Manor Museum**, housed in a 17th century farmhouse on the town's outskirts. Nearby are the **Royal Armouries** at **Fort Nelson**, where the display of artillery dating from the Middle Ages is one of the finest in the world. To the southeast lies **Gosport**, home to another of Lord Palmerston's forts, the circular Fort Brockhurst, and of the **Royal Naval Submarine Museum** located at *HMS Dolphin*.

Farnborough

Best known for the **Farnborough Air Show**, the town is also home to **St Michael's Abbey**, built in flamboyant

French style by the Empress Eugenie in honour of her husband Napoleon III. She came to live in England with her son and was joined later by her husband in exile. All three are buried in vast tombs in the mausoleum next to the Abbey.

Fordingbridge

The most famous resident of this ancient town was the bohemian painter Augustus John. Much of his colourful life was the subject of scandal, but the residents of Fordingbridge were proud of their illustrious townsman and erected a robust, rugged bronze statue of the painter by a recreation ground near the famous seven-arched bridge. The parish church has many notable features, and also well worth a visit is **Branksome China Works**, makers of fine porcelain tableware and famous animal studies.

Hamble

Famous throughout the world as a yachting centre, Hamble takes its name from the river, a mere 10 miles long, that flows past the village into **Southampton Water**. Some 3,000 vessels have berths in the **Hamble Estuary**, so there's an incredible variety of boats thronging the river during the season, anything from vintage barges to the sleekest of modern craft. To the south lies **Hamble Common**, an area of coastal heath with a wide range of habitats; along the shore are the remains of Iron Age settlements, a ruined Tudor castle and a Napoleonic gun battery.

Sailing, Hamble Estuary

Anyone interested in England's industrial heritage should travel a couple of miles north from Hamble to **Bursledon**. Ships have been built here since medieval times, the most famous being the *Elephant*, Nelson's flagship at the Battle of Copenhagen. The yard where it was built, now renamed the Elephant Boatyard, is still in business. On a rise to the north of the village stands **Bursledon Windmill**, the only working windmill in Hampshire. Built in 1814 at a cost of £800, its vanes ground to a halt during the great agricultural depression of the 1880s. Happily, all the machinery remained intact and after a lengthy restoration between 1976 and 1991, the sails are revolving once again whenever a good northerly or southerly wind is blowing, producing stoneground flour for sale.

The village can boast yet another unique industrial site. When **Bursledon Brickworks** were established in 1897 the machinery installed was at the very forefront of brickmaking technology. The works closed in 1974 but a Charitable Trust has now restored its gargantuan machines, thus preserving the last surviving example of a steam-driven brickworks in the country.

Heritage of a different kind can be found a couple of miles northwest of Hamble, at ruined **Netley Abbey**, a wonderfully serene spot surrounded by noble trees. "These are not the ruins of Netley," declared Horace Walpole in the mid-1700s, "but of Paradise". Jane Austen was equally entranced by the Abbey's romantic charm and made many visits. Dating back to 1300, the extensive ruins provide a spectacular backdrop for open-air theatre performances during the summer.

Hambledon

A village of redbrick Georgian houses, known for its wine and even better known for its cricketing connections. It was in the Hambledon Club that the rules of the game were laid down in 1774. A granite monument stands on **Broadhalfpenny Down**, where the early games were played.

Havant

Originally a Roman crossroads, the town

developed into a leading manufacturing centre; its history is explored in the town's museum. To the north lies **Stansted Park**, one of the country's most elegant stately homes, while to the southeast is the picturesque village of **Emsworth**, sometime home of the novelist PG Wodehouse.

Hayling Island

A traditional family resort for more than a century, Hayling Island manages to provide all the usual seaside facilities without losing its rural character.

Hayling is something of a Mecca for board sailors and is the place where board-sailing was invented. The **Hayling Billy Coastal Path** provides access for walkers, cyclists and riders, along with excellent views.

Highclere

Sir Charles Barry, the architect of the Houses of Parliament, was in similarly exuberant mood when engaged on the building of **Highclere Castle** for the 3rd Earl of Carnarvon. The largest mansion in the whole country is indeed a grand affair, with turrets at the angles and a huge pinnacled tower in the centre. It stands on the site of a former Palace of the Bishops of Winchester, overlooking a lovely park that is one of Capability' Brown's greatest creations. In the basement is an exhibition of ancient artefacts collected by the 5th Earl, who was with Howard Carter on the 1922 expedition that discovered the tomb of

Tutankhamun. A small museum in the basement of the Castle recalls that breathtaking moment. Another display reflects the family's interest in horse racing.

Horndean

This village has a long association with brewing, and the company of George Gale, founded in 1847, offers guided tours. To the northwest lies the lovely **Queen Elizabeth Country Park**, and nearby **Butser Ancient Farm** is a living, working reconstruction of an Iron Age farm.

Lymington

An ancient seaport and market town, once a major producer of salt - its story is told in the **St Barbe Museum**. The church in the nearby pretty village of **Boldre** has become a shrine to *HMS Hood* which was sunk by the *Bismarck* in 1941 with the loss of 1,400 lives.

Lyndhurst

The most striking building in this compact little town is the **Church of St Michael**, rebuilt in mid-Victorian times in what John Betjeman described as 'the most fanciful, fantastic Gothic style that I ever have seen'. The rebuilding coincided with the heyday of the Pre-Raphaelite movement, so the church contains some fine stained glass by Burne-Jones, produced by the firm of William Morris, as well as a splendidly lush painting by Lord Leighton of *The*

New Forest Ponies

Wise and Foolish Virgins.

In St Michael's churchyard is the Grave of Alice Liddell who, as a young girl, was the inspiration for Lewis Carroll's Alice in Wonderland. As Mrs Reginald Hargreaves, Alice lived all her married life in Lyndhurst and was very active in local affairs.

Next to the church is the **Queen's House**, originally built as a royal hunting lodge, with medieval and Tudor elements still visible. Many Kings and Queens have lodged here and the last monarch to stay, George III, graciously allowed loyal villagers to watch through the window as he ate dinner. The House is now the headquarters of the Forestry Commission and is also home to the Verderers Court, an institution dating back to Norman times which still deals with matters concerning the forest's ancient commoning rights.

Middle Wallop

The village of Middle Wallop became famous during the Battle of Britain when the nearby airfield was the base for squadrons of Spitfires and Hurricanes. Many of the old buildings have been incorporated into the **Museum of Army Flying**, which traces the development of Army Flying from the balloons and kites of pre-World War I years, through various imaginative dioramas, to a helicopter flight simulator in which visitors can test their own skills of 'hand and eye' co-ordination.

About 3 miles east of Middle Wallop, **Danebury Ring** is Hampshire's largest Iron Age hill fort, intensively occupied from about 550 BC until the arrival of the Romans.

Milford-on-Sea

This sizeable coastal village is most notable for its fine, remarkably well-preserved 13th century Church of All Saints, its grand views across The Solent to the Isle of Wight, and the odd-looking construction called **Hurst Castle**. At the centre of Hurst Castle is a squat fort built by Henry VIII to guard the Solent entrance against incursions by the French. Its tower is flanked by two long low wings added in the 1860s for gun emplacements, the square openings making them look rather like shopping arcades. The Castle was used as a garrison right up until World War II but is now in the care of English Heritage which has an on-site exhibition explaining its history.

Hurst Castle stands at the tip of a long gravel spit which stretches out across the Solent to within three quarters of a mile of the Isle of Wight coast.

Minstead

The village of Minstead offers two interesting attractions, one of which is the **Church of All Saints**. During the 18th century, the gentry and squirearchy of Minstead seem to have regarded church attendance as a necessary duty which, nevertheless, should be made as agreeable as possible. Three of the village's most affluent residents paid to have the church fabric altered so that they could each have their own entrance door leading to a private 'parlour', complete with open fireplace and comfortable chairs. The squire of Minstead even installed a sofa on which he could doze during the sermon.

Admirers of the creator of Sherlock Holmes, Sir Arthur Conan Doyle, will want to pay their respects at his grave in the churchyard here.

Minstead's other main attraction is **Furzey Gardens**, eight acres of delightful, informal landscape with extensive views over the New Forest towards the Isle of Wight. Beautiful banks of azaleas and rhododendrons, heathers and ferns surround an attractive water garden, and amongst the notable species growing here are incandescent

Chilean Fire Trees and the strange 'Bottle Brush Tree'.

Nether Wallop

The names of the three Wallops (Over, Middle and Nether) have provided a good deal of amusement to visitors over the centuries, so it's slightly disappointing to discover that Wallop is just a corruption of the Old English word *waell-hop*, meaning a valley with a stream. At Nether Wallop the stream is picturesquely lined with willow trees, while the village itself is equally attractive, with many thatched or timbered houses. The most notable building is **St Andrew's Church**, partly because of its Norman features and handsome West Tower of 1704, but also

Nether Wallop

because of its striking medieval wall paintings which provide an interesting contrast with Stanley Spencer's at Burghclere. Some 500 years old, these lay hidden for generations under layers of plaster and were only rediscovered in the 1950s. Outside St Andrew's stands an item of great interest for collectors of churchyard oddities. It's a dark grey stone pyramid, 15 feet high, with red stone flames rising from its tip. This daunting monument was erected at his own expense and in memory of himself by Francis Douce, 'Doctor of Physick', who died in 1760.

New Milton

One of New Milton's most striking buildings is the splendid **Water Tower** of 1900. Late-Victorian providers of water services seem to have enjoyed pretending that their storage towers and sewage treatment plants were really castles of the Middle Ages. They built these mock-medieval structures all around the country, but the one at New Milton is particularly imposing. Three storeys high, with a castellated parapet, the octagonal building has tall, narrow windows - ideal for Water Authority archers seeing off customers who have dared to dispute their water bills.

Devotees of vintage motorbikes will make for a very different attraction: the **Sammy Miller Museum** to the west of the town, widely regarded as one of the best of its kind in the world.

Petersfield

An appealing market town, Petersfield is dominated by the bulk of **Butser Hill**, 900 feet high and the highest point of the South Downs offering grand panoramic views over the town and even, on a clear day, to the spire of Salisbury Cathedral, some 40 miles distant.

Most of the elegant buildings around the Square are Georgian, but the **Church of St Peter** is much older, dating back to Norman times and with a fine north aisle to prove it. Just off the Square, the **Flora Twort Gallery** was once the home and studio of the accomplished artist of that name who moved to Petersfield at the end of World War I. Her delightful paintings and drawings capture life in the town over some 40 years - "reminders of some of the things we have lost" as she put it shortly before her death at the age of 91 in 1985.

From the Gallery, a short walk along Sheep Street brings the visitor to **The Spain**, a pleasant green surrounded by some of the town's oldest houses. It apparently acquired its rather unusual name because dealers in Spanish wool used to hold markets there.

Portsmouth

Portsmouth is the country's leading naval base and at **Flagship Portsmouth** several historic ships can be seen. One of them is the most famous flagship in naval history, HMS *Victory*. From the outside it's a majestic, three-masted ship; inside it's creepily claustrophobic, except for the Admiral's and Captain's spacious, mahogany-panelled quarters. Visitors can pace the very same deck from which Nelson master-minded the decisive encounter with the French navy off Cape Trafalgar in 1805. The precise spot where he fell and the place on the sheltered orlop (lowest) deck where he died are both marked by plaques.

The death of Nelson was a tragedy softened by a halo of victory: the loss of the *Mary Rose*, some 260 years earlier, was an unmitigated disaster. Henry VIII had ordered the ship, the second largest in his fleet, to be built. He was standing on Southsea Common above Portsmouth in 1545, watching the *Mary Rose* manoeuvre, when it suddenly heeled over and sank. All 700 men on board drowned. More than four centuries later, in 1982, the hulk of the *Mary Rose* was carefully raised from the seabed where it had lain for so long. Its oak frame is still drying out, the impressive remains now housed in the timber-clad **Mary Rose Museum**.

Another ship you can see at Portsmouth doesn't possess the same historical glamour as the *Victory* or the *Mary Rose*, but HMS *Warrior* merits a visit because when this mighty craft was commissioned in 1860, she was the Navy's first ironclad warship. A great advance in technology, but the

distinctions between the officers' and crew accommodation show little difference from those obtaining in Nelson's day.

Like Southampton, Portsmouth suffered badly during World War II, losing most of its 17th and 18th century buildings, but some survive, including **St George's Church** and the barn-like **Beneficial Boy's School**. One of the most interesting buildings is to be found in Southsea, the city's resort area. **Southsea Castle** was built in 1544 as one of Henry VIII's series of forts protecting the south coast from French attacks. It has been modified several times since then but the original Keep is still intact and there are good views across the Solent from the gun platforms.

Portsmouth also offers visitors a wealth of varied museums: the **Royal Armouries**, housed in the huge Victorian Fort Nelson, claims to be 'Britain's Loudest Museum', with live firings every day; the **Charles Dickens Birthplace Museum** at 393, Old Commercial Road, has been restored and furnished to show how the house looked

Portchester Castle

when the great novelist was born here in 1812; and the **D-Day Museum** in Southsea commemorates the Allied invasion of Europe in 1944.

Standing at the head of Portsmouth Harbour, **Portchester Castle** is not only the grandest medieval castle in the county but also stands within the best-preserved site of a Roman fort in northern Europe.

The medieval castle dates back to 1120 although the most substantial ruins are those of the royal palace built for Richard II between 1396 and 1399. Richard was murdered in 1399 and never saw his magnificent castle. Also within the walls of the Roman enclosure is **Portchester Church**, a superb Norman construction built between 1133 and 1150 as part of an Augustinian Priory.

Ringwood

Ringwood has expanded greatly in recent years but its centre still boasts a large number of elegant Georgian houses, both large and small. **Ringwood Meeting House**, built in 1727 and now a Museum, is an outstanding example of an early Nonconformist chapel, complete with the original, rather austere, fittings. **Monmouth House** is of about the same period and stands on the site of an earlier house in which the luckless Duke of Monmouth was confined after his unsuccessful uprising against James II. The Duke had been discovered hiding in a ditch just outside the town and despite his abject pleas to the King to spare his life he was

beheaded at Tower Hill a few days later.

Five miles west of the town stretch the great expanses of **Ringwood Forest**, which includes the **Moors Valley Country Park**. One of the most popular attractions in the Moors Valley Country Park is the **Moors Valley Railway**, a delightful narrow gauge steam railway with rails just 7¼ inches apart. The route southwards runs alongside the Moors Lake, a manmade feature which also serves as a flood diversion area when the River Moors, notorious for causing flooding in the area, is running high. The southern terminus of the railway is at Lakeside Station where there's a Visitor Centre, Information Point, Tearoom and Country Shop.

A mile or so south-east of Ringwood, in the hamlet of **Crow**, the **New Forest Owl Sanctuary** is home to the largest collection of owls in Europe, housed in more than 100 aviaries. There are flying displays, both inside and out, daily lectures to entertain visitors of all ages, a café and shop. In the hospital units Bruce Berry, founder of the sanctuary, and his dedicated staff have prepared hundreds of birds for release back into the world. The Sanctuary is open daily from March to November; weekends only during the winter.

Rockbourne

Rockbourne Roman Villa, the largest of its kind in the region, was discovered in 1942 when oyster shells and tiles were found by a farmer in the course of digging out a ferret. Excavations have revealed superb mosaics, part of the amazing Roman underground heating system and the outline of the great villa's 40 rooms. Hundreds of the objects unearthed are on show in the site's museum.

Romsey

"Music in stone", and "the second finest Norman building in England" are just two responses to **Romsey Abbey**, a majestic building containing some of the best 12th and 13th century architecture to have survived. Built between 1120 and 1230, the Abbey is remarkably complete. Unlike so many monastic buildings which were destroyed or fell into ruin after the Dissolution, the Abbey was fortunate in being bought by the town in 1544 for £100. Subsequent generations of townspeople have carefully maintained their bargain purchase. The Abbey's most spectacular feature is the soaring nave which rises more than 70 feet and extends for more than 76 feet. Among the Abbey's many treasures is the Romsey Rood which shows Christ on the cross with the hand of God descending from the clouds.

Just across from the Abbey, in Church Court, stands the town's oldest dwelling, King John's House, built around 1240 for a merchant. It has served as a royal residence but not, curiously, for King John who died some 14 years before it was built. He may though

have had a hunting lodge on the site. The house is now a museum and centre for cultural activities.

Romsey's most famous son was undoubtedly the flamboyant politician Lord Palmerston, three times Prime Minister during the 1850s and 1860s. Palmerston lived at Broadlands, just south of the town, a gracious Palladian mansion built by Lord Palmerston's father in the mid-1700s. The architect was Henry Holland, and the landscape was modelled by the ubiquitous Lancelot 'Capability' Brown. The important collections of furniture, porcelain and sculpture were acquired by the 2nd Viscount Palmerston. The house passed to the Mountbatten family and it was Lord Louis Mountbatten who first opened Broadlands to the public shortly before he was killed in 1979. The present owner, Lord Romsey, has established the Mountbatten Exhibition in tribute to his grandfather's remarkable career as naval commander, diplomat, and last Viceroy of India. To the northeast lies the **Sir**

Romsey Abbey

Harold Hillier Garden and Arboretum, which houses 11 National Plant Collections. To the northwest is **Mottisfont Abbey**, originally an Augustinian priory and subsequently a country mansion. The superb grounds contain the National Collection of old-fashioned roses and what is thought to be England's largest plane tree.

Southampton

From this historic port, Henry V set sail for Agincourt in 1415, the Pilgrim Fathers embarked on their perilous journey to the New World in 1620, and, on April 10th, 1912, the *Titanic* set off on its maiden voyage, steaming majestically into the Solent. The city's sea-faring heritage is vividly recalled at the excellent **Maritime Museum**, housed in the 14th century **Wool House**. The museum tells the story of the port from the age of sail to the heyday of the great ocean liners.

As a major sea-port, Southampton

was a prime target for air raids during World War II and suffered grievously. But the city can still boast a surprising number of ancient buildings. Substantial stretches of the medieval Town Walls have miraculously survived, its ramparts interspersed with fortifications such as the oddly-named 15th century **Catchcold Tower** and **God's House Gate and Tower**, which now houses the city's archaeological museum. Perhaps the most impressive feature of the walls is **Bargate**, one of the finest medieval city gates in the country. From its construction around 1200 until the 1930s, Bargate remained the principal entrance to the city. Its narrow archway is so low that Southampton Corporation's trams had to be specially modified for them to pass through. Inside the arch stands a statue of George III, cross-dressing as a Roman Emperor. Bargate now stands in its own pedestrianised area, its upper floor, the former Guildhall, now a Museum of local history and folklore.

Another remarkable survivor is the **Medieval Merchant's House** in French Street which has been expertly restored and authentically furnished, now appearing just as it was when it was built around 1290. One of the most popular visitor attractions in

Ocean Village Marina, Southampton

Southampton is the **Tudor House Museum & Garden**, a lovely 15th century house with an award-winning Tudor Garden complete with fountain, bee skeps and 16th century herbs and flowers.

A major development is **Ocean Village**, an imaginatively conceived waterfront complex with its own 450-berth marina, undercover shopping, excellent restaurants and a multi-screen cinema.

The city also occupies an important place in aviation history. A short step from Ocean Village, the **Hall of Aviation** presents the story of aviation in the Solent and incorporates the **RJ Mitchell Memorial Museum**. Mitchell lived and worked in Southampton in the 1930s and designed the Spitfire and the S6 Seaplane which won the coveted Scheider Trophy.

Stratfield Saye

Stratfield Saye House was just one of many rewards a grateful nation showered on the Duke of Wellington after his decisive defeat of Napoleon at Waterloo. The Duke himself doesn't seem to have been reciprocally grateful: only lack of funds frustrated his plans to demolish the gracious 17th century house and replace it with an even more impressive mansion which he intended to call Waterloo Palace. Quite modest in scale, Stratfield Saye fascinates visitors with its collection of the Duke's own furniture and personal items such as his spectacles, handkerchiefs and carpet slippers. More

questionable are the priceless books in the library, many of them looted from Napoleon's own bibliothèque. A good number of the fine Spanish and Portuguese paintings on display share an equally dubious provenance, 'relieved' during the Duke's campaign in those countries as 'spoils of war'.

Winchester

One of the country's most historic cities, Winchester was adopted by King Alfred as the capital of his kingdom of Wessex, a realm which then included most of southern England. There had been a settlement here since the Iron Age and in Roman times, as Venta Belgarum, it became an important military base. **The Brooks Experience**, located within the modern Brooks Shopping Centre, has displays based on excavated Roman remains with its star exhibit a reconstructed room from an early-4th century town-house.

When the Imperial Legions returned to Rome, the town declined until it was refounded by Alfred in the late 800s. His street plan still provides the basic outline of the city centre. A Saxon cathedral had been built in the 7th century but the present magnificent **Cathedral**, easily the most imposing and interesting building in Hampshire, dates back to 1079. Winchester Cathedral boasts the longest nave in Europe, a dazzling 14th century masterpiece in the Perpendicular style, a wealth of fine wooden carvings, and gems within a gem such as the richly decorated Bishop Waynflete's Chantry of

Westgate Museum, Winchester

Two years after Jane Austen was buried in the Cathedral, the poet John Keats stayed in Winchester and it was here that he wrote his timeless *Ode to Autumn* - "Season of mists and mellow fruitfulness" His inspiration was a daily walk past the Cathedral and College and through the Water Meadows beside the River Itchen.

The city's numerous other attractions include **The Great Hall**, the only surviving part of the medieval Castle rebuilt by Henry III between 1222 and 1486. Sumptuous medieval monuments like the effigy of William of Wykeham, founder of Winchester College, provide a striking contrast to the simple black stone floorslabs which separately mark the graves of Izaak Walton and Jane Austen.

Just south of the Cathedral, on College Street, are two other buildings of outstanding interest. No. 8, College Street, a rather austere Georgian house with a first-floor bay window, is **Jane Austen's House** in which she spent the last six weeks of her life in 1817. Right next door stands **Winchester College**, the oldest school in England, founded in 1382 by Bishop William of Wykeham to provide education for seventy 'poor and needy scholars'. Substantial parts of the 14th century buildings still stand, including the beautiful Chapel.

1236; the early-14th century Pilgrim Hall, part of the **Pilgrim School**, and originally used as lodgings for pilgrims to the shrine of St Swithun; and **Wolvesey Castle**, the residence of the Bishops of Winchester since 963. The present palace is a gracious, classical building erected in the 1680s, flanked by the imposing ruins of its 14th century predecessor which was one of the grandest buildings in medieval England. Also well worth a visit is the 15th century **Hospital of St Cross**, England's oldest almshouse. Founded in 1132 by Henri du Blois, grandson of William the Conqueror, it was extended in 1446 by Cardinal Beaufort, son of John of Gaunt. It is still home to 25 Brothers and maintains its long tradition of hospitality by dispensing the traditional Wayfarer's Dole to any traveller who requests it.

THE BARLEY MOW

THE HURST, WINCHFIELD, HOOK, HAMPSHIRE RG27 8DE
TEL: 01252 617490

> **Directions:** From Hook, take the A30 towards Hartley Wintney. After a few miles turn right signposted Winchfield Station. Pass the station and continue along this road for about 1 mile; the inn is on the left. From the M3 (J4a) take the A327 to the A30, then left through Hartley Wintney, then as above.

Brian Sprackling was for many years a loyal regular at **The Barley Mow**, but when he took it over at the beginning of 2003 its best days seemed to be behind it. But by sheer hard work and the loyalty of the locals, the good times have returned to this fine white-painted Georgian building, which is now one of the most popular pub-restaurants in the area. There's a traditional look to the black-beamed bar, with its elaborately carved brick hearth and the wealth of pictures and team photographs of the Barley Mow Cricket Club, whose ground lies next to the inn. Four real ales are on tap to quench thirsts, and the bar and restaurant menus provide plenty of choice for snackers and diners.

The man at the stoves in Kevin

Manning, a chef with lots of talent and lots of experience – and a prime mover in the revival of The Barley Mow's fortunes. Baguettes with interesting fillings like roast Mediterranean vegetables or marinated prawns in ginger and lime make super lunchtime snacks, with pâtés, curries, beer-battered cod and a splendid dish of liver, bacon and kidney served on creamed potatoes as alternatives. The evening menu, served in the comfortable à la carte restaurant, brings mouthwatering dishes such as salmon and prawn terrine, red mullet with spaghetti, herb-crusted rack of lamb and baked cod with tomatoes, bay leaf and parsley. Food is available every lunchtime from 12 to 2 and Tuesday to Saturday evenings in the restaurant, where booking is advised. Children are welcome if eating, and at all times in the beer garden. The Basingstoke Canal runs nearby with its towpath walks.

- 🕐 Lunchtime and evening (all day Sat and Sun in summer)
- 🍴 Home-cooked bar and evening restaurant meals
- 💷 Not Amex or Diners
- 🅿 Car park, beer garden
- 🎵 Themed evenings every three months
- @ email: sprax@skynow.net
- ❓ Fleet 2 miles, Hartley Wintney 2 miles, Hook 3 miles, Basingstoke 8 miles

THE BEAR & RAGGED STAFF

STONYMARSH, MICHELMERSH, NR ROMSEY, HAMPSHIRE SO51 0LB
TEL: 01794 368602

Hampshire

Directions: From Romsey take the A3057 north for about 4 miles.

The Bear & Ragged Staff is a grand old redbrick building which has developed from a country inn pure and simple to one of the best and most popular destination restaurants in the region. Open all day, every day, it has all the charm and character that its origins would suggest, with a patchwork of gnarled beams, wooden screens dividing the various sections of the bar, all kinds of brass and copper ornaments and pictures and prints of days gone by. Quality cask ales are on tap to satisfy thirsts, but for most visitors this is first and foremost an eating place, owned and overseen by ex-brewery man Jonathan Salmon and his wife. Consistent quality is the order of the day, and the menu caters for all appetites and tastes.

The large and growing band of regular customers will testify that nothing beats a leisurely couple of hours relaxing over a meal at this outstanding inn, but those with less time to spare or smaller appetites to satisfy will also find what they want on

the bar menu, which runs from traditional sandwiches to ciabatta with terrific hot fillings, ploughman's, nachos and vegetarian or chicken dippers. Blackboards announce the constantly changing daily specials, which offer a choice that is almost unrivalled, from plaice goujons, stuffed jalapeno peppers and oriental prawn fishcakes to lasagne, hickory smoked ribs, pan-fried trout, beef Wellington, steak & Murphys pie, and liver with bacon and onions. For dessert, perhaps apple and blackberry fool or chocolate fudge cake. Vegetarians will always find plenty of choice, and the top-notch food is complemented by wines from the Old and New Worlds, available by bottle or by two sizes of glass. Coffee is freshly made from the bean. The Bear & Ragged Staff has ample off-road parking and a large beer garden, and all areas are accessible to wheelchair users. The Fish Inn at Ringwood is in the same ownership.

- All day seven days
- Snacks and full restaurant menu
- All the major cards
- Ample off-road parking, large beer garden
- Mottisfont Abbey 1 mile, Sir Harold Hillier Gardens 3 miles, Romsey 4 miles

THE CROWN

THE STREET, OLD BASING, HAMPSHIRE RG24 7BW
TEL/FAX: 01256 321424

Directions: The Crown is situated next to Basing House in the centre of Old
Basing, 1 mile northeast of Basingstoke off the A30 or M3.

The modern town of Basingstoke
may be just up the road, but here
in Old Basing you could be on
another planet. The majestic
ruins of Basing House, once the
grandest private residence in the
country, bring the crowds from
near and far, but next door to the
house is another of the village's
attractions. **The Crown** was built
in three stages, the earliest in the 18th
century, and the interior has a
delightfully old-world look. One
particularly charming area is the cosy
little snug with books, newspapers and a
log-burning stove. This is just one of the
improvements made by owner Adrian
Culver, a trained chef, and manager
Sarah, who have done much to enhance
the appeal of the inn since they arrived
in October 2003.

Adrian's passion for food is evident
from a glance at his menus, which offer a
fine combination of traditional English
and modern international dishes, with
typical choices running from aubergine
millefeuille and smoked salmon timbale
for starters to tuna steak with chilli
butter, steak & ale pie, liver & onions
and rabbit and smoked bacon casserole.
Desserts such as chocolate torte or
meringue nest with raspberries and
cream keep the pleasure level high right
to the end. Food is served every session
except Sunday evening, and booking is
recommended at the weekend. London
Pride is the house real ale, and there are
usually three others, including one from
a local brewery. When Basing House is
staging its historical re-enactments, The
Crown joins in the fun with beer
festivals and hog roasts.

- 🕐 Lunchtime and evening (all day Sat
  & Sun, all day every day in summer)
- 🍴 Home cooking
- 💷 Not Amex or Diners
- 🅿 Car park
- 🎵 Real ale festivals
- ❓ Basing House next door;
  Basingstoke 1 mile, Sherborne St
  John (The Vyne) 4 miles

THE ECLIPSE INN

THE SQUARE, WINCHESTER, HAMPSHIRE SO23 9EX
TEL: 01962 865676

> **Directions:** Winchester is located a short drive from the M3 – leave at J9 or J10. Follow signs for the city centre. The Square is in the centre of the city, next to the High Street.

In the heart of historic Winchester, **The Eclipse** is open all day, every day, offering excellent hospitality to local residents and to the many visitors who come to explore the city throughout the year. For the former, it is a well-loved 'local', a place to enjoy a drink and to put the world to rights, or to take a break from business or shopping in the middle of the city. For the latter, it is a welcome spot to pause for refreshment on a tour of one of the country's most interesting and historic cities. For many years the building was the rectory of St Lawrence's Church, and it has been a public house since 1890. Behind the black and white frontage with handsome timbers and small-paned windows, original oak beams, oak settles and an open fireplace create a delightfully traditional ambience in which to relax and enjoy a drink and something to eat.

The inn is owned and run by Sarah

Kingston and Alan Dare, who work hard to provide quality food and ales and to ensure that the place retains its old-world charm, with no distractions of piped music or gaming machines. The welcome they provide is warm and genuine, and the resident pub cat is every bit as friendly as its owners. A selection of real ales, many from local brewers, is always on tap, and all the food is home-made and freshly prepared to order; the choice runs from filled rolls and panini to hearty pies and casseroles. The magnificent Cathedral is at the top of most itineraries, but Winchester has numerous other 'musts' to visit, including the College – the oldest school in England – and the Great Hall, which is just a few steps from The Eclipse.

- 🕐 11-11
- 🍴 Snacks and meals
- £ Not Amex or Diners
- 🅿 Outside seating
- ❓ All the attractions of Winchester are close by.

THE FISH INN

THE BRIDGES, WEST STREET, RINGWOOD, HAMPSHIRE BH24 2AA
TEL: 01425 473185

Hampshire

Directions: The inn is located on the western edge of Ringwood by the A31.

The Fish Inn is a top-notch country inn and a restaurant of distinction in a pleasant rural setting on the banks of the River Avon on the western edge of Ringwood. The outside of the building, with white-painted brick, immaculate thatch and a colourful profusion of tubs and hanging baskets, is matched by the interior, where wonderful old beams (some with a height warning!), slatted wooden floors, brass and copper ornaments and open fires paint a splendidly traditional picture. Owner Jonathan Salmon has put the Fish Inn firmly on the map as one of the most popular places for a meal, and one to rival most dedicated restaurant in terms of variety and quality, but it also serves admirably its former role as a place where locals and tourists can mingle over a glass or two of the exceptional cask ales always on tap, including, naturally, the excellent Ringwood Ales. In the seven

distinct eating and drinking areas of the inn an outstanding selection of superb food is served all day, every day, from sandwiches and tasty chicken or vegetarian dippers to the full range announce throughout the inn on blackboards. And what mouthwatering reading they make, with traditional, modern and continental dishes ranging from mozzarella mushrooms and cod in a salt & vinegar batter to tuna steak with plum sauce, braised lamb shank, steaks, chilli con carne and turkey with a stilton cream sauce. Desserts get a whole blackboard to themselves, and the marvellous food is complemented by wines available by bottle or two sizes of glass. Coffee freshly made from the bean rounds off a meal to remember.

The Fish Inn is in the same ownership as the Bear & Ragged Staff at Michelmersh, with the same absolute commitment to the traditional values of a country pub.

- 🕐 All day seven days
- 🍴 Snacks and full restaurant menu
- 💷 All the major cards
- 🅿 Ample off-road parking, garden
- @ web: www.thefishinn.net
- ❓ Ringwood (Meeting House Museum) 1 mile, New Forest Owl Sanctuary 2 miles, Ringwood Forest including Moors Valley Country Park 3 miles

ALDERSHOT ROAD, CHURCH CROOKHAM, NR FLEET,
HAMPSHIRE GU52 9EP
TEL: 01252 616503 FAX: 01252 810798

Directions: The inn lies on the southern outskirts of Fleet just south of the Basingstoke Canal.

Nestling among the trees in the pleasant countryside south of Fleet, **The Foresters** has been a popular inn to visit for more than a century. For long a spot favoured for its romantic atmosphere, this handsome building with a tile-roofed veranda has now become a place for lovers of good food, interesting beers and New World wines. The transformation has been achieved by managing partners Steve and Glenice Nicolopulo, who have been careful to retain the ambience and charm of a traditional English country pub while broadening its appeal. Wood plays a prominent part in the bar, with some of the walls half-panelled and a slatted bar counter, and there's a fine stone hearth.

The inn is now very much food-led, with plenty of choice available from

noon right through to 9 o'clock. Mel and Donna in the kitchen put prime fresh ingredients to excellent use on menus that range from generously filled lunchtime sandwiches and wraps (chicken Caesar is a popular choice) to feta cheese salad, salmon fishcakes, sausages served with cheddar mash, cod fillet, steaks, lamb shank with red wine and rosemary, and a hearty beef & Guinness pie. Food service stops after lunch on Sunday. Wines are taken seriously, too, and the specials of the moment are chalked up above the bar counter. A good selection of ales includes Timothy Taylor Landlord and London Pride, and the favoured lager is Staropramen brewed in Prague. The Foresters has a large car park and a delightful tree-sheltered garden with picnic benches and garden furniture.

- 🕐 All day, every day
- 🍴 Main menu served 12-9, also sandwiches 12-5
- 💷 Not Amex or Diners
- Ⓟ Car park, garden
- @ email: info@foresters.fsnet.co.uk
- ❓ Fleet 1 mile, Aldershot 3 miles

THE FOREST INN

LYNDHURST ROAD, ASHURST, HAMPSHIRE SO40 7DU
TEL: 023 8029 2331

> **Directions:** From J3 of the M27 take the M271 towards Southampton. After about 2 miles take the A35 towards Lyndhurst; Ashurst is 5 miles along this road.

The Forest Inn, a long, low building set back from the road, is a popular country local and an ideal spot to take a break from a journey along the A35. It's a place with a growing reputation for the quality and variety of the food as well as for the friendly welcome accorded to one and all by hosts Geoff and Mandy Hart. The ambience in the bars and the non-smoking restaurant is comfortably traditional, with flagstone floors, lots of wood, open fires, bricks, beams and decorative features that include brass and copperware, ceramics and old agricultural implements. Mandy oversees the running of the kitchen, where she and her helpers produce a variety of dishes, many of them just that little bit different and all of them equally

delicious: parma ham with figs and honey, darnes of mackerel, Dover sole with wild mushrooms, four-cheese and bacon tartlet.

The inn fields darts teams in the local league and hosts regular quiz nights and occasional live music evenings. Families are always welcome, and Ashurst, which stands on the A35 3 miles from Lyndhurst and a similar distance from Southampton, is a place with several family attractions. Most notable among these are the New Forest Butterfly Farm in Langley Wood; Longdown Dairy Farm, home to the National Dairy Council Museum Collection; and the Otter, Owl and Wildlife Conservation Park. And the Forestry Commission's camping site at Ashurst offers visitors the opportunity of camping in the heart of the forest – a very pleasant prospect, with wildlife all around and the Forest Inn close at hand!

- 🕐 Lunchtime and evening every day
- 🍴 Snacks and full meals
- £ All the major cards
- 🅿 Off-road parking, beer garden
- 🎵 Darts, quiz nights, occasional live music evenings
- ❓ Longdown Dairy Farm, National Dairy Council Museum, New Forest Butterfly Farm, Otter, Owl & Wildlife Conservation Park all close by; Walking and riding in the New Forest; Furzey Gardens 5 miles, Beaulieu 7 miles

THE GEORGE INN

THRUXTON, NR ANDOVER, HAMPSHIRE SP11 8LZ
TEL/FAX: 01264 772480

Hampshire

> **Directions:** The inn lies just off the A303 1 mile west of Andover.

When Debbie and Michael arrived at the end of 2003 to take charge of **The George Inn**, they brought with them many years' experience in the trade. Behind the smart white-painted frontage, the George has a delightfully welcoming air, and the wood-panelled bar counter, the beams, the hops, the feature brick wall and the fine old rustic tables and chairs all add up to a picture of traditional charm. The inn also has considerable outdoor appeal, with a vine-decked patio leading up to a large lawned beer garden with a children's play area; there's also ample parking front and rear. London Pride, Ringwood Best and two regularly changing guests make up the real ale quota, and food is served lunchtime and evening every day except

Tuesday, when the inn is closed.

The lunchtime bar menu provides ciabatta sandwiches, jacket potatoes, ploughman's platters and tasty specials such as bacon and emmental tart or pork, brie and grape pie, while the evening menu, listed on blackboards, tempts with the likes of chicken livers with bacon and pine nuts, cold seafood platter, steak & mushroom pie, lasagne and home-cooked ham with egg and chips. Most diners find it hard to resist desserts like jaffa orange sponge or chocolate and brandy torte. The George has long been a favourite pit stop for visitors to nearby Thruxton motor racing circuit, built on a World War II airfield and host to events that include Formula 3, Touring Cars, Superbikes, Trucks and Karts. Another attraction close by is the Hawk Conservatory and Country Park at Weyhill.

- Lunchtime and evening (all day Fri, Sat & Sun, also all day Wed-Mon in summer); closed all Tuesdays
- Bar and restaurant menus
- Not Amex
- Car park, beer garden, patio with vines, children's play area
- Thruxton motor racing circuit 1 mile, Andover 1 mile, Weyhill (Hawk Conservatory & Country Park) 1 mile

THE GREEN DRAGON

LONDON ROAD, LIPHOOK, HAMPSHIRE GU30 7AN
TEL: 01428 723276

Directions: The inn is located centrally in Liphook, where the A3 meets the B2131 and B3004.

Easy to find in the centre of Liphook, **The Green Dragon** started life in the 17th century as a coaching inn, with stables at the rear and a smithy on the premises. The archway that once led from the street to the stables now leads to the car park at the back, where there is

also a beer garden. Inside, black beams and stone features take the eye, and the bar is a convivial spot for relaxing with a glass of Courage Best, Abbot ale or one of the excellent choice of other draught and bottled beers, lagers, stouts and ciders. Andrew and Eve Ellis, who took charge of the Green Dragon in February 2004, are both chefs, with many years' experience in catering, and they set great

store by the food served here.

Wholesome, tasty snacks and main dishes are available throughout most of the opening hours, and the triple layer sandwiches and hot baguettes served with chips are meals in themselves. Home-made burgers, scampi and chips, and sausage & bacon puffs are other typical choices, with apple spotted dick or rhubarb and orange pudding ending a meal in style. With a couple of days' notice the enterprising Andrew and Eve will prepare a dish of the customer's choice, and the many plans they have for the inn include hog roasts, barbecues and other summer events. Pool and darts are played in the bar, and major sporting fixtures are shown on a big-screen TV.

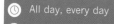

- All day, every day
- Home cooking
- All the major cards
- Car park, beer garden
- Pool, darts, Sky TV, summer barbecues
- Haslemere 3 miles, Petersfield 6 miles

THE GREEN DRAGON AT BROOK

Hampshire

BROOK, NR LYNDHURST, HAMPSHIRE SO43 7HE
TEL: 023 8081 3359

Directions: From J1 of the M27 take the B3078 north to Brook (less than 1 mile).

In a delightful rural setting by a stream spanned by a hump-backed bridge, **The Green Dragon** at Brook has a very long and interesting history. The oldest parts date back to the 15th century, when it was the home of a wheelwright and coffin-maker, but for the last 200 years it has been a charming country inn. This well-established tradition of hospitality is being carried on by experienced licensees Pete and Sandy Smith. Behind the attractive white-painted, thatch-roofed exterior the look is traditional, with beams, exposed brick, brassware, pictures and prints, but the most intriguing feature is the display of 'bends' of leather bearing the imprints of the iron brands that denoted the owners of animals with common rights to graze on New Forest land – the connection with the nearby forest remains strong, and in

summer it's not unusual to see forest ponies gathering in the forecourt.

Food is a very important part of the Green Dragon's business, and the printed menu and the daily specials offer an impressive choice, from filled fresh-baked rolls and jacket potatoes to spicy chicken wings, pasta with a variety of sauces, cod in a salt and vinegar batter, seafood crumble pie and giant Yorkshire puddings filled with liver & bacon casserole or sausage & onion casserole. The daily fresh fish choice is always a popular order, and the inn featured as a finalist in recent Seafood Pub of the Year awards. To accompany all this excellent food are good cask ales and an extensive wine list with helping tasting notes; six wines are available by the glass (two sizes). The Green Dragon has a patio garden and plenty of off-road parking.

- Lunchtime and evening every day
- Bar snacks and full meals
- Not Amex or Diners
- Off-road parking, patio garden
- Bar billiards, occasional live music evenings
- Minstead (13th church, Furzey Gardens, Rufus Stone) 2 miles, Lyndhurst 6 miles

THE HARE & HOUNDS

CHARLTON DOWN, ANDOVER, HAMPSHIRE SP11 0JA
TEL: 01264 735503

Directions: The inn lies off the A343 about 2 miles north of Andover, half a mile south of Wildhern village.

Set back from the road in delightful rural surroundings, **The Hare & Hounds** is a real English country pub offering bags of character, the warmest of welcomes and great food and drink. The facade is part red brick, part pebbledash, and the traditional inn sign of hares and hounds sitting down round a table together is an indication of the really friendly and relaxed atmosphere that visitors will find within. The inn is run by experienced publicans Nick Jeffree and his mother Sheila, and it's Sheila whose hearty home cooking is one the inn's chief assets. Everything on the menu is freshly prepared and full of flavour, and the Sunday roasts bring a loyal clientele from miles around. The bar area and the non-smoking restaurant are at one end of the main public room, while at the other end

the locals are busy playing pool or darts: pub games are a serious business here, and the inn fields teams for darts, pool and cribbage in the local leagues. Quiz nights are another regular feature, along with meat draws, all of which establish the Hare & Hounds as a real pillar of the local community. Visitors will find ample off-road parking, and the inn has a pleasant enclosed beer garden with seats for 30. The finest way of generating a thirst and an appetite is to take advantage of the miles of well-established footpaths in the parish, enjoying a landscape and seeing a variety of wildlife that have changed little down the years. Andover, a short drive to the south, has many interesting places to see, including the striking Guildhall, the town museum and the Church of St Mary, whose interior was modelled on Salisbury Cathedral.

- Lunchtime and evening every day
- Home cooking including Sunday roasts
- £ All the major cards
- P Off-road parking, enclosed garden
- Darts, pool, cribbage – teams in local leagues; quiz nights, meat draws
- ? Lots of local walks with great views; Andover (St Mary's Church, Guildhall, museums) 2 miles

THE KINGS ARMS

ST THOMAS STREET, LYMINGTON, HAMPSHIRE SO41 9NB
TEL: 01590 672594

Directions: From the north the A337 Southampton Road runs right into Lymington; close to the centre of town, St Thomas's Street runs off this road to the left.

Lymington is an ancient seaport and market town that was once an important centre for the manufacture of salt and the building of boats. The broad High Street that leads up from the quay is a hive of activity on Saturdays, when the market that was established in the 13th century is still held, This street leads into St Thomas's Street, where **The Kings Arms** stands, a handsome old redbrick building with a white-painted upper section. Lynda Smith and her son Paul took over here in February of 2002, and they have done a great job in transforming a rather forlorn old people's local into a cheerful, thriving pub that appeals to all ages, to locals and to the many visitors attracted to the town. This they have achieved with the help of Stella, their good-natured Irish wolfhound-cum-lurcher rescue dog, and with the occasional presence of the

friendly ghost Penny, who restricts her appearances to late at night.

The inn is noted for its cask ales, many from local breweries, served straight from the original stillage, and an extensive menu of home-cooked dishes is served in the non-smoking restaurant. Weekly specials add to the choice, and the Sunday roast is always popular. During the week, a £5 express menu caters for lunchers in a hurry, and the lighter snacks include pizzas, Cornish pasties and a superb selection of sandwiches. The Kings Arms is also a very convenient base for getting to know Lymington, and for guests staying overnight there's an en suite double room and an en suite family room (a double bed and 2 single beds). Both have a TV and tea tray, and the tariff includes a choice for breakfast – full English or scrambled eggs with smoked salmon.

- 🕐 11·11 (Sun 12-10.30)
- 🍴 Home cooking
- 🛏 3 rooms en suite
- 🅿 Car park
- 🎵 Darts, Sky TV, monthly live entertainment
- ❓ St Barbe Museum in town; Beaulieu Motor Museum 5 miles, New Forest 5 miles

THE KINGS HEAD

QUAY HILL, LYMINGTON, HAMPSHIRE SO41 3AR
TEL: 01590 672709 FAX: 01590 688453

Hampshire

Directions: From J1 of the M27 or from Lyndhurst take the A337 to Lymington, then the B3054 into the centre of town. The inn is on Quay Hill, near the riverfront.

The Kings Head is a lovely old white-painted brick building with dark blue window surrounds, a slate roof, colourful hanging baskets and a pub sign resembling a king in a pack of cards. Dating back some 300 years, it retains much of old-world appeal, with original beams from old warships, wood panelling and a log fire. The walls are hung with photographs and prints of old sailing vessels, and the talk in the bar often turns to seafaring matters, as the inn is very popular with sailing folk. Landlord Paul Grafton is not short of a few good tales himself, and the atmosphere created by Paul, his staff and his customers is invariably cheerful and convivial; ever since his arrival 12 years ago the pub transformed itself from an unloved local into one of the best and friendliest hostelries in the area,

frequently commended in the local and the national press.

Five real ales – the choice changes regularly – do an admirable job of quenching thirsts, and in the 60-cover restaurant an award-winning chef produces high-quality dishes on a tempting menu that's supplemented by daily specials. The Kings Head is situated very close to the estuary, a short walk from the railway station and just minutes from Lymington's main shopping streets. This ancient seaport and market town has much to interest the visitor, including St Barbe Museum, which tells the story of the area between the New Forest and the Solent with special reference to the salt producing and boatbuilding industries; it also houses a renowned art gallery.

- 🕐 11-2.30 & 6-11, all day Sat & Sun
- 🍴 Home cooking
- 💷 All the major cards
- 🅿 Patio
- ❓ St Barbe Museum in town; ferry to Isle of Wight 1 mile, New Forest 5 miles, Beaulieu Motor Museum 5 miles

THE LUZBOROUGH HOUSE

LUZBOROUGH LANE, ROMSEY, HAMPSHIRE SO51 9AA
TEL: 01794 523816

Hampshire

Directions: From the end of the M3 or from J3 or J4 of the M27 take the A27 in the direction of Romsey. Between roundabouts on the south side of town the A27 is called Luzborough Lane, and the inn is located in this stretch.

Easily found on the A27 on the southern edge of Romsey, **The Luzborough House** is a delightful old redbrick building separated from the main A27 by a side road and a splendid old wall, also of red brick. Inside, exposed brick, old beams and wooden floors continue the traditional look, and sturdy wooden pillars and pew-style seats create separate sections in the open-plan bar. Kevin Daley and his staff have a warm welcome for both drinkers and diners, both of whom will find an excellent selection from which to choose. In the non-smoking conservatory restaurant overlooking the garden a fine range of food is served, with the emphasis on freshness, quality and variety. Herb & garlic bread piled with olives and roasted cherry tomatoes is a

tasty appetiser for two to share, and the printed menu and daily specials present a truly mouthwatering choice, from crab gratin or moules marinière to pastas and salads (served in starter or main course sizes), steaks, glazed ham hock, bouillabaisse, halibut with roasted sweet peppers, best end of lamb with rosemary gravy and, to finish, a lovely lemon tart with lemon and honey marmalade. The regular themed dinner evenings are always popular occasions, as are the weekly quiz nights. The inn has ample off-road parking and a large, attractive garden with lawns, shrubs, borders and plenty of picnic tables to make the most of the summer. The main road location makes The Luzborough House very accessible to motorists, and the many attractions of Romsey are very close by.

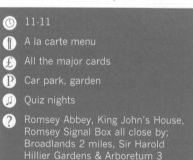

- 🕐 11-11
- 🍴 A la carte menu
- £ All the major cards
- Ⓟ Car park, garden
- 🎵 Quiz nights
- ❓ Romsey Abbey, King John's House, Romsey Signal Box all close by; Broadlands 2 miles, Sir Harold Hillier Gardens & Arboretum 3 miles, Mottisfont Abbey 4 miles

THE OAK

SMANNELL, NR ANDOVER, HAMPSHIRE SP11 6JJ
TEL: 01264 336102 FAX: 01264 332453

Directions: Smannell lies 2 miles north of Andover off the A343.

Smannell is a tiny hamlet a couple of miles north of Andover, and **The Oak** is very much part of its social life. This is especially true since the arrival of tenants Simon and Kim and chef Carly, who all arrived here in February 2004. During their first few months they have breathed new life into The Oak, whose redbrick facade is inlaid with white stone panels – a feature of other buildings in the vicinity. The inside of this former private house on a corner site has been totally refurbished, with period and modern elements combining harmoniously and attractive features that include a brick hearth and supporting columns, high wooden stools and country furniture. Behind the inn are a large car park and a splendid beer garden, where barbecues are planned for balmy summer Sunday evenings.

Food is very important part of the business, and Carly does visitors proud with a variety of lunchtime dishes and evening meals that really do offer something for everyone. Baguettes, burgers, jacket potatoes and salads make tasty quick snacks, and other choices for lunch include chilli con carne, fish & chips, Thai vegetable curry, scampi and an excellent home-made steak & ale pie. In the evening, steaks are a popular order, and the specials board also tempts with such delights as calamari with soy sauce, breast of duck with caramelised apple, lamb shank in mint and rosemary suace, salmon in a white wine sauce and an unusual and very delicious brie and red berry tart. The Oak has become a very popular place for a meal, so it's advisable to book to be sure of a table in the non-smoking restaurant. To enjoy with the food or own there own are well-kept real ales – Wadworth 6X, Henrys IPA and guests – and plenty of wines by bottle or glass.

- Lunchtime and evening
- Home cooking
- Not Diners
- Car park, garden
- Barbecue summer Sunday evenings
- Andover 2 miles, Longparish 5 miles

THE SHIP INN

MAIN ROAD, BISHOPS SUTTON, ALRESFORD, HAMPSHIRE SO24 0AQ
TEL: 01962 732863

Directions: From Winchester take the A31 east towards Alton, pass through New Alresford on to the B3047; 1 mile to Bishops Sutton.

On a corner site in the village of Bishops Sutton, **The Ship Inn** is very much a family affair, with Bob and Mandy Bennett at the helm and daughter Rebecca (Becca) the queen of the kitchen. The sign outside the pink-painted brick building has a different ship under full sail on each side, and the maritime theme is continued prominently inside, with numerous seafaring paintings and prints and nautical memorabilia. A splendid brick hearth boasts a handsome copper hood, and another is adorned with copper pans; the charmingly traditional scene is completed by a feature stone and brick wall, a slatted wooden serving counter, some pew-style seats, rustic wooden tables and row upon row of china mugs.

The Bennetts have made The Ship a favourite port of call for many locals, who have been impressed by the friendliness of the leaseholders, the range of real ales (Ringwood Best is the favourite) and by Becca's excellent food. Her menu of tried and tested pub classics runs from garlic mushrooms and deep-fried brie with cranberry sauce to omelettes, burgers, scampi, cod and plaice, and her super home-made pies – perhaps steak & stilton or steak & ale; sandwiches, baguettes, jacket potatoes and ploughman's platters for lighter or quicker meals. There's always a generous choice of vegetarian dishes – lasagne, curry, kiev, sweet & sour vegetables, nut roast – and children have their own menu. The non-smoking restaurant has 22 covers, and in addition there's small room for private parties of up to 12. Booking is recommended to be sure of a table on Saturday evening and for Sunday's roast lunch.

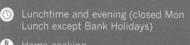

- Lunchtime and evening (closed Mon Lunch except Bank Holidays)
- Home cooking
- Not Diners
- Beer garden
- Themed food evenings, occasional live music

THE STAR INN

THE HORSEFAIR, ROMSEY, HAMPSHIRE SO51 8EZ
TEL: 01794 516353

Directions: The inn is centrally located in Romsey 1 minute from the Abbey.

In the heart of historic Romsey, just a minute's walk from the Abbey, **The Star Inn** is both a convivial local and an excellent base for exploring the town and the many places of interest in the region. Built in the 17th century and originally a weaver's cottage, it was later extended to become the tap for the local Strongs Brewery, and behind the smart black-and-white frontage the look is firmly traditional, with slatted floors, panelling, bespoke stools and tables and chairs and a log burning fire in a big brick hearth.

The inn has been run since the autumn of 2002 by Dawn Whalen and her family, who have made many friends with their ready friendliness and the excellent hospitality they extend to everyone who passes through the doors. In the 40-cover non-smoking dining area all tastes and appetites are satisfied with a daily changing selection of dishes that run from light snacks and sandwiches to full meals and the popular Sunday roasts. Real ale connoisseurs have a choice of four well-kept brews, and tea and coffee are also available. Entertainment includes weekly folk music nights and weekly quizzes, and for visitors staying overnight the inn has four guest bedrooms – two twins and two family rooms – with en suite facilities, TVs and tea trays. The Abbey is just one of many historic buildings to visit in Romsey, a thriving market town on the River Test, and to the south is one of the region's most important country houses, Broadlands, the seat of the Mountbatten family.

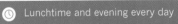

- Lunchtime and evening every day
- Snacks and full meals
- All the major cards
- 4 en-suite rooms
- Beer garden
- Darts, weekly quiz, weekly folk music
- Many historic buildings to see in Romsey. Just south is Broadlands, home of the Mountbatten family.

THE WHEATSHEAF AT BRAISHFIELD

BRAISHFIELD ROAD, BRAISHFIELD, NR ROMSEY,
HAMPSHIRE SO51 0QE
TEL: 01794 368372

Directions: Braishfield is reached by a minor road north of Romsey (4 miles).

Within easy reach of the M3 and M27, **The Wheatsheaf** is a superb country inn with experienced hosts in Peter and Jenny Jones. Drinkers and diners get an equally warm welcome, and Peter and Jenny have always striven to take pub food away from the ordinary and into a fusion of different styles of cooking. Wine and beer are no less important than the food, and a wide range of hand-pulled ales, lagers, wines and soft drinks is available. The bar areas are a real delight, with slatted wooden floors, beams, wood panelling, open fires and a wealth of prints, vintage posters, copper and brass ornaments, pretty lamps and old farming implements. The bars and the lovely garden are ideal to enjoy a drink, but what puts The Wheatsheaf in a class of its own is the outstanding food.

The menu would grace any top-class restaurant, and the reputation built up by Jenny and her team extends far beyond the local towns and villages. Making a final decision on what to order is a problem that faces many a diner, but everything is terrific, from the basket of bread with marinated garlic, red pepper & chilli jelly and herb olive oil to the liqueur coffee that rounds off a meal to remember. In between come classics like Caesar salad or steak & kidney pudding, and more unusual items such as saffron risotto with leeks and wild mushrooms, Shetland blue mussels, crispy shredded duck, fillet of royal bream, smoked lamb with a kumquat and brandy sauce, pan-fried breast of guinea fowl, cheese and leek sausages with creamy mash and carrot crisps, and rhubarb & lemon sponge pudding. Starters and main courses are matched on the menu with suggested appropriate wines.

- ⏰ 11-11
- 🍴 Snacks and full menu
- £ All the major cards
- Ⓟ Car park, garden
- @ website:
  www.wheatsheafbraishfield.co.uk
- ❓ Mottisfont Abbey 3 miles, Sir Harold Hillier Gardens & Arboretum 1 mile, Romsey 4 miles, Winchester 6 miles

THE WHITE HART

THE STREET, EVERSLEY, HAMPSHIRE RG27 0PJ
TEL: 0118 973 2817   FAX: 0118 973 2819

> **Directions:** The inn is located on the main street of Eversley, on the A327 10 miles south of Reading.

Built in 1643 and once at the heart of a working farm, **The White Hart** is everything a country pub should be, with character aplenty in its convivial bars. Wonderful old beams, a fire blazing in a brick hearth, woodblock floors, hand-crafted furniture, small-paned windows and pictures of the inn in days gone by create a great ambience, and a choice of well-kept real ales satisfies country thirsts. At lunchtime, tasty snacks are served, from soup and paté to sandwiches, toasties, jacket potatoes, ploughman's platters and daily hot specials. But the White Hart is probably best known for its close connection with the world of Rugby Union. It is the home base of the Marauders Sevens team, who regularly meet here and organise their fixtures. Dewi Morris and

Jeremy Guscott are just two of the many famous players who have donned Marauders shirts down the years. More familiar pub games also have their place here, including darts, cribbage and shove-halfpenny, and brains are taxed by regular quiz nights.

Eversley, which stands on the A327 about 10 miles south of Reading, was the home of Charles Kingsley, author of *The Water Babies* and *Westward Ho!*. His life is commemorated in a hall in the village and he is buried in the local churchyard. The area around the inn is great walking country, and close by are the Finchampstead Ridges, offering wonderful views across the Blackwater Valley, and the wooded beauty spot of California Country Park, home to 34 different species of tree and the habitat of a wide variety of animals, birds and plants.

- 🕐 Every lunchtime and evening
- 🍴 Lunchtime snacks and daily specials
- 💷 All the major cards
- 🅿 Off-road parking
- 🎵 Darts, quiz nights, cribbage, shove-halfpenny, rugby events
- @ e-mail: seawhitehart@aol.com
- ❓ Great walking country, esp. Finchampstead Ridges 2 miles, Arborfield 4 miles

THE WHITE HART

20 COLLEGE STREET, PETERSFIELD, HAMPSHIRE GU31 4AD
TEL: 01730 262270 FAX: 01730 231619

Directions: Petersfield is located just off the A3; the White Hart is on the eastern edge of town on the Midhurst road.

Phil and Lynne Beckett welcome visitors to **The White Hart**, which they have transformed from near-neglect when they arrived in 2000 into the delightful pub that it is today. The atmosphere in the bars is very warm and friendly, and the inn is the ideal spot to unwind and relax over a drink and a meal. Three real ales are always on tap, along with a good choice of draught and bottle beers and lagers and a selection of wines, and an extensive menu of home-cooked food is served in the conservatory restaurant that overlooks the garden. The cooking is supervised by Lynne, who keeps her customers happy with a daily changing choice of meat, poultry and vegetarian options – and above all, the superb fish dishes for which the inn has become particularly well known. The Sunday roast is another highlight, and the inn has function room that can be booked

🕐 12-11

🍴 Home cooking, Sunday roasts

£ All the major cards

P Off-road parking, garden, children's play area

♫ Quiz nights, annual charity roast

? Museums and galleries in Petersfield, Butser Hill 2 miles

for small parties or other special occasions. This is very much a pub for all the family, and the enclosed secure garden has an excellent children's play area where the little ones can burn up energy in safety.

There's plenty to see in the appealing market town of Petersfield, and among the main attractions are an equestrian statue of William III clad in Roman costume, the Teddy Bear Museum, the Physic Garden and the justly renowned Flora Twirt Gallery filled with charming local scenes drawn and painted by the eponymous artist over a period of 40 years ands left by her to Hampshire County Council on her death in 1985. There's also good walking hereabouts, and the energetic can head for nearby Butser Hill, the highest point of the South Downs, to take some exercise and enjoy spectacular views.

SOUTH HARTING, NR PETERSFIELD, HAMPSHIRE GU31 5QB
TEL: 01730 825355

Directions: From Petersfield take the B2146 to South Harting (about 3 miles). The inn is on the main street of the village.

The White Hart is a stunning country inn set in beautiful gardens on the main street of a village on the edge of the South Downs. The white-painted frontage with tall redbrick chimneys and lots of greenery promises much, and the interior does it more than justice, with an open log fire that never goes out, lots of cosy nooks and crannies and a wealth of pictures, prints and brass ornaments. Mine hosts Vell and Samantha have built up a reputation for hospitality and good food and drink that has spread well beyond the surrounding towns and villages. In the two main bars, an impressive selection of drinks is served, from teas and coffees to real ales, lagers, wines and speciality malt whiskies. Even before alcohol is served the inn is busy doing a breakfast trade, and food remains the main orientation for the rest of the day.

Thick-cut sandwiches with interesting fillings such as goat's cheese with sun-dried tomatoes or roast beef and horseradish and a garnish of chips and salads are almost meals in themselves, while typical main dishes on the ever-changing menu include salmon wrapped in prosciutto served with herby lentils, slow-cooked half-shoulder of lamb or venison steak with garlic mash and a redcurrant jus. Children can have smaller portions or dishes from their own menu, and few diners can resist desserts like treacle tart or spiced pear in red wine. House wines are served by the bottle or by small or regular glass – a typical thoughtful touch from hosts who always put the customer first. With its lovely setting and easy access, The White Hart is a perfect choice for a party or other celebration; the function room can accommodate 60, and Vell and Samantha and their staff are on hand to see that a special occasion really is special.

- 🕐 12-11 (also for breakfast)
- 🍴 Bar and restaurant menus
- 💷 All the major cards
- 🅿 Off-road parking, garden, function room
- ❓ Uppark (National Trust) 2 miles, Buriton 3 miles, Petersfield 3 miles

Hampshire

THE WHITE HORSE

16 KEYHAVEN ROAD, MILFORD-ON-SEA,
HAMPSHIRE SO41 0QY
TEL: 01590 642360

Directions: Milford is on the B3058 5 miles west of Lymington – turn left off the A337 at Everton. The inn is on the eastern edge of Milford on the road towards Keyhaven

Milford-on-Sea is a coastal village between Lymington and Christchurch, and at its very eastern edge stands **The White Horse**. A substantial 18th century building, its brick facade is painted white, with black window surrounds and shutters. The inn is run by Pat and Oggie who took over here 15 years ago. Original timbers add to the traditional look in the bar and lounge, where a good selection of ales and wines is always available. Well-loved pub favourites are the mainstay of the menu and the specials board, and the chef puts a premium on finding the best local produce. Wednesday and Thursday are curry nights, when there's a special offer on meals for two with a choice of five curries and a carafe of red or white wine.

The beer garden has seats for 30, and there's plenty of off-road parking space. For all its early life the White Horse was the last building on the eastern edge of Milford, whose attractions include the 13th century Church of All Saints, great views across The Solent and the odd-looking Hurst Castle with one of Henry VIII's forts at its centre. A pleasant way of building up a thirst and an appetite is to explore the castle, which stands at the end of a spit jutting out into the Solent to within ¾ of a mile from the Isle of Wight. There are plenty of other good walks in the vicinity of the inn, while for motorists Lymington is a short drive to the east, Christchurch a similar distance to the west, with Bournemouth just beyond.

- 🕐 11-3 & 5.30-11
- 🍴 Traditional home cooking, curry nights
- £ All major cards accepted
- Ⓟ Off road parking, beer garden
- ❓ Hurst Castle 1 mile, Lymington 5 miles, Christchurch 5 miles, Bournemouth 7 miles

THE YEW TREE

HOLLINGTON CROSS, ANDOVER ROAD, HIGHCLERE, NR NEWBURY,
BERKSHIRE RG20 9SE
TEL: 01635 253360

Directions: From the M4 J13 take the A34 to Newbury then the A343 Andover
road to Highclere and Hollington Cross.

The Yew Tree is a fine 17th century building in a pleasant setting close to Highclere Castle. A splendid old yew tree does indeed stand by the inn, along with other plants in tubs or flower beds. The immaculate white-painted, slate-roofed frontage leads into an equally delightful interior with low beams and three open fireplaces. Mine host is Eric Norberg, who has run hotels, restaurants, bars and clubs in his native Sweden and all over Europe for the last 30 years. His passion is food and drink, which is good news for his many regular customers and for the visitors who pass this way throughout the year. London Pride and frequently changing guest beers head the drinks list, which also includes an outstanding selection of spirits from around the world.

The daily changing menu includes both familiar classics and less usual pub dishes, from pheasant terrine and Eric's special gravid lax to crayfish and herb risotto, a 1lb 4oz rib of beef, pork with prunes and armagnac, and steamed sea bass with bok choi, spring onions, ginger, chilli and red pepper salsa. Super desserts and excellent Illy coffee round off a memorable meal, which is accompanied by wines expertly selected from vineyards around the world. Finally, there's a tempting list of digestifs with all the familiar names and many more besides – some 27 in all! Highclere Castle is one of many places of interest in the vicinity of the Yew Tree, which is a great base for tourists and for visitors to nearby Newbury races. Comfortable, well-appointed overnight accommodation comprises four double rooms and two twins, all with en suite facilities, TV and tea/coffee trays.

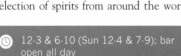

- 🕐 12-3 & 6-10 (Sun 12-4 & 7-9); bar open all day
- 🍴 Home cooked snacks and meals
- 💷 Not Diners
- 🛏 6 bedrooms, all en suite
- 🅿 Car park, patio
- @ email: eric.norberg@theyewtree.net
- ❓ Highclere Castle 2 miles, Burghclere (Sandham Memorial Chapel) 2 miles, Newbury 6 miles

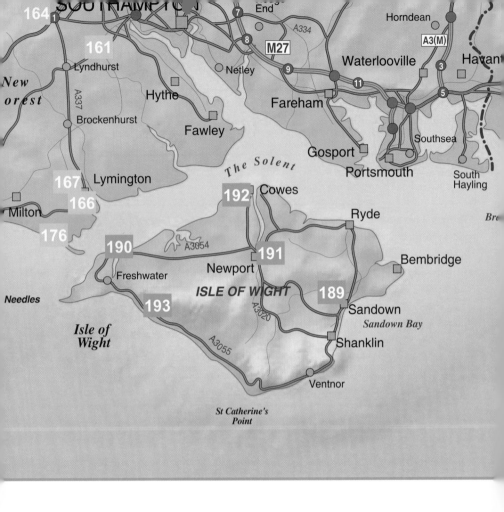

Please note all cross references refer to page numbers

ISLE OF WIGHT

The Isle of Wight has adopted a motto which declares: "All this beauty is of God". It echoes the poet John Keats' "A thing of beauty is a joy for ever", the first line of his poem *Endymion* which he wrote while staying on the island in the hope that its crisp country air would improve his health.

It was comparatively recently that the largest isalnd off the British coast became popular as a resort. This was partly because for centuries, right up until the 1600s, the island was a first port of call for pestiferous French raiders who made the islanders' lives a misery with their constant incursions.

Compton Bay

The turning point came in the 1840s when Queen Victoria and Prince Albert bought an estate near East Cowes, demolished an existing house, and Albert designed and built an Italianate mansion he named Osborne House. A few years later, the Poet Laureate, Alfred, Lord Tennyson, bought Farringford on the eastern side of the island. Socially, the Isle of Wight had arrived.

The Isle of Wight is a paradise for walkers, with hundreds of miles of footpaths and trails, and it's also a popular place for cyclists, while for those who want to do no more than laze and bathe it has no fewer than 23 major beaches.

PLACES OF INTEREST

Bembridge

The most easterly point of the island, Bembridge was itself an island until the reclamation of the huge inland harbour of Brading Haven in the 1880s. The story of that major work is one of many aspects of the town's history featured in the **Bembridge Maritime Museum** which also displays ship models, artefacts from shipwrecks, and diving equipment, as well as action videos of underwater footage and lifeboat rescues. A fascinating exhibition of life in Bembridge, past and present, is portrayed in photographs and artefacts at the **Bembridge Roy Baker Heritage Centre** in Church Road. Also well worth a visit is the **Bembridge Windmill** (National Trust). Dating from around 1700, it is the only windmill to have survived on the island, with much of its wooden machinery still intact.

Brading

For what is little more than a large village, Brading is remarkably well stocked with visitor attractions, among them a diminutive **Town Hall** with whipping post and stocks outside, and a fine church housing some striking tombs of the Oglander family. The most ancient of the village's sights is the **Brading Roman Villa** which in the 3rd century was the centre of a rich and prosperous farming estate. It covers some 300 square feet and has fine mosaic floors with a representation of Orpheus charming wild animals with his lyre.

The oldest surviving house on the island is now home to the **Isle of Wight Waxworks**, an all-weather family attraction displaying scenes and characters from island history. Close by, The **Lilliput Antique Doll & Toy Museum** exhibits more than 2,000 dolls and toys, ranging across the centuries from around 2000 BC to 1945. The collection also includes dolls' houses, tinplate toys, trains, rocking horses, and many unusual and rare playthings.

On the edge of the village stands **Morton Manor**, a lovely old house, dating back to 1249, largely rebuilt in 1680, set in one of the finest gardens in England. The landscaped grounds feature rose and Elizabethan sunken gardens, ponds and cascades, and many mature specimen trees including the largest London Plane you're ever likely to see. Other attractions include the Stable Shop, licensed tearooms, a safe children's play area with a traditional Elizabethan turf maze, and even a vineyard. In fact, Brading has two vineyards: the other is the well-known Adgestone Vineyard, planted in 1968 and the oldest on the island.

A mile or so northwest of the village, **Nunwell House & Gardens** should definitely not be missed. The picturesque house has been a family home since 1522 and is of great historic and architectural interest. It was here that Sir John Oglander, an ancestor of the present owner, was host to Charles I on his last night of freedom and modern day visitors can still see the Parlour Chamber in which they met.

Some of the grandest views on the island can be enjoyed from **Brading Down**, just west of the village on the minor road that leads to Downend. From Downend, it's less than a mile to **Arreton Manor** which claims, with some justification, to be the most beautiful and intriguing house on the Isle of Wight. There was a house on this site long before Alfred the Great mentioned Arreton in his will of 885 AD and the manor was owned by successive monarchs from Henry VIII to Charles I. The present house was built during the reigns of Elizabeth and James I and is a superb example of the architecture of that period, with mellow stone walls and Jacobean panelling complemented by furniture from the same era. Perhaps the most appealing aspect of Arreton is that indefinable atmosphere of a house that has been lived in for centuries. Other attractions include a **Museum of Childhood**, **Lace Museum**, **National Wireless Museum**, gift shop, tea-rooms and picnic area.

A mile or so southwest of Arreton Manor stands another grand old house, **Haseley Manor**. In the mid-1970s, it was a deserted and decaying shell but in a heroic work of restoration has been saved by Raymond and Krystyna Young. They have furnished and decorated the rooms in period, adding audio-visual tableaux explaining the different eras. Visitors can also watch a film showing how the mammoth task of restoration was carried out. Inside the house, there's an indoor play area for small children, a working pottery where children can try their hand at the slippery craft, tea-room and gift shop. Outside, the attractions include magnificent herb, flower and water gardens, a children's farm and adventure playground, and a picnic area.

Calbourne

The most enchanting part of this village is **Winkle Street**, which has a row of charming old cottages opposite the village stream and an ancient sheepwash. Close by, in a lovely landscaped valley, is one of the Island's major attractions, the **Water Mill & Museum of Rural Life**. The mill is the last survivor of the many that once stood on the Island, and exhibits in the Museum include old agricultural machinery, domestic bygones, a vintage fire engine and a giant gun that was originally intended to protect the Needles approach to Portsmouth.

Carisbrooke

John Keats wrote: "I do not think I shall ever see a ruin to surpass **Carisbrooke Castle**". The castle is set dramatically on a sweeping ridge and it's quite a steep climb up from the picturesque village to the massive Gatehouse. This was built in 1598 but the oldest parts of the castle date back to Norman times, most notably the mighty keep which, apart from Windsor, is the most perfect specimen of Norman architecture in Britain.

Carisbrooke Castle

monument in Newport church where the Princess was buried. The effigy, in pure white Carrara marble, bears an inscription stating that it had been erected "as a token of respect for her virtues, and of sympathy for her misfortunes by Victoria R 1856".

More cheerful aspects of a visit to the Castle include the Donkey Centre. Donkeys walking a treadmill were once used to turn the huge 16th century wheel in the Wellhouse to draw water from a well 161 feet deep. A light at the bottom of the well gives some idea of its depth. Before donkeys were trained to raise the water, the task was performed by prisoners and nowadays visitors are invited to have a go at walking the treadmill themselves.

Also within the Castle grounds are a **Coach House Exhibition** and **Victorian Island Exhibition**, the **Isle of Wight Museum** and a tea room.

During the season costumed guides conduct visitors around the noble ruins. The most poignant of their stories concern Charles I and his youngest daughter, Elizabeth. Charles was imprisoned here in the months before his trial and the guides will point out the mullion window through which he unsuccessfully attempted to escape. After the King's execution, Cromwell's Council of State ordered that his daughter Elizabeth, 'for her own safety', should also be incarcerated at Carisbrooke. The 14 year old implored them not to send her to her father's former prison, but they were adamant. Elizabeth was a sickly child and less than a week after her arrival at the Castle she 'was stricken by fever and passed away, a broken-hearted child of fourteen'. The story touched the heart of Queen Victoria, who set up a

Cowes

The origins of Cowes as the most famous yachting resort in the world go back to the early 1800s. It was then a rather ordinary port whose main business was shipbuilding. In 1811, the Duke of Gloucester came to stay and as part of the rather limited entertainment on offer he watched sailing contests between local fishermen. The Duke's patronage led to amateur gentlemen running their own contest and founding a club. The Prince Regent joined the club in 1817 and on his accession as George IV it was first re-christened the **Royal Yacht Club**, and then the **Royal Yacht Squadron**. Nowadays, **Cowes Week** has become the premier yachting event of the year and also a fixture in the social calendar.

Sailing off Cowes

Across the River Medina, **East Cowes** is most famous for **Osborne House**, a clean-cut, Italianate mansion designed and built by Prince Albert in 1846. Queen Victoria loved "dear beautiful Osborne" and so did her young children. They had their very own house in its grounds, a full-size Swiss Cottage, where they played at housekeeping, cooking meals for their parents, and tending its vegetable gardens using scaled-down gardening tools. In the main house itself, visitors can wander through both the State and private apartments which are crammed with paintings, furniture, ornaments, statuary and the random bric-a-brac that provided such an essential element in the decor of any upper-class Victorian home. Osborne House possessed a special place in the Queen's affections. It had been built by the husband she adored with an almost adolescent infatuation: together they had spent many happy family days here. After Albert's premature death from

typhoid in 1861, she often returned to Osborne, her staff instructed to lay out the Prince's clothes in his dressing-room each night, and the Queen herself retiring to bed with his nightshirt clasped in her arms. In 1901 she returned to Osborne for the last time, dying here in her 83rd year.

Freshwater

Freshwater and the surrounding area are inextricably linked with the memory of Alfred, Lord Tennyson. In 1850, he succeeded Wordsworth as Poet Laureate, married Emily Sellwood, and shortly afterwards moved to **Farringford**, just outside Freshwater. Tennyson was an indefatigable walker and, however foul the weather, would pace along nearby High Down dramatically arrayed in a billowing cloak and a black, broad-brimmed sombrero. After his death, the area was re-named Tennyson Down and a cross erected high on the cliffs in his memory. There are more remembrances of the great poet in the **Church of All**

Freshwater Bay

lighthouse and past the line of jagged slabs of gleaming chalk towering some 200 feet high. The sea has gouged deep caves out of the cliffs. Two of them are known as Lord Holmes' Parlour and Kitchen, named after a 17th century Governor of the Island who once entertained his guests in the 'Parlour' and kept his wines cool in the 'Kitchen'.

Saints in Freshwater town where Lady Tennyson is buried in the churchyard and a touching memorial inside commemorates their son Lionel, "an affectionate boy", who died at the age of 32 while returning from India.

As Tennyson grew older, he became increasingly impatient with sightseers flocking to Farringford hoping to catch sight of the now-legendary figure. He moved to his other home at Blackdown in Sussex, where he died in 1892.

About a mile south of the town, Freshwater Bay was once an inaccessible inlet, much favoured by smugglers. It was here that Tennyson persuaded his great friend the pioneer photographer Julia Margaret Cameron to settle. Her home was **Dimbola Lodge**, which now attracts thousands of visitors with its permanent exhibition of her work and that of other distinguished photographers. From the Bay there are regular cruises around the island's most spectacular natural feature, the **Needles**. The boat trip takes you through the swirling waters around the

The Needles are undoubtedly at their most impressive when viewed from the sea, but they are still a grand sight from the land. There are some particularly striking vistas from the **Needles Old Battery**, a Victorian coastal fort standing 250 feet above the sea. Visitors pass through a long tunnel and emerge onto a platform with panoramic views. The **Needles Pleasure Park** at Alum Bay also has good views and offers a wide range of family entertainments, a chairlift from the clifftop to the beach, boat trips to the lighthouse, a glass-making studio and many other attractions.

Newport

Set around the River Medina, Newport has a history going back to Roman times. Excavations in 1926 uncovered the well-preserved remains of a **Roman Villa**, a 3rd century farmhouse in which one side of the building was given over entirely to baths. Visitors can follow the bather's progress through changing room, cold

The Needles

room, warm and hot rooms with underfloor heating systems, and integral cold and hot plunge baths. A Roman style garden has been re-created in the grounds and provides an interesting insight into the wealth of new plants the Romans introduced into Britain.

Newport received its first charter back in 1190 but the growth of the small town received a severe setback in 1377 when it was completely burnt to the ground by the French. Recovery was slow and it wasn't until the 17th century that Newport really prospered again. Indirectly, this was also due to the French since the island was heavily garrisoned during the Anglo-French wars of that period. Supplying the troops with provisions and goods brought great wealth to the town.

Some striking buildings have survived, among them **God's Providence House**, built in 1701 and now a tea room; John Nash's elegant Town Hall of 1816; an 18th century brewers warehouse near the harbour which now houses the **Quay Arts Centre**, incorporating a theatre, two galleries, a craft shop, café and bar; and a charming **Tudor Old Grammar School**. One of the old riverside warehouses is home to the **Classic Boat Museum**, and next door is the **Isle of Wight Bus Museum**.

To the northwest of Newport, **Parkhurst Forest** offers miles of woodland walks, while over to the northeast, at **Wootton, Butterfly World and Fountain World** is home to hundreds of exotic butterflies flying free inside a beautifully landscaped indoor garden with ponds, streams, fountains and waterfalls. Other attractions include an Italian water garden, a Japanese water garden with Koi Carp, a restaurant, garden centre and shop.

Ryde

For many visitors to the Island, Ryde is the arrival point and **Ryde Pier** was one of the first to be built. The town has five miles of sandy beaches and all the usual seaside attractions. The pieris served by an electric railway that runs to Sandown and Shanklin, operated by electric trains retired from service on the Northern Line of London Transport. The line connects with the Isle of Wight Steam Railway at Smallbrook Junction. To the east of Ryde lies **Flamingo Park**, home to colonies of exotic birds.

Isle of Wight

Sandown

"A village by a sandy shore" was how a
guide-book described Sandown in the
1870s. Since then, its superb position on
sweeping Sandown Bay has transformed
that village into the island's premier
resort. Now a lively town, Sandown
offers its visitors every kind of seaside
attraction. There are miles of flat, safe
sands where a Kidzone safety scheme
operates during the season, a traditional
Pier complete with theatre, colourful
gardens, a Sunday market, abundant
sporting facilities, and even pleasure
flights from the nearby airfield. On the
edge of the town, the **Isle of Wight
Zoological Gardens** specialises in
breeding severely endangered exotic
species and is home to the UK's largest
variety of Royal Bengal, Siberian and
Chinese tigers. The Zoo is also a World
Health Organisation centre for
venomous snakes, their venom extracted
for use in antidotes for snake bites.

In Sandown's High Street, the
Museum of Isle of Wight Geology is
especially popular with children who
love its life-sized dinosaurs - the Isle of
Wight is renowned for the number and
quality of the dinosaur remains that have
been discovered here. The museum, "120
million years in the making", has
excellent displays on all aspects of the
island's geology. As part of its
educational programme, museum staff
will advise you on the best places to look
for fossils and, when you return with your
discoveries, will identify them for you.

Shanklin Chine

Shanklin

Like Sandown, Shanklin was just a small
village a century or so ago. The old
village has survived intact, a charming
little complex of thatched houses
standing at the head of the **Shanklin
Chine**. The famous Chine is a
spectacular ravine some 300 feet deep
and 180 feet wide, noted for its waterfalls
and rare flora. There's a Nature Trail to
follow or you can join a guided tour. The
Heritage Centre includes an interesting
exhibit on PLUTO (the Pipe Line Under
The Ocean) secretly constructed
during World War II to transport fuel
from the island to the Continent during
the D-Day landings. There's also a

memorial to the soldiers of 40 Commando who trained in this area for the disastrous assault on Dieppe in 1942.

The old village stands on a 150ft cliff from which the ground slopes gently down to the safe, sheltered beach, with its long, seafront esplanade. With its scenic setting, many public gardens, and healthy climate, Shanklin has appealed to many celebrities. Charles Darwin was particularly fond of the town, the American poet Longfellow fell in love with it, and John Keats was a familiar figure in Sandown throughout the summer of 1818. The grassy open space known as Keats Green commemorates his stay here during which he wrote some of his best-known poems.

Shorwell

Pronounced 'Shorell' by the locals, the village of Shorwell has no fewer than three venerable manor houses within its boundaries. **West Court**, **Wolverton**, and **North Court** were built respectively during the reigns of Henry VIII, Elizabeth I, and James I. They possess all the charm you would expect from that glorious age of English architecture but sadly none of them is open to the public. However, you can visit St Peter's Church to gaze on its mesmerisingly beautiful 15th century wall-painting and admire its 500-year-old stone pulpit covered by an elaborate wooden canopy of 1620.

This small village has yet another attraction. **Yafford Mill** is an 18th century water mill in full working order. It's surrounded by ponds and streams, and the paddocks are home to rare cattle, sheep and pigs, a collection of antique farm machinery, a steam engine and narrow-gauge railway. There are also waymarked nature walks, a playground, picnic area, gift shop, tea gardens and licensed bar.

Ventnor

Along the southeastern corner of the island stretches a 6-mile length of ragged cliffs known as Undercliffe. Clinging to the slopes at its eastern end, Ventnor has been described as 'an alpinist's town' and as 'a steeply raked auditorium with the sea as the stage'. Promoted as a spa town in the 1830s, its distinguished visitors have included a young Winston Churchill and an elderly Karl Marx.

Ventnor Heritage Museum houses a fascinating collection of old prints, photographs and working models relating to the town's history, while **Ventnor Botanical Gardens** shelters some 10,000 plants in 22 acres of grounds, including many rare and exotic trees, shrubs, alpines, perennials, succulents and conifers. There's a picnic area and children's playground, and during August the Gardens host open-air performances of Shakespeare plays. Above the town, **St Boniface Down**, at 785 feet the highest point on the island, provides some dizzying views across coast and countryside.

A mile or so to the west, in neighbouring St Lawrence, The **Isle of Wight Rare Breeds and Waterfowl Park**, set in 30 acres of coastal farmland, operates as a survival centre for more than 40 breeds of rare farm animals. The Park is also home to over 100 species of waterfowl and poultry, there's a guinea pig 'village' and chipmunk 'mansion', special children's areas, a unique temperate waterfall house, lakeside cafeteria and gift shop.

About 3 miles inland from Ventnor, **Appuldurcombe House** is now a sad shell of a once-imposing 18th century mansion, but the ornamental grounds landscaped by 'Capability' Brown provide an enchanting setting for walks and picnics. It also contains an **Owl and Falconry Centre** where daily flying displays and courses in falconry are held. The **Isle of Wight Donkey Sanctuary** is nearby, as is the village of **Godshill** with its magical **Model Village** and the **Nostalgia Toy Museum**.

Yarmouth

A regular ferry links this picturesque little port to Lymington on the mainland. It was once the principal port on the island which was why Henry VIII ordered the building of **Yarmouth Castle** in the 1540s. It was garrisoned until 1885 but is now disused, though much remains. The town also boasts a quaint old **Town Hall**, a working pier, and a 13th century church rather unhappily restored in 1831. It's worth going inside to see the incongruous statue on the tomb of Sir Robert Holmes, Governor of the Island in the mid-17th century. During one of the endless conflicts with the French, Sir Robert had captured a ship on board which was a French sculptor with an unfinished statue of Louis XIV. He was travelling to Versailles to model the King's head from life. Sir Robert decided that the elaborate statue of the King (in full French armour) would do nicely for his own tomb. The sculptor was ordered to replace the Royal head with Sir Robert's. No doubt deliberately, the artist made a poor fist of the job and the head is decidedly inferior to the rest of the statue.

One mile west of this appealing little town, **Fort Victoria Country Park**, owned by the Isle of Wight Council, is one of the major leisure complexes on the island.

THE CASTLE

FITZROY STREET, SANDOWN, ISLE OF WIGHT PO36 8HY
TEL/FAX: 01983 403169

Directions: Sandown lies just off the main A3055 on the east side of the island. The Castle Inn is located 1 minute from the seafront.

Sandown is the island's leading holiday resort town, with miles of safe, flat sands, a traditional pier, museums, gardens, a railway station and all the expected leisure and family attractions. The Castle is a neat redbrick building nestling between white-fronted neighbours a minute's walk from the seafront and close to the shops and other facilities of the town. Patriotic flags and hanging baskets make a colourful sight on the facade, while the look is agreeably traditional in the open-plan bar. This is a real 'locals' pub, with a strong following among the residents, but it is also a favourite with the many visitors who crowd the island in the summer on day trips or holidays. Mine hosts Penny and Dave, prominent figures in the life of the island (he's a local councillor) are always happy to advise tourists of the best way to spend their time. One of the best ways is of course to linger at The Castle, where the

hospitality continues throughout the year. Food is served at lunchtime, the choice spanning familiar favourites such as sandwiches, jacket potatoes, potato wedges and basket meals based on chicken, scampi and goujons of plaice. Among the most popular thirst-quenchers are well-kept real ales, including one from the local Ventnor brewery, one from George Gale in Hampshire and one from Archers of Swindon.

The Castle has off-road parking, a garden and a children's room, and it also offers a comfortable and very convenient base for an island holiday. The two guest bedrooms, both recently refurbished to a commendably high standard, have en suite facilities, TV and tea/coffee trays. Apart from all the amenities expected of a thriving seaside town, Sandown has other attractions, including a zoo and the fascinating Museum of Isle of Wight geology complete with life-size dinosaurs.

- 🕐 12·11
- 🍴 Snacks and meals
- 🅿 Off-road parking
- 🎵 Pool, darts, petanque, cribbage, shove-halfpenny
- ❓ Sandown Zoo, Museum of Isle of Wight Geology; Shanklin Chine 2 miles, Nunwell House at Brading 3 miles

THE KINGS HEAD

QUAY STREET, YARMOUTH, ISLE OF WIGHT PO41 0PB
TEL: 01983 760351

Directions: The inn is located close to the seafront in Yarmouth.

Robert and Michelle Jackson have the welcome mat out for visitors to **The Kings Head**, a 16th century pub in a prime position opposite the harbour. Inside, exposed brick, old beams, copper and brass ornaments, wood panelling, stone floors, rustic table and chairs and well-chosen prints and pictures create a lovely intimate and relaxing ambience in which singles, couples, families and groups are all made to feel equally at ease. Food is an important part of the business at this delightful pub, served every day from 12 to 2.30 and from 6 to 9.30. Fresh fish dishes such as sea bass with a tarragon sauce or lemon sole with mixed peppers and dill are a speciality, and other choices run from lunchtime sandwiches and baguettes to chargrilled burgers (inclduing a vegetarian version), chilli con carne, sizzling fajitas, Italian stone-baked pizzas and daily specials such as crab au gratin, and duck breast with

raspberry sauce. To accompany the excellent cooking or to enjoy on their own are three real ales and a good selection of wines.

In fine weather, tables an chairs are set out on the patio. Yarmouth is a fascinating and picturesque little place with old stone quays, narrow streets and attractive old houses. On of the most interesting buildings, but one that is easy to miss down by the ferry, is Yarmouth Castle, built by Henry VIII in 1547 after the town had been sacked by the French. A climb to the top is rewarded with a fine view of the comings and goings of vessels in the Solent. Just outsdie town is Fort Victoria, whose multiple attractions include a leisure complex, beaches, an aquarium, a planetarium and the largest model railway layout in Britain.

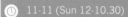

- 🕐 11-11 (Sun 12-10.30)
- 🍴 Home cooking (fresh fish a speciality)
- 💷 All the major cards
- 🅿 Beer garden
- ❓ Fort Victoria Country Park 1 mile, Freshwater 3 miles, The Needles 5 miles

THE OLD STAG INN

2 COWES ROAD, NEWPORT, ISLE OF WIGHT PO30 5TW
TEL: 01983 522709

Directions: From the centre of Newport, take the A3020 towards Cowes. After about a mile and a half you pass the hospital on the right; the inn is a little further on, also on the right.

Built originally as a coaching inn, **The Old Stag Inn** acquired its present name as recently as 1999, having been called at first The Stag and later encumbered with the unlikely name of The Cask & Custard Pot. Behind the distinguished redbrick facade, the spacious bars are attractively furnished and decorated with a wealth of old prints, bygones and local memorabilia. The very welcoming and enthusiastic hosts Stuart and Kevin have made their inn a very popular spot for food, which is served every day from noon right through to 9 o'clock in the evening.

The extensive menu and the specials board cater for all tastes and appetites, with dishes ranging from jacket potatoes, deli-size salads and moules marinière to salmon haollandaise, pan-fried mackerel, beef stroganoff, braised lamb shank and chicken breast in a variety of styles - plain, cajun, garlic or bacon & brie. There are always lots of vegetarian main courses, and children can their own menu or have smaller portions of many dishes on the main menu. The Old Stag is very much part of the local community, and good conversation over a glass or two of real ale goes along with darts, pool, chess and various card games - not forgetting the regular quiz nights. Pétanque is played in the garden, where tables and chairs are set out to make the most of fine days and there is a large car park at the rear. There's plenty for the visitor to see in and around Newport, including important Roman remains, the elegant John Nash town hall and a thriving arts centre. Just outside town, Carisbrooke Castle is one of the island's major attractions.

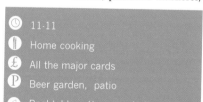

- 🕐 11-11
- 🍴 Home cooking
- 💷 All the major cards
- 🅿 Beer garden, patio
- 🎱 Pool table, pétanque, darts
- @ email: stuartbrock@wight365.net
- ❓ Newport 2 miles, Carisbrooke Castle 2 miles, Parkhurst Forest 1 mile

THE PORTLAND INN

2 WORSLEY ROAD, GURNARD, ISLE OF WIGHT PO31 8JN
TEL: 01983 292948

Directions: The inn stands on the B3325 1 mile from Cowes.

The Portland Inn stands on a corner site in Gurnard, which lies on the southern outskirts of Cowes. Behind the neat cream and white exterior, the look is pleasingly traditonal, with beams, framed pictures and prints and a very handsome wood-clad serving area in the L-shaped main bar. The pub has recently been taken over by Malcolm van Erp, who has enhanced its reputation as a favourite spot where local residents and visitors are equally welcome. Real ales are always available, along with a good selection of beers and lagers, cider, wines and spirits, teas and coffees. Straightforward, value-for-money pub dishes are served during the daytime. Children are allowed in the 40-cover dining area, and of course in the beer garden, a popular spot in summer, when barbecues are a regular event.

It's a very sociable place, with good conversation supplemented by pool, Darts and Sky TV for the big sporting events and also quiz nights. Cowes really comes alive during Cowes Week, a rendezvous for sailors from all over the world and a firm fixture in the social calendar. But Cowes has plenty to attract the visitor throughout the year, including museums, a super model railway exhibition and Queen Victoria's beloved Osborne House. Gurnard is also well placed for some of the island's other attractions, including excellent walking in Parkhurst Forest. The whole island is a paradise for walkers, with hundreds of miles of footpaths and trails; it's also very popular with cyclists, while for those who want to do little but laze and bathe there are no fewer tha 23 major beaches.

- 11-11
- Daytime bar food
- All the major cards
- Beer garden, summer barbecue
- Pool table, TV for sports, quiz nights
- Cowes 1 mile, Osborne House 3 miles, Parkhurst Forest 2 miles, Newport 5 miles

THE SUN INN

HULVERSTONE, ISLE OF WIGHT PO30 4EH
TEL: 01983 741124

> **Directions:** Hulverstone lies just to the west of Brook on the A3055 on the southwest coast of the island.

Just beyond Brook in a beautiful and peaceful past of the island, The Sun Inn brings its own special brand of sunshine to visitors throughout its long opening hours. Owners Chris and Kate have been on the island for 10 years and were previously connected with another pub, the White Lion at Arreton. Hospitality is way of life at The Sun, and its reputation for the warmth of its welcome and the excellence of its food and drink make it a favourite choice not only with residents on all parts of the island but also with the many visitors from the mainland. The white-painted, thatch-roofed inn stands on its own in a quiet country setting, and the views from the large garden extend to the sea and the cliff chalks along the coast at Tennyson Down. Inside, the bar has a traditional look, with flagstone floors and pictures of the island in days gone by. A good

variety of fine ales (including some from the island's brewery) and wines is always available, and good-value meals are served from a menu of familiar favourites supplemented by daily specials. A measure of the Sun's popularity is the opening of a new 80-cover restaurant in time for the summer rush of 2004. The garden tables are in great demand when the sun shines, and the inn has plenty of off-road parking.

This part of the Isle of Wight is particularly serene and beautiful, and there are lovely walks in the vicinity of the inn, along the coast or up on Brighstone Down at 700 feet the highest point on the island. There are many visitor attractions within an easy drive of the Sun, notably the Dinosaur Farm Museum at Brighstone, the National Trust's Mottistone Manor Garden, Dimbola Lodge at Freshwater, Alum Bay with its multi-coloured sands and The Needles, the island's best-known landmark.

🕐 12·11

🍴 Bar and restaurant menus

£ All the major cards

Ⓟ Car park, large garden

@ email: cthesuninn@aol.com

❓ Brighstone Down 2 miles, Dinosaur Farm 5 miles, Tennyson Monument 3 miles, The Needles 4 miles

215 **The Benett Bar**, Tisbury, Salisbury

216 **The Black Horse**, Cherhill, Calne

217 **The Black Horse**, West Tytherley, Salisbury

218 **The Bug & Spider and Marsh View Hotel**, Calne

219 **The Bustard Inn**, Shrewton, Salisbury

220 **The Cat Tavern**, Salisbury

221 **The Cross Inn**, Tisbury

222 **The Crown Inn**, Cholderton, Salisbury

223 **The Duke of York**, Holloway, Malmesbury

224 **The Fountain Inn**, Whiteparish, Salisbury

225 **The Foxham Inn**, Foxham, Chippenham

226 **The French Horn**, Pewsey

227 **The Old Inn**, Allington, Salisbury

228 **The Oliver Cromwell**, Bromham, Devizes

229 **The Red Lion**, Upavon, Pewsey

230 **The Riverside Inn**, Bradford-on-Avon

231 **The Royal Oak**, Corsley Heath, Warminster

232

The Silver Plough, White Hill, Pitton

233 **The Swan Inn**, Enford, Pewsey

234 **The Wheatsheaf**, Wilton, Salisbury

235 **The White Bear Inn**, Devizes

236 **The White Horse**, Biddestone, Chippenham

237 **The Wyndham Arms**, Dinton, Salisbury

Please note all cross references refer to page numbers

WILTSHIRE

Wiltshire is a county rich in the monuments of prehistoric man; it also has one of the highest concentrations of historic houses and gardens in the country. It's a great place for walking and cycling, with wide open spaces, woodland and downland and a number of chalk streams that are home to a huge variety of wetland wildlife. And the county has its own very special surprises in the shape of the famous white horses, the intriguing crop circles and, above all, the great and ancient stone circles, rich in history and mystery and legend. Pretty villages abound, and the area in and around the distinguished town of Marlborough takes in some of the most renowned prehistoric sites in the country, as well as monuments to Wiltshire's industrial past.

Stourhead Gardens

Wiltshire

Salisbury and south Wiltshire are a part of traditional England, with 6,000 years of history, and a delight for visitors from all over the world. The jewel in the crown of the county is

Stonehenge, near Amesbury

Salisbury, at the confluence of the Rivers Avon, Wylye, Bourne and Nadder, with its glorious Cathedral, a masterpiece of the Early English style. Elsewhere in the region are the chalk downs and river valleys, the stately homes and picturesque villages, the churches, the ancient hill forts and, above all, Stonehenge, one of the great mysteries of the prehistoric world.

The region's more recent, industrial heritage is also evident in many forms, from brewing at Devizes to Wilton's carpet factory.

Queen Elfrida founded an abbey here in 979 in atonement for her part in the murder of her son-in-law, Edward the Martyr, at Corfe Castle. Henry II rebuilt the abbey's great Church of St Mary and St Melor, whose tall central tower is the only structure to survive from the pre-Norman monastery. A mile to the north of Amesbury, the A345 passes along the eastern side of **Woodhenge**, a ceremonial monument even older than Stonehenge. It was the first major prehistoric site to be discovered by aerial photography, its six concentric rings of post holes having been spotted as cropmarks by Squadron Leader Insall in 1925. Like Stonehenge, it seems to have been used as an astronomical calendar. When major excavation was carried out in the 1920s, a number of neolithic tools and other artefacts were found, along with the skeleton of a three-year-old child whose fractured skull suggested some kind of ritual sacrifice.

Two miles west of Amesbury at the junction of the A303 and A344/ A360 stands **Stonehenge** itself, perhaps the greatest mystery of the prehistoric world, one of the wonders of the world, and a monument of unique importance. The World Heritage Site is surrounded by the remains of ceremonial and domestic structures, many of them accessible by road or public footpath. The great stone blocks of the main ring are truly massive, and it may be that the stones in the outer rings - rare bluestones from the Preseli Hills of west Wales - had to be transported over 200 miles. Stonehenge's orientation on the rising and setting sun has always been one of its most remarkable features, leading to theories that the builders were from a sun-worshipping culture or that the whole structure is part of a huge astronomical calendar ... or both. The mystery remains, and will probably remain for ever.

Avebury

A 28-acre World Heritage Site is the centre of the **Avebury Stone Circles**, the most remarkable ritual megalithic monuments in Europe. A massive bank and ditch enclose an outer circle and two inner circles of stones. The outer circle of almost 100 sarsen stones (sand and silica) encloses two rings with about 40

Avebury Stone Circles

stones still standing. Archaeologists working on the site have recently found the remains of a long-vanished avenue of stones leading south towards Beckhampton. This discovery seems to vindicate the theory of the 18th century antiquary William Stukeley, who made drawings of the stone circles with this avenue marked. The stones in the avenue had disappeared so completely (perhaps destroyed out of some superstition in the Middle Ages) that few believed Stukeley. The research team from Southampton, Leicester and Newport Universities uncovered a series of subterranean features which appear to be buried stones and the sockets in which they were set. Two large stones, known as Adam and Eve, had always been known about on this route, but there were no further traces until the team's discoveries in 1999. The **Avebury Stones** bear testimony to the enormous human effort that went into their construction: some of the individual stones weigh 40 tons and all had to dragged from Marlborough Downs. Many of the archaeological finds from the site are displayed in Avebury's **Alexander Keiller Museum**, which also describes the reconstruction of the site by Keiller

in the 1930s.

Avebury has a gem from Elizabethan times in **Avebury Manor**, which stands on the site of a 12th century priory. The house and its four-acre walled garden, which features a wishing well, topiary, a rose garden and an Italian walk, are owned by the National Trust.

Box

Bath stone is still quarried at this delightful spot, which is best known for one of the foremost engineering feats of its time, **Box Tunnel**. The 1.8 mile railway tunnel took five years to excavate and when completed in 1841 was the longest such tunnel in the world.

Bradford-on-Avon

A historic market town at a bridging point on the Avon, which it spans with a superb nine-arched bridge with a lock-up at one end. The town's oldest building is the **Church of St Lawrence**, believed to

Kennet & Avon Canal, Bradford-on-Avon

have been founded by St Aldhelm around 700. It 'disappeared' for over 1,000 years, when it was used variously as a school, a charnel house for storing the bones of the dead, and a residential dwelling. It was re-discovered by a keen-eyed clergyman who looked down from a hill and noticed the cruciform shape of a church. Another of the town's outstanding buildings is the mighty **Tithe Barn**, once used to store the grain from local farms for Shaftesbury Abbey.

Off the A363 on the northern edge of town, **Barton Farm Country Park**, which once served Shaftesbury Abbey, offers delightful walks in lovely countryside by the River Avon and the Kennet & Avon Canal.

Half a mile south of town by the River Frome is the Italian-style **Peto Garden** at **Iford Manor**. Famous for its romantic, tranquil beauty, its steps and terraces, statues, colonnades and ponds, the garden was laid out by the architect and landscape gardener Harold Ainsworth Peto between 1899 and 1933. He was inspired by the works of Lutyens and Jekyll to turn a difficult hillside site into "a haunt of ancient peace".

Broad Chalke

A Saxon village where the 17th century diarist has a small estate. A warden of the parish church, he was also a keen angler, and wrote of his beloved River Ebble: *"There are not better trouts in the Kingdom of England than here."* The designer and photographer Sir Cecil Beaton spent his final years in Broad

Chalke and is buried in All Saints churchyard.

Calne

A former weaving centre in the valley of the River Marden; the prominent wool church reflects the prosperity of earlier times. One of the memorials in the church is to Dr Ingenhousz, who is widely credited with creating a smallpox vaccination before Jenner.

A short distance from Calne, to the west, stands **Bowood House**, built in 1625 and now a treasury of Shelborne family heirlooms, paintings, books and furniture. In the Bowood Laboratory, Dr Joseph Priestley, tutor to the 1st Marquess of Lansdowne's son, conducted experiments that resulted in the identification of oxygen. The house is set in lovely Capability Brown grounds with a lake and terraced garden. The mausoleum was commissioned in 1761 by the Dowager Countess of Shelborne as a memorial to her husband and was Robert Adam's first work for them. A separate woodland garden of 60 acres, with azaleas and rhododendrons, is open from late April to early June.

The **Atwell Motor Museum**, on the A4 east of Calne, has a collection of over 70 vintage and classic cars and motorcycles from the years 1924 to 1983.

Castle Combe

The loveliest village in the region, and for some the loveliest in the country, Castle Combe was once a centre of the

Castle Combe

Oldbury Castle is another of Wiltshire's famous white horses. This one was built in 1790 under the instruction of Dr Christopher Alsop, known as 'the mad doctor'. For some years the horse's eye, four feet across, was filled with upturned bottles which sparkled in the sunlight.

prosperous wool trade, famed for its red and white cloth, and many of the present-day buildings date from the 15th and 16th centuries, including the Perpendicular Church of St Andrew, the covered market cross and the manor house, built with stones from the Norman castle that gave the village its name. One of the Lords of the Manor in the 14th century was Sir John Fastolf, who was reputedly the inspiration for Shakespeare's Falstaff.

Cherhill

Cherhill was a stop on the London-Bristol coaching route, and, for a time in the 18th century, one which caused passengers some trepidation. The Cherhill gang regularly held up and robbed the coaches, and the fact they carried out their crimes wearing nothing at all made identification more than a little tricky.

On the chalk ridge south of the village by the ancient earthwork of

Chippenham

This historic settlement on the banks of the Avon was founded around 600 by the Saxon king Cyppa. It became an important administrative centre in King Alfred's time and later gained further prominence from the wool trade. It was a major stop on the London-Bristol coaching run and is served by the railway between the same two cities. Buildings of note include the Church of St Andrew (mainly 15th century) and the half-timbered Hall, once used by the burgesses and bailiffs of the Chippenham Hundred and latterly a museum (the **Chippenham Museum and Heritage Centre** is now in the Market Place). At Hardenhuish Hall on the edge of town, John Wood the Younger of Bath fame built the Church of St Nicholas; completed in 1779, it is notable for its domed steeple and elegant Venetian windows.

In the flood plain to the east of Chippenham stands the 4½-mile footpath known as **Maud Heath's Causeway**. This remarkable and ingenious walkway consisting of 64 brick and stone arches was built at the end of the 15th century at the bequest of Maud Heath, who spent most of her life as a poor pedlar trudging her often muddy way between her village of Bremhill and Chippenham. She died a relatively wealthy woman, and the land and property she left in her will provided sufficient funds for the upkeep of the causeway, which is best seen near the hamlet of Kellaways. A statue of Maud, basket in hand, stands overlooking the flood plain at Wick Hill.

Clench Common

A lovely part of the world for walking or cycling. The Forestry Commission's West Woods, particularly notable for its bluebells in May, has a picnic site. The **Wansdyke Path**, a long earthwork of a single bank and ditch, forms part of the wood's boundary. Also nearby is Martinsell Hill, topped by an ancient fort. Downland to the east of the fort is particularly beautiful in early spring and summer.

Codford St Peter & Codford St Mary

Sister villages beneath the prehistoric remains of **Codford Circle**, an ancient hilltop meeting place which stands 617 feet up on Salisbury Plain. The church in Codford St Peter has one of Wiltshire's finest treasures in the form of a 9th

century Saxon stone carving of a man holding a branch and dancing. East of Malmpit Hill and visible from the A36 is a rising sun emblem carved by Australian soldiers during World War 1. In the military cemetery at Codford St Mary are the graves of Anzac troops who were in camp here. Anzac graves may also be seen at nearby Baverstock.

Corsham

"Corsham has no match in Wiltshire for the wealth of good houses," asserted no less an authority than Nikolaus Pevsner. Many of the town's fine buildings are linked to the prosperity that came from the two main industries of cloth-weaving and stone-quarrying. **Corsham Court**, based on an Elizabethan house dating from 1582, was bought by Paul Methuen in 1745 to house a fabulous collection of paintings and statuary. The present house and grounds are principally the work of Capability Brown, John Nash, Thomas Bellamy and Humphrey Repton - a top-pedigree setting for the treasures inside, which include paintings by Caravaggio, Fra Lippo Lippi, Reynolds, Rubens and Van Dyke, and furniture by Chippendale. Among other important buildings in Corsham are a row of 17th century Flemish weavers' cottages, an old market house and the superb almshouses built in 1668 by Dame Margaret Hungerford. A unique attraction is the Underground Quarry Centre, the only shaft stone mine open to the public in the world, opened in 1810 and reached by 159 steps. Helmets, lamps and an experienced guide are provided for this fascinating underground tour that tells the story of Bath stone from rock face to architectural heritage.

Cricklade

The only Wiltshire town on the Thames was an important post on the Roman Ermin Street and had its own mint in Saxon times. It has many buildings of interest, notably the Church of St Sampson, with its cathedral-like four-spired tower, where a festival of music takes place each September; the famous school founded by the London goldsmith Robert Jenner in 1651; and the fancy Victorian clock tower. Nearby **North Meadow** is a National Nature Reserve where the rare snakeshead fritillary grows.

Crofton

The eastern end of the Vale of Pewsey carries the London-Penzance railway and the Kennet & Avon Canal, which reaches its highest point near Crofton. The site is marked by a handsome Georgian pumping station which houses the renowned **Crofton Beam Engines**. The most venerable dates from 1812 and is the oldest working beam engine in the world.

Devizes

At the western edge of the Vale of Pewsey, Devizes is the central market town of Wiltshire. The town was founded in 1080 by Bishop Osmund, nephew of William the Conqueror. The bishop was responsible for building a timber castle between the lands of two powerful manors, and this act brought about the town's name, which is derived from the Latin 'ad divisas', or 'at the boundaries'. After the wooden structure burnt down, Roger, Bishop of Sarum, built a stone castle in 1138 that survived until the end of the Civil War, when it was demolished. Bishop Roger also built two fine churches in Devizes. Long Street is lined with elegant Georgian houses and also contains the Wiltshire Archaeological and Natural History Society's **Devizes Museum**, which has a

Devizes Castle

splendid collection of artefacts from the area, and a gallery with a John Piper window and regularly changing exhibitions.

Devizes Visitor Centre is based on a 12th century castle and takes visitors back to medieval times, when Devizes was home to the finest castle in Europe and the scene of anarchy and unrest during the struggles between Empress Matilda and King Stephen. An interactive exhibition shows how the town came to be at the centre of the 12th century Civil War and thrived as a medieval town.

Many more of the town's finest buildings are situated in and around the old market place, including the Town Hall and the Corn Exchange. Also here is an unusual **Market Cross** inscribed with the story of Ruth Pierce, a market stall-holder who stood accused, in 1753, of swindling her customers. When an ugly crowd gathered round her, she stood and pleaded her innocence, adding "May I be struck dead if I am lying". A rash move, as she fell to the ground and died on the spot.

Devizes stands at a key point on the Kennet & Avon Canal, and the **Kennet & Avon Canal Museum** tells the complete story of the canal in fascinating detail. Many visitors combine a trip to the museum with a walk along the towpath, which is a public footpath. Each July the Canalfest, a weekend of family fun designed to raise funds for the upkeep of the canal, is held at the Wharf, which is also the starting point,

on Good Friday, of the annual Devizes-Westminster canoe race.

Dinton

Two National Trust properties to visit near this lovely hillside village. **Little Clarendon** is a small but perfectly formed Tudor manor house; **Philipps House** is a handsome white-fronted neo-Grecian house with a great Ionic portico. The work of the early 19th century architect Jeffrey Wyattville, it stands in the beautiful grounds of Dinton Park.

East and West Kennet

West Kennet Long Barrow, one of Britain's largest neolithic burial tombs, is situated a gentle stroll away from the twin villages. The tomb is of impressive proportions - 330 feet long, 80 feet wide and 10 feet high - and is reached by squeezing past some massive stones in the semicircular forecourt.

Easton Grey

Here the southern branch of the River Avon is spanned by a handsome 16th century bridge with five stone arches. A manor house has overlooked the village since the 13th century, and the present house, with a classical facade and an elegant covered portico, dates from the 18th century. It was used as a summer retreat by Herbert Asquith, British Prime Minister from 1908 to 1916, and in 1923 the Prince of Wales was in residence during the Duke of Beaufort's hunting season at Badminton.

Highworth

The name is appropriate, as the village stands at the top of a 400-foot incline, and the view from **Highworth Hill** takes in the counties of Wiltshire, Gloucestershire and Oxfordshire. There are some very fine 17th and 18th century buildings round the old square, and the parish church is of interest: built in the 15th century, it was fortified during the Civil War and was attacked soon after by Parliamentarian forces under Fairfax. One of the cannonballs which struck it is on display outside. The church contains a memorial to Lieutenant Warneford, who was awarded the VC for destroying the first enemy Zeppelin in 1915.

Imber

The part of Salisbury containing the village of Imber was closed to the public in 1943 for use by American troops and has been used as a firing range by the Army ever since. The evicted villagers were told that they could return to Imber after the War, but the promise was not kept and the village has remained uninhabited.

Lacock

The National Trust village of Lacock is one of the country's real treasures. The quadrangle of streets - East, High, West and Church - holds a delightful assortment of mellow stone buildings, and the period look (no intrusive power cables or other modern-day eyesores)

keeps it in great demand as a film location. Every building is a well-restored, well-preserved gem, and overlooking everything is **Lacock Abbey**, founded in 1232 by Ela, Countess of Salisbury in memory of her husband William Longsword, stepbrother to Richard the Lionheart. In common with all monastic houses, Lacock was dissolved by Henry VIII, but the original cloisters, chapter houses, sacristy and kitchens survive.

Much of the remainder of what we see today dates from the mid-16th century, when the abbey was acquired by Sir William Sharington. He added an impressive country house and the elegant octagonal tower that overlooks the Avon. The estate next passed into the hands of the Talbot family, who held it for 370 years before ceding it to the National Trust in 1944.

The most distinguished member of the Talbot family was the pioneering photographer William Henry Fox Talbot, who carried out his experiments in the 1830s. The **Fox Talbot Museum** commemorates the life and achievements of a man who was not just a photographer but a mathematician, physicist, classicist, philologist and transcriber of Syrian and Chaldean cuneiform. He also remodelled the south elevation of the abbey and added three new oriel windows. One of the world's earliest photographs shows a detail of a latticed oriel window of the abbey; made in 1835 and the size of a postage stamp, it is the earliest known example of a photographic negative. Fox Talbot's grave is in Lacock cemetery.

Longleat

Longleat House, the magnificent home of the Marquess of Bath, was built by an ancestor, Sir John Thynne, in a largely symmetrical style, in the 1570s. The inside is a treasure house of old masters, Flemish tapestries, beautiful furniture, rare books.....and Lord Bath's murals. The superb grounds of Longleat House were landscaped by Capability Brown and now contain one of the country's best known venues for a marvellous day out. In the famous **Safari Park** the Lions of Longleat, first introduced in 1966, have been followed by a veritable Noah's Ark of exotic creatures, including elephants, rhinos, zebras and white tigers. The park also features safari boat rides, a narrow-gauge railway, children's amusement area, garden centre and the largest hedge maze in the world.

Longleat House

Lover

In the vicinity of this charmingly-named village is the National Trust's **Pepperbox Hill** topped by an early 17th century octagonal tower known as **Eyre's Folly**. Great walking, great views.

Ludwell

Near the village is the National Trust-owned **Win Green Hill**, the highest point in Wiltshire, crowned by a copse of beech trees set around an ancient bowl barrow. From the summit there are wonderful views as far as the Quantock Hills to the northwest and the Isle of Wight to the southeast.

Lydiard Tregoze

On the western outskirts of Swindon, **Lydiard Park** is the ancestral home of the Viscounts Bolingbroke. The park is a delightful place to explore, and the house, one of Wiltshire's smaller stately homes, is a real gem, described by Sir Hugh Casson as "a gentle Georgian house, sunning itself as serenely as an old grey cat". Chief attractions inside include the little blue Dressing Room devoted to the 18th century society artist Lady Diana Spencer, who became the 2nd Viscountess Bolingbroke. St Mary's

Church, next to the house, contains many monuments to the St John family, who lived here from Elizabethan times. The most striking is the **Golden Cavalier**, a life-size gilded effigy of Edward St John in full battledress (he was killed at the 2nd Battle of Newbury in 1645).

Malmesbury

England's oldest borough and one of its most attractive. The hilltop town is dominated by the impressive remains of the **Benedictine Malmesbury Abbey**, founded in the 7th century by St Aldhelm. In the 10th century, King Athelstan, Alfred's grandson and the first Saxon king to unite England, granted 500 acres of land to the townspeople in gratitude for their help in resisting a Norse invasion. Those acres are still known as King's Heath and are owned by 200 residents who are descended from those far-off heroes. Athelstan made Malmesbury his capital and he is buried in the abbey, where several centuries later a monument was put up in his honour.

The abbey tower was the scene of an early attempt at human-powered flight when in the early part of the 11th century Brother Elmer strapped a pair of wings to his arms, flew for about 200 yards and crashed to earth, breaking both legs and becoming a cripple for the rest of his long life. The flight of this intrepid cleric, who reputedly forecast the Norman invasion following a sighting of Halley's Comet, is commemorated in a stained glass window. The octagonal **Market Cross** in the town square is one of many interesting buildings that also include the Old Stone House with its colonnade and gargoyles, and the arched Tolsey Gate, whose two cells once served as the town jail.

In the **Athelstan Museum** are displays of lace-making, costume, rural life, coins, early bicycles and tricycles, a manually-operated fire engine, photographs and maps. Personalities include a local notable, the philosopher Thomas Hobbes.

A more recent piece of history concerns the **Tamworth Two**, the pigs who made the headlines with their dash for freedom. Their trail is one of many that can be followed in and around the town

Marlborough

Famous for its public school and its broad high street, Marlborough is situated in the rural eastern part of Wiltshire in the upland valley of the Kennet, which flows through the town. It was once an important staging post on the coaching run from London to Bath and Bristol, and the presence of the A4 means that it still has easy links both east and west. Its main street, one of the finest in the country, is dignified by many Tudor houses and handsome Georgian colonnaded shops, behind which are back alleys waiting to be explored. St Mary's Church, austere behind a 15th century frontage, stands in **Patten Alley**, so named because pedestrians had to wear pattens (an overshoe with a metal sole) to negotiate the mud on rainy days. The porch of the church has a ledge where churchgoers would leave their pattens before entering. Other buildings of interest include those clustered round The Green (originally a Saxon village and the working-class quarter in the 18th and 19th centuries); the turn-of-the-century Town Hall looking down the broad High Street; and the ornate 17th century Merchant's House, now restored as a museum.

Marlborough College was founded in 1843 primarily for sons of the clergy. The Seymour family built a mansion near the site of the Norman castle. This mansion was replaced in the early 18th century by a building which became the Castle Inn and is now C House, the oldest part of the College.

Pewsey

In the heart of the beautiful valley that bears its name, this is a charming village of half-timbered houses and thatched cottages. It was once the personal property of Alfred the Great, and a statue of the king stands at the crossroads in the centre. The parish church, built on a foundation of sarsen stones, has an unusual altar rail made from timbers taken from the San Josef, a ship captured by Nelson in 1797.

Attractions for the visitor include the old wharf area and the **Heritage Centre**. In an 1870 foundry building it contains an interesting collection of old and unusual machine tools and farm machinery. The

original **Pewsey White Horse**, south of the village on Pewsey Down, was cut in 1785, apparently including a rider, but was redesigned by a Mr George Marples and cut by the Pewsey Fire Brigade to celebrate the coronation of King George VI. **Pewsey Carnival** takes place each September, and the annual Devizes to Westminster canoe race passes through **Pewsey Wharf**.

A minor road runs past the White Horse across Pewsey Down to the isolated village of **Everleigh**, where the Church of St Peter is of unusual iron-framed construction. Rebuilt on a new site in 1813, it has a short chancel and narrow nave, an elegant west gallery and a neo-medieval hammerbeam roof.

Salisbury

The glorious medieval city of Salisbury stands at the confluence of four rivers, the Avon, Wylye, Bourne and Nadder. Originally called New Sarum, it grew around the present Cathedral, which was

Salisbury High Street and Gate

Cathedral Close, Salisbury

built between 1220 and 1258 in a sheltered position two miles south of the site of its windswept Norman predecessor at Old Sarum. Over the years the townspeople followed the clergy into the new settlement, creating a flourishing religious and market centre whose two main aspects flourish to this day.

One of the most beautiful buildings in the world, **Salisbury Cathedral** is the only medieval cathedral in England to be built all in the Early English style - apart from the spire, the tallest in England which was added some years later and rises to an awesome 404 feet. The Chapter House opens out of the cloisters and contains, among other treasures, one of the four surviving originals of Magna Carta. The oldest working clock in Britain and possibly in the world is situated in the fan-vaulted north transept; it was built in 1386 to strike the hour and has no clock face. The Cathedral is said to contain a door for each month, a window for each day and a column for each hour of the year. A small statue inside the west door is of Salisbury's 17th century **Boy Bishop**: it was a custom for choristers to elect one of their number to be bishop for a period lasting from St Nicholas Day to Holy Innocents Day (6-28 December). One year the boy bishop was apparently literally tickled to death by the other choristers; since he died in office, his statue shows him in full bishop's regalia.

The Close, the precinct of the ecclesiastical community serving the Cathedral, is the largest in England and contains a number of museums and houses open to the public. **Salisbury Museum**, in the 17th century King's House, is home of the Stonehenge Gallery and the winner of many awards for excellence. Displays include Early Man, Romans and Saxons, the Pitt Rivers collection, Old Sarum, ceramics, costume, lace, embroidery and Turner watercolours. A few doors away is **The Royal Gloucestershire, Berkshire and Wiltshire Museum** housed in a 13th century building called the Wardrobe, which was originally used to store the bishop's clothes and documents. The museum tells the story of the county regiments since 1743 and the exhibits include Bobbie the Dog, the hero of Maiwand, and many artefacts from foreign campaigns. The house has a riverside garden with views of the famous water meadows. The historic **Medieval Hall** is the atmospheric setting for a 30-minute history of Salisbury in sound and pictures.

Silbury Hill

Mompesson House, a National Trust property, is a perfect example of Queen Anne architecture notable for its plasterwork, an elegant carved oak staircase, fine period furniture and the important Turnbull collection of 18th century drinking glasses. In the Market Place is the **John Creasey Museum** and the **Creasey Collection of Contemporary Art**, a permanent collection of books, manuscripts, objects and art. Also in the Market Place, in the library, is the Edwin Young Collection of 19th and early 20th century oil paintings of Salisbury and its surrounding landscape. There are many other areas of Salisbury to explore on foot and a short drive takes visitors to the ruins of **Old Sarum**, abandoned when the bishopric moved into the city. Traces of the original cathedral and palace are visible on the huge uninhabited mound, which dates back to the Iron Age. Old Sarum became the most notorious of the 'rotten boroughs', returning two Members of Parliament, despite having no voters,

until the 1832 Reform Act stopped the cheating. A plaque on the site commemorates Old Sarum's most illustrious MP, William Pitt the Elder.

Savernake Forest

The ancient woodland of **Savernake Forest** is a magnificent expanse of unbroken woodland, open glades and bridle paths. King Henry Vlll hunted wild deer here and married Jane Seymour, whose family home was nearby. Designated an SSSI (Site of Special Scientific Interest), the forest is home to abundant wildlife, including a small herd of deer and 25 species of butterfly.

Silbury Hill

The largest man-made prehistoric mound in Europe, built around 2800BC, standing 130 feet high and covering five acres. Excavation in the late 1960s revealed some details of how it was constructed but shed little light on its purpose. Theories include a burial place for King Sil and his horse and a hiding place for a large gold statue built by the Devil on his way to Devizes.

Steeple Ashton

The long main street of this village is lined with delightful old buildings, many featuring half-timbering and herringbone brickwork. The Church of St Mary the Virgin, without a steeple since it was struck by lightning in 1670, houses the **Samuel Hey Library**, whose highlight is the early 15th century Book of Hours.

Stourton

The beautiful National Trust village of Stourton lies at the bottom of a steep wooded valley and is a particularly glorious sight in the daffodil season. The main attraction is, of course, **Stourhead**, one of the most famous examples of the early 18th century English landscape movement. The lakes, the trees, the temples, a grotto and a classical bridge make the grounds a paradise in the finest 18th century tradition, and the gardens are renowned for their striking vistas and woodland walks as well as a stunning selection of rare trees and specimen shrubs, including tulip trees, azaleas and rhododendrons. The house itself, a classical masterpiece built in the 1720s in Palladian style for a Bristol banker, contains a wealth of

Grand Tour paintings and works of art, including furniture by Chippendale the Younger and wood carvings by Grinling Gibbons. On the very edge of the estate, some three miles by road from the house, the imposing King Alfred's Tower stands at the top of the 790ft Kingsettle Hill. This 160ft triangular redbrick folly was built in 1772 to commemorate the King, who reputedly raised his standard here against the Danes in 878.

Swindon

Think Swindon, think the Great Western Railway. Think GWR, think Isambard Kingdom Brunel. The largest town in Wiltshire, lying in the northeast corner between the Cotswolds and the Marlborough Downs, was an insignificant agricultural community before the railway line between London and Bristol was completed in 1835.

Stourhead Gardens

Swindon Station opened in that year, but it was some time later, in 1843, that Brunel, the GWR's principal engineer, decided that Swindon was the place to build his locomotive works. Within a few years it had grown to be one of the largest in the world, with as many as 12,000 workers on a 320-acre site that incorporated the Railway Village; this was a model development of 300 workmen's houses built of limestone extracted from the construction of Box Tunnel. This unique example of early-Victorian town planning is open to the public as the **Railway Village Museum**.

The **Great Western Railway Museum** moved from the same site in Faringdon Road in the autumn of 1999 to a new home in the former GWR works, with a new name, a great deal more space and a host of new interactive exhibits. **STEAM** has a superb collection of locomotives (6000 *King George V* is the star), nameplates, signalling equipment and an exhibition of the life and achievements of Brunel; it also focuses on the human aspect of a hard industry, telling the story of the men and women who built and repaired the locomotives and carriages of God's Wonderful Railway for seven generations. The last locomotive to be built at the works was 92220 *Evening Star*, a powerful 2-10-0 freight engine destined to have all too short a working life. Engineering work continued on the site until 1986, when the works finally closed. The site now also contains the **National Monuments Record Centre** - the public archive of the Royal Commission on the Historical Monuments of England, with 7 million photographs, documents and texts.

There's lots more to Swindon than the legacy of the GWR: it's a bustling and successful commercial town with excellent shopping and leisure facilities and plenty of open spaces. One such is **Coate Water Country Park** on the Marlborough road.

Trowbridge

The county of town of Wiltshire, and another major weaving centre in its day. A large number of industrial buildings still stand, and the Town Council and Civic Society have devised an interesting walk that takes in many of them. The parish church of St James, crowned by one of the finest spires in the county, contains the tomb of the poet and former rector George Crabbe, who wrote the work on which Benjamin Britten based his opera *Peter Grimes*. Trowbridge's most famous son was Isaac Pitman, the shorthand man, who was born in Nash Yard in 1813.

Warminster

The largest centre of population is a historic wool, corn-trading and coaching town with many distinguished buildings, including a famous school with a door designed by Wren. In addition to the 18th and 19th century buildings, Warminster has a number of interesting monuments: the Obelisk with its feeding troughs and pineapple top erected in

1783 to mark the enclosure of the parish; the Morgan Memorial Fountain in the Lake Pleasure Grounds; and *Beyond Harvest*, a statue in bronze by Colin Lambert of a girl sitting on sacks of corn. Warminster's finest building is the Church of St Denys, mainly 14th century but almost completely rebuilt in the 1880s to the design of Arthur Blomfield. The **Dewey Museum**, in the public library, displays a wide range of local history and geology. To the west of town is the 800ft **Cley Hill**, an Iron Age hill fort with two Bronze Age barrows. Formerly owned by the Marquess of Bath, the Hill was given to the National Trust in the 1950s and is a renowned sighting place for UFOs. (The region is also noted for the appearance of crop circles and some have linked the two phenomena.)

On the northern edge of Warminster, **Arn Hill Nature Reserve** forms a circular walk of two miles through woodland and open downland.

West Overton

The area between Marlborough and Avebury sees the biggest concentration of prehistoric remains in the country. The scattered community of West Overton stands at the foot of **Overton Hill**, the site of an early Bronze Age monument called **The Sanctuary**. These giant standing stones are at the southeastern end of West Kennet Avenue, an ancient pathway which once connected them to the main megalithic circles at Avebury. Overton Hill is also

the start point of the Ridgeway long-distance path, which runs for 80 miles to the Chilterns. Just off this path is **Fyfield Down**, now a nature reserve, where quarries once provided many of the great stones that are such a feature of the area. **Devil's Den** long barrow lies within the reserve. The local legend that Satan sometimes appears here at midnight attempting to pull down the stones with a team of white oxen has not in recent times been corroborated.

Westbury

Westbury, at the western edge of the chalk downlands of **Salisbury Plain**, was a major player in the medieval cloth and wool trades, and still retains many fine buildings from the days of great prosperity, including some cloth works and mills. It was formerly a 'rotten borough' and returned two MPs until 1832. Scandal and corruption were rife, and the **Old Town Hall** in the market place is evidence of such goings-on, a gift from a grateful victorious candidate in 1815. This was Sir Manasseh Massey Lopes, a Portuguese financier and slave-trader who 'bought' the borough to advance his political career.

All Saints Church, a 14th century building on much earlier foundations, has many unusual and interesting features, including a stone reredos, a copy of the Erasmus Bible and a clock with no face made by a local blacksmith in 1604. It also boasts the third heaviest peal of bells in the world.

On the southern edge of town is

another church well worth a visit. Behind the simple, rustic exterior of St Mary's, Old Dilton, are a three-decker pulpit and panelled pew boxes with original fittings and individual fireplaces. Just west of Westbury, at Brokerswood, is Woodland Park and Heritage Centre, 80 acres of ancient broadleaf woodland with a wide range of trees, plants and animals, nature trails, a lake with fishing, a picnic and barbecue area, a tea room and gift shop, a museum, a play area and a narrow-gauge railway.

By far the best-known Westbury feature is the famous **Westbury White Horse**, a chalk carving measuring 182 feet in length and 108 feet in height. The present horse dates from 1778, replacing an earlier one carved to celebrate King Alfred's victory over the Danes at nearby Ethandun (Edington) in 878. The white horse is well looked after, the last major grooming being in 1996. Above the horse's head are the ruins of Bratton Castle, an Iron Age hill fort covering 25 acres.

Westbury White Horse

The third oldest borough in England, once the capital of Saxon Wessex. It is best known for its carpets, and the **Wilton Carpet Factory** on the River Wylye continues to produce top-quality Wilton and Axminster carpets. Visitors can tour the carpet-making exhibition in the historic courtyard then go into the modern factory to see the carpets made on up-to-date machinery using traditional skills and techniques. Alongside the factory is the Wilton Shopping Village offering high-quality factory shopping in a traditional rural setting.

Wilton House is the stately home of the Earls of Pembroke. When the original house was destroyed by fire in 1647, Inigo Jones was commissioned to build its replacement. He designed both the exterior and the interior, including the amazing Double Cube Room, and the house was further remodelled by James Wyatt. The art collection is one of the very finest, with works by Rembrandt, Van Dyke, Rubens and Tintoretto; the furniture includes pieces by Chippendale and Kent. There's plenty to keep children busy and happy, notably the Wareham Bears (a collection of 200 miniature costumed teddy bears), a treasure hunt quiz and a huge adventure playground. There's a Tudor kitchen, a Victorian laundry and 21 acres of landscaped grounds with parkland, cedar trees, water and rose gardens and an elegant Palladian bridge.

The **Church of St Mary and St Nicholas** is a unique Italianate church built by the Russian-born Countess of Pembroke in 1845. The lavish interior is resplendent with marble, mosaics, richly carved woodwork and early French stained glass.

Wootton Bassett

A small town with a big history. Records go back to the 7th century, and in 1219 King Henry lll granted a market charter (the market is still held every Wednesday). The most remarkable building in Wootton is the **Old Town Hall**, which stands on a series of stone pillars, leaving an open-sided ground-floor area that once served as a covered market. The museum above contains a rare ducking stool, silver maces and a mayoral sword of office.

A section of the **Wilts & Berks Canal** has been restored at **Templars Fir**. In May 1998 about 50 boats of all kinds were launched on the canal and a day of festivities was enjoyed by all. The railway station, alas, has not been revived after falling under the Beeching axe in 1966.

Wootton Rivers

An attractive village with a real curiosity in its highly unusual church clock. The Jack Sprat Clock was built by a local man from an assortment of scrap metal, including old bicycles, prams and farm tools, to mark the coronation of King George V in 1911. It has 24 different chimes and its face has letters instead of numbers.

Wroughton

Wroughton Airfield, with its historic Second World War hangars, is home to the **National Museum of Science and Industry's** collection of large aircraft, and the road transport and agricultural collection.

Nearby **Clouts Wood Nature Reserve** is a lovely place for a ramble, and a short drive south, by the Ridgeway, is the site of **Barbury Castle**, one of the most spectacular Iron Age forts in southern England. The open hillside was the scene of a bloody battle between the Britons and the Saxons in the 6th century; the Britons lost and the Saxon kingdom of Wessex was established under King Cealwin. The area around the castle is a country park.

THE BENETT BAR

THE BENETT ARMS HOTEL, HIGH STREET, TISBURY, NR SALISBURY,
WILTSHIRE SP3 6HD
TEL: 01747 870428

Wiltshire

Directions: From the A30, about 5 miles northeast of Shaftesbury, take the minor road on the left to Ansty and Tisbury (3 miles)

Part of the Benett Arms Hotel, but run independently from it, **The Benett Bar** is a focal point in the social life of Tisbury. The mid-Victorian building, which takes its name from a notable local family, has a splendidly traditional look, and the scene inside is set by black beams running up white walls, a wood-panelled main bar counter,

thatch for the bar in the games area - where pool and darts are played - and everywhere lots of bric-a-brac including wagon wheels hanging from the ceilings.

Owners Alan and Colette took over in April 2003, enhancing its status as one of the town's most popular meeting places. They share the cooking, and they tell the customers what dishes are available at any time. The Sunday roasts

are always popular, so booking is definitely recommended. The regular real ales are London Pride and Ringwood Best, joined by a frequently changing guest ale. The village of Tisbury is well worth taking time to explore, and among the notable buildings are one of the longest tithe barns in the country and the 12th century Church of St John the Baptist, which contains some splendid monuments to the Arundell family of nearby Wardour Castle. This castle, one of the most romantic ruins in England, is a venue for regular special events during the summer. Another attraction within easy reach is Farmer Giles Farmstead at Teffont Magna, one of the most popular choices in the region for a family day out.

- 🕐 11-3 & 6-11 (all day Fri, Sat & Sun)
- 🍴 Home cooking (no written menu); Sunday roast
- 🅿 Small front and side parking areas
- 🎵 Pool table, darts, jukebox
- ❓ Old Wardour Castle 3 miles, Farmer Giles Homestead 5 miles, Dinton Park Gardens 6 miles

Wiltshire

THE BLACK HORSE

MAIN ROAD, CHERHILL, NR CALNE, WILTSHIRE SN11 8QT
TEL: 01249 813365   FAX: 01249 819069

Directions: From the M4 (J16) take the A3102 heading towards Calne. On reaching Calne, take the A4 heading out towards Marlborough. The inn is situated approximately 3 miles to the east of Calne on the left hand side of the A4.

The village of Cherhill was once a stop on the London-Bristol coaching route. Today's travellers can be sure of a warm reception and excellent hospitality if they break their journey at the **Black Horse**. The inn has a large car park and a beautiful beer garden. The proprietor of this neatly maintained old building is Arthur Hall MBE, who came into the licensed trade after a long career as a military man. He and his staff welcome visitors into a very pleasant bar with a log fire, traditional decor and furnishings, where it is a real pleasure to relax with a pint of one of their many real ales or a glass of wine. The wine list offers a fine choice, with many wines available by the glass (two sizes), a perfect complement to the first-class food served every lunchtime and evening. The main menu's change

seasonally and there is a Chef's Special board that changes weekly offering a large variety of choice. Equal attention is paid to preparation and presentation, and both of these menus cater very well for the vegetarians amongst us. Arthur also organises theme evenings to feature cuisines from around the world. South of the village is the ancient earthwork of Oldbury Rings and one of Wiltshire's most famous white horses cut into the chalk next to the Landsdown Monument. There are many other interesting sights in the locality, notably the Avebury Stone Circle, one of the most remarkable ritual megalithic monuments in Europe. Many villages had their gangs of highway robbers in the 17th and 18th centuries, but Cherhill's were just that little bit different – they carried out their dastardly deeds completely naked!

- 🕐 11am -11pm
- 🍴 Home cooking including Sunday roasts
- 💷 All major cards accepted
- 🅿 Off-road parking, large garden area
- ❓ Avebury Stone Cicle 4 miles, Oldbury Castle, Landsdown Monument and White Horse 1 mile, Calne Motor Museum 3 miles, Bowood House 4 miles.

THE BLACK HORSE

THE VILLAGE, WEST TYTHERLEY, NR SALISBURY, WILTSHIRE SP5 1NF
TEL: 01794 340308

> **Directions:** From Salisbury take the A30 road towards Stockbridge and turn right at Middle Winterslow; follow signs through Winterslow to West Tytherley.

A warm and friendly welcome from Martin, Gail and their staff awaits visitors to **The Black Horse**, a 17th century coaching inn with a delightfully traditional look and ambience. The scene in the bars is set by gleaming brassware, displays of china, log burning fires in great brick hearths and a mixture of rustic and pew-style seating. Gail does the cooking, combining classics such as cod with chips and mushy peas or the popular Sunday roasts with some unusual twists. Three real ales are always available, along with a wide range of draught and bottled beers and an extensive wine list. One of the dining areas is designated non-smoking.

Special occasions such as Valentine's

Day bring themed menus, and the inn has a skittle alley which doubles as a function room to cater for private parties. There's also a room for darts and pool, while outside are large gardens with plenty of picnic tables, an enclosed patio and a children's play area. Easily reached by minor roads off the A30 Salisbury-Stockbridge road, the Black Horse is a great base for walking, cycling and touring, with country lanes and little villages to explore, along with easy access to Salisbury. The inn's two guest bedrooms – a double and a twin – provide quiet, comfortable overnight accommodation followed by a good breakfast to start the day. Gail has returned to the village after growing up in West Tytherley, so she is a fund of knowledge about the places to visit around the inn.

- 🕐 11.30-2.30 (Sat to 4) & 6.30-11 (Sat from 6), Sun 12-4 & 7-10.30; summer times vary
- 🍴 Home cooking including Sunday roasts
- 💷 Major cards except Amex & Diners
- 🛏 1 twin, 1 double for B&B
- 🅿 Car park, garden, children's play area, function room
- 🎵 Skittles alley, pool & darts room
- ❓ Walking, cycling, Salisbury 10 miles, Stockbridge 8 miles

THE BUG & SPIDER AND MARSH VIEW HOTEL

221 OXFORD ROAD, CALNE, WILTSHIRE SN11 8AW
TEL: 01249 813318 FAX: 01249 813300

Directions: The Bug & Spider lies 1 mile north of Calne on the Oxford Road A 3102.

Public house, hotel and restaurant: the **Bug & Spider** and **Marsh View Hotel** offers this versatile package in a convenient location in the Wiltshire countryside just north of Calne. The Bug & Spider is a traditional pub catering for both local residents and the many motorists who pass this way on leisure trips or on business. It has a convivial bar serving snacks, fine ales, premium lagers and the usual range of wines and spirits, providing hospitality, conversation, music, darts, a big TV screen for watching major sporting events and even the newspapers to read. A well-planned development adjacent to the Bug houses the Marsh View Hotel & Restaurant.

The hotel offers 12 en suite guest rooms

including one suitable for disabled guests. Rooms are available for single, twin or family occupancy and each has a TV and DVD/CD player, and fax, email and answerphone facilities make the hotel a short-term office for business people. A conference room has recently been added to the amenities, and the beer garden and adventure playground are available to users of both pub and hotel. In the restaurant, chef-patron Quenton Hartlett produces lunchtime and evening snacks and meals to remember on a regularly changing à la carte dinner menu supplemented by daily market specials – people really pressed for time can order ahead and find their meal waiting for them. The hotel is an ideal base for exploring this area, whose attractions include Calne itself, a former weaving centre with a fine medieval church, the elegant Bowood House and Lacock Abbey.

- All day every day
- Home cooking on a varied menu
- £ Major cards
- 12 en suite rooms, 1 suitable for disabled guests
- P Car park, courtyard
- Darts, large screen TV
- @ email:q.b.hartlett@btopenworld.com
- ? Calne 1 mile, Bowood House 3 miles, Lacock Abbey 8 miles, Salisbury Plain 15 miles

THE BUSTARD INN

THE BUSTARD HAMLET, SHREWTON, NR SALISBURY, WILTSHIRE
TEL: 01980 620345

Directions: The inn is on Salisbury Plain in the Bustard Hamlet 2 miles north of Shrewton off the A360.

In a remote location on Salisbury Plain, **The Bustard Inn** offers visitors the best of several worlds - great walking and wide-open spaces, access to some of the most historic sights in the country, and a delightful escape from the bustle of city life. Delightfully and unpretentious, it is in the excellent care of Roy Harris, who earlier ran it for seven years. When he left, the spirit of the place seemed to leave with him, but when he returned with Sharon Maton in September 2003 the old spark came alive again and its very special appeal was restored. Sharon, a professional chef, is queen of the kitchen, producing splendid dishes every session except Sunday evening.

The bar menu and the à la carte provide a first-class choice, and the steaks and the roasts are particular popular; booking is recommended on Friday and Saturday evenings, Sunday lunch and all Bank Holidays. The non-smoking restaurant has 26 covers, and the inn has a super 100-seat function room - a splendid venue for a meeting, a special occasion or a celebration. Wadworth 6X, the local Bustard Ale and a rotating guest make up the real ales on tap, and on a bright summer's day there's nothing to match chatting with friends and sipping a glass or two in the lovely lawned garden with its strudy wooden table and chairs, its colourful borders and a charming little well. Overnight accommodation comprises four upstairs bedrooms, available all year round and let on a room only basis. The inn takes its name from the bird which has recently been reintroduced on the Plain after a lengthy absence.

- 🕐 Lunchtime and evening (all day at leaseholder's discretion)
- 🍴 Bar menu and à la carte
- 🛏 4 upstairs bedrooms available all year
- 🅿 Off-road parking, garden
- ❓ Stonehenge 4 miles, Woodhenge 6 miles, Salisbury 10 miles

Wiltshire

THE CAT TAVERN

115 SOUTH WESTERN ROAD, SALISBURY, WILTSHIRE
TEL: 01722 327955

Directions: The inn stands at the junction of South Western Road and Fisherton Street adjacent to the railway station.

The Cat Tavern is situated just off St Pauls roundabout, which is on the ring road on the western side of the city. It's easy to spot with its rich red colour scheme and assorted cat motifs, and inside there's a pleasing variety of decor and moods, from the old panelled bar counter to the main eating area with an easy-on-the-eye blue and yellow colour scheme. Cats naturally appear in various decorative forms, along with brass ornaments, potted plants, old maps and an eclectic mix of tables and chairs.

The Cat serves hearty, freshly prepared food throughout the day, starting with a full English breakfast from 8 o'clock and ranging from sandwiches to steaks. Coffee, tea and hot chocolate are available as well as 2 or 3 real ales, proper cider and a selection of wines, and for those in a hurry food and drink can be ordered to take away. Live music sessions are held on Sundays, and there's a weekly quiz. The Cat is also an excellent choice as a base for anyone visiting Salisbury either as a tourist or on business: it has six guest bedrooms – three singles and three twins, with TV, tea trays and adjacent shower rooms. Salisbury has an almost endless variety of things to see and do, from the magnificent Cathedral and several museums to excellent shopping and art galleries.

- 🕐 8am-11pm
- 🍴 Home cooking from breakfast onwards
- 🛏 6 B&B rooms with adjacent showers
- 🅿 Cash machine on the premises
- 🎵 Weekly quiz, Sunday live music
- ❓ All the attractions of Salisbury are within easy reach

THE CROSS INN

THE QUARRY, TISBURY, WILTSHIRE SP3 6PS
TEL: 01747 871328

Directions: From the A30, about 5 miles northeast of Shaftesbury, take the minor road on the left to Ansty and Tisbury (3 miles).

A lane to the north of Ansty descends into the lovely valley of the upper Nadder to the historic community of Tisbury, where one of the most distinctive buildings is **The Cross Inn**. An old stone inn of unusual angles on a corner site, it has a magnificent thatched roof that reaches down almost to the ground floor windows (and it's a two-storey building). The inn is run in friendly, homely style by Colin and Heather, and the bars, with their beams, panelling and rustic furniture, are delightful spots to meet the regulars over a glass or two of real ale. In this charmingly traditional ambience, Heather produces a selection of generously served home-cooked dishes

that include a choice of two meats as the centrepiece of here Sunday lunches.

The Cross is very much at the heart of village life; darts, pool and cribbage are the favourite games, and there are regular music and light entertainment evenings and popular fund-raising parties. The inn has a beer garden with tables and chairs, and an adjacent car park. The thatch on its roof, splendid though it is, definitely takes second place to the thatch that tops the best-known building in the village: this is one of the largest surviving tithe barn in England, with 5,400 square feet of thatch covering the whole of its 200ft long roof. Tisbury also has a lovely old riverside church (Rudyard Kipling's parents are buried in the churchyard) and has also managed to keep its main-line railway service.

- 🕐 11-11
- 🍴 Home cooking including Sunday roasts
- 💷 All the major cards
- 🅿 Car park, beer garden
- 🎵 Darts, pool, cribbage, regular music and light entertainment
- @ email: tisburycross@aol.comTisbury
- ❓ Tithe Barn; Old Wardour Castle 3 miles, Farmer Giles Homestead 5 miles, Dinton Park Gardens 6 miles

Wiltshire

THE CROWN INN

CHOLDERTON, NR SALISBURY, WILTSHIRE SP4 6NW

TEL/FAX: 01980 629247

Directions: From the A303 take the A338 towards Salisbury; Cholderton is about 1 mile along this road. The inn is at the south end of the village.

'Just a thoroughly nice pub' is the unanimous verdict on **The Crown Inn,** a fine old building with a superb thatched roof complemented by a charming thatched wishing well on the front patio. Easy to find on the main A338 at the south end of the village, this traditional country pub complete with beams, brasses and a welcoming log fire is a lovely place to pause on a journey or to seek out for the excellent hospitality offerd by the new tenants Gordon and Mandy.

Ringwood Best and Spitfire are the resident real ales, along with rotating guest ales, and Gordon's good honest pub dishes are available throughout opening hours. The regular curry nights are always popular. Children are welcome, and they even have their own menu.

There's also an area for them to play in the large garden, beyond which is an even larger paddock where car boot sales are held. The small village of Childerton lies beside the River Avon close to the Hampshire border, with the expanse of Salisbury Plain to the north and east. This is great walking country, and Salisbury itself is a short drive down the A338. Amesbury, Stonehenge and Woodhenge lie to the west, while in the other direction lie Thruxton motor racing circuit and the town of Andover. Closer than all these is one of the county's premier family attractions - Cholderton Rare Breeds Farm Park, whose residents include poultry of all kinds, sheep and 50 different breeds of rabbit. High-season highlights include the famous 'Pork Stakes' pig races.

- 🕐 Lunchtime and evening (all day during BST)
- 🍴 Snacks and full meals
- £ Not Amex or Diners
- Ⓟ Car park, garden
- ❓ Rare breeds Farm 1½ miles, Stonehenge 7 miles, Salisbury 13 miles

THE DUKE OF YORK

HOLLOWAY, MALMESBURY, WILTSHIRE SN16 9HX
TEL: 01666 823229

Directions: The inn stands near the A429 Cirencester road just north of Malmesbury.

Standing in its own grounds close to the Cirencester road north of Malmesbury, **The Duke of York** offers excellent hospitality throughout the day. Food is taken very seriously here, and landlord Wayne Cosens is also the chef. He was formerly a butcher, so diners can be sure that the meat and indeed all the other produce

used is of the best quality. Classics such as whitebait, prawn cocktail and garlic mushrooms precede meat, fish and vegetarian options on the main menu, and the Sunday roasts always bring in the crowds. Only the hungriest or serious trenchermen accept the Duke of York challenge to finish off one or other of

two giant plates, one involving 1lb of cod and 1lb of plaice with all the trimmings, the other a mind-boggling mixed grill with steak, lamb, pork, sausages, eggs, chips, onion rings, tomatoes, mushrooms and peas: the reward is a free meal on the next visit!

The inn has one main bar, a 20-cover non-smoking eating area and a 100-cover function room. Pool, darts and skittles are the favourite pub games, and there's live music at the weekend. The Duke of York has ample car parking space and a beer garden, and a pleasant riverside walk leads to the gardens of Malmesbury Abbey. The remains of the Abbey dominate England's oldest borough, and the splendid old octagonal Market Cross is just one of many interesting buildings in the town.

- 🕐 12-11
- 🍴 Home cooked snacks and meals including Sunday roasts
- 💷 All the major cards
- 🅿 Off-road parking, beer garden, function room
- 🎵 Pool, skittles, darts
- ❓ Riverside walks to Abbey garden, Market Cross, Athelstan Museum and other sights of Malmesbury; Cotswold Water Park 6 miles, Westonbirt Arboretum 8 miles

Wiltshire

THE FOUNTAIN INN

THE STREET, WHITEPARISH, NR SALISBURY, WILTSHIRE SP5 2SG
TEL: 01794 884266 FAX: 01794 884447

Directions: From Salisbury take the A36 southbound; after about 6 miles turn left on to the A27 for Whiteparish.

Steve behind the bar and Juliet in the kitchen make an excellent partnership at **The Fountain Inn**, and in their 15 years here they have built up a strong following among the local community. Their inn, white-painted and green shuttered on a corner site in the village of Whiteparish, is also an ideal spot for visitors to pause, being on a main road and very accessible from both Salisbury and Romsey. At the front is the comfortable open-plan bar, where there's always a selection of cask ales to enjoy, while to the rear is the restaurant. The ambience throughout is just right for a fine old country inn, with beamed ceilings, ancient ships' timbers and small-paned windows contributing to the

traditional look.

The Fountain is very much food-orientated, and the daily changing list of dishes chalked up on blackboards provides customers with pleasant problems in choosing what to order. Typical choices range from home made soups to pan-fried sardines for starters, to classic cod cooked in beer batter, home-made pies, creole chicken and minted lamb steaks for main courses. Meals are served with a choice of four different potatoes together with fresh vegetables or salad. The theme evenings are also always very popular occasions. The Fountain Inn is surrounded by open countryside, with great walking and terrific views, and the six guest bedrooms, all with en suite facilities, TVs and tea trays, provide an ideal base for both country-lovers and visitors to nearby Salisbury and Romsey.

- 🕐 Both sessions every day
- 🍴 Home cooking with regular theme evenings
- 💷 All the major cards
- 🛏 6 en suite rooms
- Ⓟ Car park, garden
- 🎵 Darts, dominoes
- @ website: 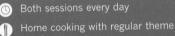 www.the-fountain-inn.com
- ❓ Great walking and great views in the surrounding countryside; Salisbury 10 miles, Romsey 6 miles

THE FOXHAM INN

FOXHAM, NR CHIPPENHAM, WILTSHIRE SN15 4NQ
TEL: 01249 740665

Directions: From J17 of the M4 follow signs to Sutton Benger; turn left at T-junction through Sutton Benger and Christian Malford. Follow signs to the inn on this road.

Tucked away down country lanes, **The Foxham Inn** is well worth seeking out for the excellent hospitality provided by chef-patron Iain Murray-Clarke and his wife Louise. The beautiful redbrick building is made even more lovely by creepers, greenery and flowers in tubs and wooden troughs, and the promise of the outside is more than fulfilled within, where a log fire in a brick hearth, panelling and pine benches and tables all play their part in creating a really warm and welcoming scene. This is definitely a place to relax and when the weather's kind it's a perfect spot to enjoy a drink in the open air. Whatever the weather, visitors to this outstanding inn can look forward to enjoying super home-cooked food complemented by top-class ales and well-chosen wines (plenty available by the glass).

In the bar and non-smoking restaurant Iain's menu and his daily specials board offer mouthwatering choices that take their inspiration from near and far: garlicky wild mushrooms topped with Brie, liver and bacon with sage gravy and mash, chicken and prawn Singapore noodles with prawn crackers, beer-battered haddock and chips with mushy peas, a lovely vegetarian dish of griddled halloumi with citrus couscous, roasted vegetables and salsa, steaks served plain or with a choice of green peppercorn, Stilton, garlic butter or Dijon mustard sauce with caramelised brown sugar topping. Special menus are produced for notable dates in the calendar, including food and wine evenings. This is a really exceptional country pub where it's easy to forget that busy Chippenham and Calne are just a short drive away.

- Tues-Fri 12-2.30 & 7-11, Sat/Sun 12 -3, Sat 7-11, Sun 7-10.30
- Bar snacks and full menu
- All except Amex and Diners
- Car park
- Theme nights, food & wine evenings
- website: www.thefoxhaminn.co.uk
- Chippenham 5 miles, Calne 5 miles

THE FRENCH HORN

MARLBOROUGH ROAD, PEWSEY, WILTSHIRE SN9 5NT
TEL: 01672 562443 FAX: 01672 562785

Directions: The French Horn is situated on the A345 1 mile north of Pewsey.

Close to the Kennet & Avon Canal on the northern outskirts of the attractive town of Pewsey, the **French Horn** has built up an enviable reputation for its food, drink and hospitality. That reputation extends far outside the region, as the inn has earned entries in the most prestigious guides, and for many visitors no stay in the region is complete without a meal at the French Horn. Barrie and Pauline Ineson and their staff always aim to provide the best, which includes a choice of three Cask Marque real ales, quality wines and the best and freshest of seasonal and wherever possible local ingredients for the wide choice of dishes. These range from light snacks and bar meals, which include some South African dishes, to a full à la carte menu, and everything is home-made and cooked to order. The restaurant and family room are non-smoking areas, but smoking is allowed in the bar.

Hanging baskets and window boxes adorn the redbrick facade, while inside, open log fires, copper and brass ornaments, pictures and prints create a very welcoming and traditional ambience. At the rear of the inn is a beer garden with tables and chairs overlooking the Canal and with an enclosed children's play area. Pewsey is a delightful village of half-timbered houses and thatched cottages that was once the property of King Alfred. A statue of the King stands at the crossroads in the centre of the village, and other attractions in and around Pewsey include the Heritage Centre and one of the most famous of Wiltshire's white horses cut in chalk.

🕐 Mon-Thurs 11.30-3 & 6-11, Fri&Sat 11.30-11, Sun 12-10.30

🍴 Home cooking

£ All the major cards

Ⓟ Off-road parking, canalside garden, children's play area, function room

@ email: info@french-horn.co.uk website: www.french-horn.co.uk

❓ Golf; in Pewsey: Heritage Centre, Pewsey Wharf; Pewsey White Horse 2 miles

THE OLD INN

TIDWORTH ROAD, ALLINGTON, NR SALISBURY, WILTSHIRE SP4 0BN
TEL: 01980 610421

> **Directions:** The Old Inn lies on the A338 Salisbury-Swindon road about 7 miles northeast of Salisbury.

Standing on the main A338 seven miles north of Salisbury, **The Old Inn** is equally popular as a much-loved 'local' and as a magnet for a considerable passing trade. Jonathan and Jane Baker left London and bought the lease in July 2003, since when they have applied their many years of management experience in enhancing the inn's attractions and the service offered to their customers. Jane is the chef, personally supervising the menus and the purchasing. Everything is prepared and cooked on the premises, and there's always a good selection of traditional pub dishes and a range of children's meals. At the weekend the bistro-style menu incorporates all the home-made dishes, and the Sunday roasts are great favourites.

Open fires keep things cosy in the bar, which has a non-smoking area for diners. The inn serves a full range of lagers, bitters, wines and spirits, with two or three regularly changing guest ales and a very reasonably priced house wine. Summer barbecues are a popular feature in the summer, and throughout the year the live music evenings are guaranteed to bring in the crowds. The Old Inn is located in the pretty Bourne Valley, a very pleasant part of the world for walking, and many of the country's leading places of historic interest are within an easy drive, including Stonehenge and Woodhenge, Old Sarum and all the splendours of the city of Salisbury. Also close by are Cholderton Rare Breeds Farm Park, Wilton Shopping Village and the Museum of Army Flying.

- ⊙ Summer: open all day, closed Monday; Winter: 12-3 & 6-11, all day weekends, closed Monday
- 🍴 Not Amex
- £ Visa, Mastercard, Delta, Switch
- Ⓟ Car park, beer gardens, children's pets area
- ♫ Darts, fruit machines, live music evenings
- @ email: jonny-baker@btinternet.com
- ❓ Cholderton Rare Breeds Farm 3 miles, Amesbury 3 miles, Salisbury 7 miles

THE OLIVER CROMWELL

71 ST EDITH'S MARSH, BROMHAM, NR DEVIZES,
WILTSHIRE SN15 2DF
TEL: 01380 850293 FAX: 01380 859620

Wiltshire

Directions: Take the A342 northwest out of Devizes towards Chippenham. The inn lies 3 or 4 miles along this road on the right.

The Oliver Cromwell is a 17th century former coaching inn standing on the A342 between Devizes and Chippenham. It was known as The Bell until 1978, when its name was changed to recognise the involvement of Cromwell in this part of the world during the English Civil War. Bob and Pam brought many years' experience in the trade when they took over the reins in 2001, and thanks to their efforts their fine old inn has established itself as one the region's most popular places to visit for a drink or a meal.

The promise of the outside, with its cream-painted stonewalls, its slate roof and its pretty red flower troughs, is more than fulfilled within, where black beams, exposed stone walls, a massive stone hearth and old implements and armoury create a delightfully traditional atmosphere. A skittle alley can be used as a function room or an extension to the non-smoking restaurant. Three real ales are always on tap, and quality home cooking is on offer every session. The choice runs from baguettes, salads and ploughman's platters to steaks, lamb tagine, Thai chicken curry and specials such as cod with a black olive tapenade, Madras beef curry or chicken, mushroom and sweetcorn lasagne. Children are very welcome, and they have a particularly tempting menu of their own. The garden, with picnic benches and a children's play area, commands splendid views across the fields to Roundway Hill in the distance. This was the scene in July 1643 of a violent battle which cost hundreds of lives and resulted in a decisive win for the Royalists.

- 🕐 Lunchtime and evening (all day Sat & Sun)
- 🍴 Home cooking on varied menus
- 💷 Not Amex or Diners
- 🅿 Car park, beer garden with children's play area, function room (skittle alley)
- ❓ Devizes 4 miles, Lacock 5 miles, Roundway Hill 5 miles

THE RED LION

EAST CHISENBURY, UPAVON, NR PEWSEY, WILTSHIRE SN9 6AQ
TEL: 01980 671124   FAX: 01980 671136

Directions: The village of East Chisenbury is located off the A345 2 miles south of Upavon.

The huge red beast painted on the snowy-white end wall leaves motorists in no doubt that they have arrived at **The Red Lion**. This lovely old building has a thatched roof and a thatched entrance, while exposed brick is a major feature in the stylishly modernised bar area. Leaseholders Simon and Jacqui brought plenty of experience and enthusiasm when they took over in September 2003, and they have made East Chisenbury a place to head for when looking for the best in hospitality, eating and drinking.

A good range of draught ales is always on hand to quench thirsts, but The Red Lion is above all known for its food. Simon is the chef, and his à la carte menu, specials board, fish board and Sunday lunch board are all compiled using the best and freshest of ingredients, many of them from local suppliers. Food is served in the 28-cover non-smoking restaurant and throughout the pub, but such is the popularity of The Red Lion that booking is essential at the weekend. The Sunday menu is guaranteed to bring in the crowds, offering a choice of traditional roasts along side light lunches and dishes such as pork steak rolled in mixed herbs, cod in beer batter or ham, eggs and chips - the last is ideal for late risers! This truly outstanding inn is located in the delightful village of East Chisenbury, just south of Upavon and short drive from Pewsey with its famous White Horse.

- Lunchtime and evening; closed Mondays, also Sun eve in winter
- Home cooking
- Not Amex or Diners
- Car park, beer garden
- Upavon 2 miles, Pewsey 6 miles

THE RIVERSIDE INN

49 ST MARGARET'S STREET, BRADFORD-ON-AVON,
WILTSHIRE BA15 1DE
TEL: 01225 863526 FAX: 01225 868082

Directions: The inn is located by the River Avon in the heart of Bradford-on-Avon.

The aptly named **Riverside Inn** is an imposing three-storey building in local stone. It was originally the home of a wealthy merchant, and in its time it has also been the home of the Conservative Club, the town library and the headquarters of a rowing club. It became an inn and hotel in 1981, and since 1996 it has been owned and personally run by Peter and Alison Eveleigh. The traditionally appointed bar boast many attractive features, including slatted wooden floors and a huge hearth topped by a black beam hung with brass ornaments. Wadworth 6X is the house regular, and high-qaulity food is served from noon right through to 9 o'clock Monday to Saturday and on Sunday lunchtime, also Sunday evening in the summer. Alison does the cooking, and her printed menu and the daily specials board guarantee that there's always something to please everyone. The Riverside Inn also has 11 well-appointed guest bedrooms. The inn is also a popular venue for parties, meetings and gatherings for all special occasions, and it has yet another string to its bow, the Black Cat Club. This is Bradford-on-Avon's biggest and brightest live music venue, with late-night licences on Thursday, Friday and Saturday nights. Bradford is a historic market town and there's plenty for the visitor to see in and around it, including the ancient Church of St Lawrence, a mighty tithe barn, Barton Farm Country Park and the Italian-style Peto Garden at Iford Manor.

 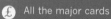

- 🕐 11-11
- 🍴 Home cooking
- 💷 All the major cards
- 🛏 11 en suite bedrooms including a family room
- Ⓟ Private car parking available
- ♫ Quiz nights Sun in winter; live music (The Black Cat Club) Thurs, Fri & Sat nights
- @ e-mail: info@riversideboa.co.uk

  Web: www.riversideboa.co.uk
- ❓ All the attractions of Bradford are nearby

THE ROYAL OAK

CORSLEY HEATH, NR WARMINSTER, WILTSHIRE BA12 7PR
TEL/FAX: 01373 832238

Directions: Corsley Heath is on the A362 3 miles east of Frome.

Nearly 400 years and once thought to have been a monks' retreat, **The Royal Oak** is a fine old stone building in a lovely country setting. The front of the inn overlooks a pretty green, while at the back tables and benches are set out for enjoying a drink in the sunshine. Inside, Jane and Nigel have created an ambience of great charm and

character, with country furniture, real fires, pictures and prints, brass and copper ornaments and an art deco mirror all contributing to the traditional scene. Wooden screens create little snugs, and the superb Stables Restaurant is decorated in the warmest of pinks.

Nigel is a professional chef, and since arriving in 2002 has made The Royal Oak one of the most sought after eating places in the area. The bar and restaurant menus present an across the board choice that runs from light snacks to fillet, rump, sirloin, ribeye or 16oz T-bone steaks from locally reared cattle, served plain or with a pepper, Diane or port & stilton sauce. Other typical dishes might include trout terrine, spaghetti bolognese and roast duck with a port and red plum sauce, with lattice apple pie or lemon crunch to round off a meal to remember. Booking is advisable at the weekend. Three real ales - Wadworth 6X, IPA and a guest - haed the drinks list. The Royal Oak has a pool table, skittle alley and dartboard, and in the back garden there's an area where children can play in safety. Corsley Heath is a short drive from Frome and Warminster and from Longleat House with its treasure-filled rooms, its Capabilty Brown grounds and its world-famous safari park.

- 🕐 11-11
- 🍴 Bar and à la carte menus
- £ Not Amex or Diners
- Ⓟ Car park, garden with children's play area, patio
- 🎵 Pool table, skittle alley
- ❓ Cley Hill 2 miles, Longleat 2 miles, Frome 3 miles, Warminster 3 miles

THE SILVER PLOUGH

WHITE HILL, PITTON, WILTSHIRE SP5 1DU
TEL: 01722 712266 FAX: 01722 712262

Wiltshire

> **Directions:** Pitton lies 3 miles east of Salisbury off the A30.

Originally a farmhouse, and an inn since the 1950s, **The Silver Plough** at Pitton has a reputation for hospitality and good food and drink that has spread far beyond the region. Its immaculate white frontage is flanked by trees, shrubs and topiary, and picnic tables are set on the lawn. The interior is equally stunning, with lovely old country furniture, a thatched servery and a wealth of ornaments adorning the walls and hanging from the beams. There are also many sporting trophies and mementoes relating to the previous career of landlord Hughen Riley, who runs the inn with his wife Joyce - this is the tenth inn they have run for the Hall & Wodehouse brewery. Hughen played professional football for Rochdale, Bury, Crewe and Bournemouth, and after hanging up his boots he became a professional chef.

His superb cooking can be enjoyed every lunchtime and every evening. Fresh seasonal produce is to the fore in dishes that range from classics such as steak & kidney pie or ham hock with parsley sauce to pheasant & rabbit casserole, sea bass with a fennel sauce or quorn & mushroom stroganoff with herby rice. Four real ales are always available, along with an extensive wine list that includes some country fruit wines. A charity quiz is held on the first Wednesday of each month, and the inn has a skittle alley that can be used for parties. At the back of this truly outstanding inn is a modern bungalow block with two self-contained en suite guest bedrooms. Staying here is a pure delight, providing the opportunity to sample more of the wonderful food and at the same time offering an ideal base for touring the region.

- 🕐 Lunchtime and evening
- 🍴 Home cooking
- £ Not Amex or Diners
- 🛏 21 en suite rooms
- Ⓟ Car park front and rear, garden
- 🎵 Quiz first Wednesday each month
- @ web: www.silverploughpitton.co.uk
- ❓ Salisbury 3 miles

THE SWAN INN

LONG STREET, ENFORD, NR PEWSEY, WILTSHIRE SN9 6DD
TEL/FAX: 01980 670338

Wiltshire

> **Directions:** From the A303 14 miles west of Andover turn right on to the A345 towards Devizes and Marlborough. Enford is about 7 miles along this road.

The sign of a white swan on a gibbet straddling the road tells drivers that they have arrived at this lovely old pub. Part redbrick, part painted white, with a thatched roof and a little lawn at the front, **The Swan Inn** is everything a traditional country pub should be, and leaseholders Paul and Clare Jackson are maintaining and enhancing a reputation for hospitality that has been attracting generations of locals and visitors from further afield. Exposed brick, old beams, pictures, prints and an assortment of ornaments and bric-a-brac paint a delightfully traditional scene and create a perfect ambience for relaxing with a glass of the excellent locally brewed Heelstone Bitter.

Paul's cooking is the number one attraction here, and his menus provide a fine choice for all tastes and appetites. Filled baguettes, Welsh rarebit, omelettes and the special 4oz steak & mushroom baguette are highlights on the bar menu, while typical dishes on the regularly changing main menu might include the day's curry and the day's pie, tuna with fennel and lemon, lamb shish kebab and, to finish in grand style, a delicious sticky date pudding. This outstanding food is served every session, and booking is recommended at the weekend. The little village of Enford is situated in the heart of Salisbury Plain on the banks of the River Avon. Stonehenge and Woodhenge are an easy drive away, and the famous white horse at Pewsey is also close by.

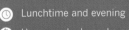

- ⏱ Lunchtime and evening
- 🍴 Home cooked snacks and meals
- £ Not Diners
- Ⓟ Garden, patio
- ❓ Salisbury Plain all around; Woodhenge 4 miles, Stonehenge 6 miles

THE WHEATSHEAF

1 KING STREET, WILTON, NR SALISBURY, WILTSHIRE SP2 0AX
TEL: 01722 742267

Directions: The inn is located on the edge of Wilton, 2 miles from Salisbury on the A36 Warminster road.

Hospitality is a way of life at **The Wheatsheaf**, in Wilton, where Steve McKinney and his team give a warm welcome to their regulars and to the many visitors who come to Salisbury, Wilton and the area as tourists or on business, for refreshment or to stay overnight.

Beams, wood panelling and an open fire give a traditional look to the bars and restaurant atea, which are open all day for the service of drinks and food – starting with morning coffee and moving on to hot and cold food available at lunch-time and in the evening. The cooking is definitely a major attraction here, and the blackboards advertise specials of the day including locally produced foods, such as Old Forge Farm sausages and Lyburn Farm cheeses, and home-cooked traditional fare.

Wilton is known the world over for its carpets, and there are organised tours round the Carpet Factory, situated next door in the popular Wilton Shopping Village. Wilton House, home of the Earl of Pembroke, with its fabulous paintings, magnificent architecture and living history, is just around the corner too.

The Wheatsheaf is a good base from which to explore Wilton - the ancient capital of Wessex, Salisbury , Stonehenge and the surrounding rural area. It's easy to find, located on the A36 between Salisbury and Warminster.

The Wheatsheaf's comfortable en suite bedrooms are equipped with TV and tea/coffee-making facilities. Behind the Wheatsheaf are the car park and a riverside garden alongside the River Wylye, where you can enjoy eating, drinking and feeding the ducks.

- 11-11
- Hot and cold meals, morning coffee, seasonal cream teas
- All the major cards
- En suite bedrooms for B&B
- Car park, riverside garden
- Darts
- At Wilton: Wilton Shopping Village, Wilton Carpet factory, Wilton House, Italianate Church

THE WHITE BEAR INN

MONDAY MARKET STREET, DEVIZES, WILTSHIRE SN10 1DN
TEL: 01380 727588

Directions: If coming from the M4, leave at J17 and take the A350 through Chippenham to Melksham, then the A365 for about 2 miles. Turn left on to the A361 to Devizes. The inn is close to the centre of town.

The White Bear is a historic inn on the site of the town's medieval market place. Formerly called The Talbot, and owned by St Mary's Church, it retains an old-world look with small-paned windows, beams, plank flooring, copper and brass ornaments, prints and glassware. The main bar is open-plan, and there's a snug smaller bar and a non-smoking eating area. Landlady Susan Westcott-Clark brought years of experience in the trade when she took over this handsome corner site, and in her short time here she has enhanced the inn's reputation as a local meeting place, as somewhere to find good food and drink and a base for both leisure and business visitors to Devizes. The food is everything the hungry visitor could want

– unpretentious, generously served, appetising and great value for money – and the choice ranges from snacks and salads to chunky pies and pasties and satisfying meat and chicken dishes. Two real ales are always on tap to quench thirsts. For overnight guests there are four comfortable bedrooms with TV, tea/coffee-makers and en suite or shared facilities.

At the western edge of the Vale of Pewsey, Devizes is the central market town of Wiltshire and is full of interesting buildings to explore. Many of the town's finest old buildings lie close to the White Bear, and its location at a key point on the Kennet & Avon Canal adds great interest: the Canal Museum and the Devizes Locks Discovery Trail should not be missed, and the Wharf, from where the Trail starts, hosts a weekend of fun each July.

- 🕐 11-2.30 & 6-11 Mon,Tues, Wed. 11-11 Thurs-Sat, 11-10.30 Sun.
- 🍴 Home-cooked snacks and meals
- £ All the major cards
- 🛏 4 B&B rooms, some en suite
- 🎵 Darts
- @ email: westcottclark@aol.com
- ❓ Close to all the attractions of Devizes, including towpath walks on Kennet & Avon Canal, Canal Museum, Devizes Museum, Visitor Centre

THE WHITE HORSE

BIDDESTONE, NR CHIPPENHAM, WILTSHIRE SN14 7DG
TEL: 01249 713305

Wiltshire

Directions: From the M4 J17 take the A350 to the roundabout before the
Chippenham bypass, then on to the A420 at the next roundabout. After about 2
miles take a left turn on to a minor road to Biddestone (1 mile).

Three miles from the busy market town of
Chippenham, Biddestone is a lovely village
where Cotswold-stone cottages, old
farmhouses and a 17th century manor
cluster round the green. **The White
Horse**, a 500-year-old white-painted stone
building with a slate roof and small-paned
windows, sits very happily in these peaceful
surroundings and is very much part of the
local community. Tony Hard, who
acquired the lease at the end of 2003 after
managing the inn for 15 years, knows his
customers well, and an open fire in the bar
creates a very pleasant ambience in which
to enjoy a chat and a drink – a choice of
real ales is always available, along with
other beers both draught and bottle and a
good wine list. All kinds of tastes and
appetites are taken care of by a daily
changing selection of home-cooked dishes
that taste as good as they sound: cheesy

melters, luxury salmon fishcakes, smokin'
Joe chicken, ocean pie, orchard pork,
vegetable jambalaya. The non-smoking
restaurant area has 56 covers, with many
more outside when the weather is fine.
The White Horse is a place for all the
family, with a large garden where children
can romp in safety, and a little pets corner.

The inn is close enough to the M4 to
provide a good opportunity for a welcome
break on a long journey, but the lovely
setting and the excellent welcome make it
well worth seeking out as a destination in
its own right. Notable among the local
places of interest is the town of Corsham,
where the wealth of good house greatly
impressed none other than Pevsner. A
unique attraction here is the Underground
Quarry Centre, the only shaft stone mine
in the world that's open to the public.

- 12-2.30 & 6-11
- Home cooking
- £ All the major cards
- Ⓟ Off-road parking, garden, pets corner
- @ email: ahard@freeserve.co.uk
- ? Corsham (Corsham Court, Quarry Centre) 3 miles, Chippenham 3 miles

THE WYNDHAM ARMS

HINDON ROAD, DINTON, NR SALISBURY, WILTSHIRE SP3 5EG
TEL: 01722 716999

> **Directions:** The village of Dinton stands on the B3089, off the A30 9 miles west of Salisbury.

Standing on a site partly occupied by a much older building, **The Wyndham Arms** is a mid-1930s hostelry with a distinctive white-painted frontage. During its relatively short life it has had several names, including The Swordsman and The Waggoners Rest, and it acquired its present name only about 6 or 7 years ago. It has been run since 2002 by Helen and Duncan Bendermacher, who have made it a popular place for both local customers and the many tourists who pass this way. Excellent food is the chief attraction, served every session except Sunday evening. The snack and restaurant menus provide a very good choice of dishes, with classics such as lasagne, macaroni and steaks alongside Thai green chicken curry, vegetable balti and Oriental king prawns with a BBQ sauce.

Wednesday is steak night, when they offer a special price for a starter + steak or a steak + pudding; this is always a popular occasion, so booking is definitely recommended. Diners can eat anywhere, including the non-smoking restaurant area with 22 covers, and children are very welcome. Three well-kept real ales are always on tap - Ringwood Best, Wadworth 6X and a rotating guest.

For those who want to tarry in this lovely hilltop village, Bed & Breakfast accommodation is available close by. And tarrying is a very good plan, as there are two National Trust properties in the vicinity. One is Little Clarendon, a Tudor house whose ground-floor rooms are furnished with vernacular oak pieces; the other is the neo-Grecian Philipps House, which stands in the landscaped grounds of Dinton Park.

- Lunchtime and evening, all day Sat & Sun
- Snacks and full menu
- Not Amex or Diners
- Car park, beer garden
- Quiz Sunday night
- Little Clarendon (NT) 2 miles, Dinton Park (NT) 2 miles, Wilton 5 miles, Salisbury 9 miles

ALPHABETICAL LIST
OF PUBS AND INNS

W

Y

Alphabetical List of Pubs and Inns

SPECIAL INTEREST LISTS

Accommodation

Accommodation

WILTSHIRE

SPECIAL INTEREST LISTS

All Day Opening

BUCKINGHAMSHIRE

The Black Horse	Great Missenden	25
The Green Man	Eversholt	29
The Old Beams	Shenley lodge, Milton Keynes	32
The Old Red Lion	Great Brickhill	35
The Old White Swan	Beaconsfield	36
The Watts Arms	Hanslope, Wolverton	40
The Whip Inn	Lacey Green, Princes Risborough	41

OXFORDSHIRE

The Bell at Charlbury	Charlbury	67
The Fox & Hounds	Uffington	74
The Fox & Hounds	Watlington	75
The George & Dragon	Chacombe, Banbury	78
The Golden Pheasant	Burford	79
The Griffin Inn	Chipping Warden	80
The Isis Tavern	Iffley Lock	81
The Morning Star	Cholsey, Wallingford	83
The Romany Inn	Bampton	93
Sturdy's Castle	Tackley	98
The White Hart	Old Headington	101
The White House	Bladon, Woodstock	102
Woodstock Arms	Woodstock	103

BERKSHIRE

The Duke of Connaught	Windsor	127
The New Inn	Stratfield Saye, Reading	129

HAMPSHIRE

The Bear & Ragged Staff	Michelmersh, Romsey	156
The Eclipse Inn	Winchester	158
The Fish Inn	Ringwood	159
The Foresters	Church crookham, Fleet	160
The Green Dragon	Liphook	163
The Kings Arms	Lymington	166
The Luzborough House	Romsey	168
The Wheatsheaf at Braishfield	Braishfield, Romsey	172
The White Hart	Petersfield	174
The White Hart	South Harting, Petersfield	175

All Day Opening

ISLE OF WIGHT

WILTSHIRE

SPECIAL INTEREST LISTS

Childrens Facilities

SPECIAL INTEREST LISTS

Credit Cards Accepted

BUCKINGHAMSHIRE

The Black Horse	Great Missenden	25
The Black Horse	Lacey green	26
The Cock & Rabbit	Great Missenden	27
Gatehangers Inn	Ashendon, Aylesbury	28
The Green Man	Eversholt	29
The Horse & Jockey	Tylers Green	30
The Lowndes Arms	Whaddon , Milton Keynes	31
The Old Beams	Shenley lodge, Milton Keynes	32
The Old Bell	Wooburn green	33
The Old Queens Head	Penn	34
The Old Red Lion	Great Brickhill	35
The Old White Swan	Beaconsfield	36
The Peacock	Bolter End, High Wycombe	37
The Seven Stars	Dinton, Aylesbury	39
The Whip Inn	Lacey Green, Princes Risborough	41

OXFORDSHIRE

The Bell at Charlbury	Charlbury	67
The Carpenters Arms	Witney	68
The Coach & Horses	Adderbury, Banbury	69
The Cricketers	Warborough, Wallington	70
The Crown at Nuffield	Nuffield, Henley-on-Thames	71
The Duke of Cumberland's Head	Clifton, Deddington	72
The Fox & Hounds	Uffington	74
The Fox & Hounds	Watlington	75
The Fox Inn	Tiddington	76
The Gate Inn	Upper Brailes, Banbury	77
The George & Dragon	Chacombe, Banbury	78
The Golden Pheasant	Burford	79
The Griffin Inn	Chipping Warden	80
The Isis Tavern	Iffley Lock	81
The Morning Star	Cholsey, Wallingford	83
The New Inn	Wroxton Heath, Banbury	84
The Old Anchor Inn	Abingdon	85
The Packhorse Inn	Milton Hill, Abingdon	86
The Plough Inn	East Hendred	87
The Red Cow	Chesterton	88
The Red Lion	Islip	89

Credit Cards Accepted

The Red Lion Inn	Cropredy, Banbury	92
The Romany Inn	Bampton	93
The Saye & Sele Arms	Broughton, Banbury	94
The Seven Stars	Marsh Baldon	95
Six Bells on the Green	Warborough, Wallingford	96
The Star Inn	Sparsholt	97
Sturdy's Castle	Tackley	98
The Vines Restaurant & Country House Hotel	Black Bourton	99
The White Hart	Eynsham	100
The White Hart	Old Headington	101
The White House	Bladon, Woodstock	102
Woodstock Arms	Woodstock	103

BERKSHIRE

The Bladebone Inn	Bucklebury	124
The Coach & Horses	Beedon, Newbury	125
The Crown & Garter	Inkpen, Hungerford	126
The Duke of Connaught	Windsor	127
The Fox & Hounds	Farley Hill, Reading	128
The New Inn	Stratfield Saye, Reading	129
Tally Ho	Hungerford Newtown	130
Ye Olde Red Lion	Chieveley, Newbury	131

HAMPSHIRE

The Barley Mow	Winchfield, Hook	155
The Bear & Ragged Staff	Michelmersh, Romsey	156
The Crown	Old Basing	157
The Eclipse Inn	Winchester	158
The Fish Inn	Ringwood	159
The Foresters	Church crookham, Fleet	160
The Forest Inn	Ashurst	161
The George Inn	Thruxton, Andover	162
The Green Dragon	Liphook	163
The Green Dragon at Brook	Brook, Lyndhurst	164
The Hare & Hounds	Charlton Down, Andover	165
The Kings Head	Lymington	167
The Luzborough House	Romsey	168
The Oak	Smannell, Andover	169
The Ship Inn	Bishops Sutton, Alresford	170

Credit Cards Accepted

The Star Inn	Romsey	171
The Wheatsheaf at Braishfield	Braishfield, Romsey	172
The White Hart	Eversley	173
The White Hart	Petersfield	174
The White Hart	South Harting, Petersfield	175
The White Horse	Milford-on-Sea	176
The Yew Tree	Highclere, Newbury	177

ISLE OF WIGHT

The Kings Head	Yarmouth	190
The Old Stag Inn	Newport	191
The Portland Inn	Gurnard	192
The Sun Inn	Hulverstone	193

WILTSHIRE

The Black Horse	Cherhill, Calne	216
The Black Horse	West Tytherley, Salisbury	217
The Bug & Spider and Marsh View Hotel	Calne	218
The Cross Inn	Tisbury	221
The Crown Inn	Cholderton, Salisbury	222
The Duke of York	Holloway, Malmesbury	223
The Fountain Inn	Whiteparish, Salisbury	224
The Foxham Inn	Foxham, Chippenham	225
The French Horn	Pewsey	226
The Old Inn	Allington, Salisbury	227
The Oliver Cromwell	Bromham, Devizes	228
The Red Lion	Upavon, Pewsey	229
The Riverside Inn	Bradford-on-Avon	230
The Royal Oak	Corsley Heath, Warminster	231
The Silver Plough	White Hill, Pitton	232
The Swan Inn	Enford, Pewsey	233
The Wheatsheaf	Wilton, Salisbury	234
The White Bear Inn	Devizes	235
The White Horse	Biddestone, Chippenham	236
The Wyndham Arms	Dinton, Salisbury	237

SPECIAL INTEREST LISTS

Garden, Patio or Terrace

BUCKINGHAMSHIRE

The Black Horse	Great Missenden	25
The Black Horse	Lacey green	26
The Cock & Rabbit	Great Missenden	27
The Green Man	Eversholt	29
The Horse & Jockey	Tylers Green	30
The Lowndes Arms	Whaddon , Milton Keynes	31
The Old Beams	Shenley lodge, Milton Keynes	32
The Old Bell	Wooburn green	33
The Old Queens Head	Penn	34
The Old White Swan	Beaconsfield	36
The Peacock	Bolter End, High Wycombe	37
The Rothschild Arms	Aston Clinton, Aylesbury	38
The Seven Stars	Dinton, Aylesbury	39
The Watts Arms	Hanslope, Wolverton	40

OXFORDSHIRE

The Bell at Charlbury	Charlbury	67
The Carpenters Arms	Witney	68
The Cricketers	Warborough, Wallington	70
The Crown at Nuffield	Nuffield, Henley-on-Thames	71
The Duke of Cumberland's Head	Clifton, Deddington	72
The Dun Cow	Hornton, Banbury	73
The Fox & Hounds	Uffington	74
The Fox & Hounds	Watlington	75
The Fox Inn	Tiddington	76
The Gate Inn	Upper Brailes, Banbury	77
The George & Dragon	Chacombe, Banbury	78
The Griffin Inn	Chipping Warden	80
The Isis Tavern	Iffley Lock	81
The Lamb & Flag	Hailey, Witney	82
The Morning Star	Cholsey, Wallingford	83
The New Inn	Wroxton Heath, Banbury	84
The Old Anchor Inn	Abingdon	85
The Packhorse Inn	Milton Hill, Abingdon	86
The Plough Inn	East Hendred	87
The Red Cow	Chesterton	88
The Red Lion	Islip	89
The Red Lion Inn	Chalgrove	91

Garden, Patio or Terrace

The Red Lion Inn	Cropredy, Banbury	92
The Romany Inn	Bampton	93
The Saye & Sele Arms	Broughton, Banbury	94
The Seven Stars	Marsh Baldon	95
Six Bells on the Green	Warborough, Wallingford	96
Sturdy's Castle	Tackley	98
The Vines Restaurant & Country House Hotel	Black Bourton	99
The White Hart	Eynsham	100
The White Hart	Old Headington	101
The White House	Bladon, Woodstock	102
Woodstock Arms	Woodstock	103

BERKSHIRE

The Bladebone Inn	Bucklebury	124
The Coach & Horses	Beedon, Newbury	125
The Crown & Garter	Inkpen, Hungerford	126
The Duke of Connaught	Windsor	127
The Fox & Hounds	Farley Hill, Reading	128
The New Inn	Stratfield Saye, Reading	129

HAMPSHIRE

The Barley Mow	Winchfield, Hook	155
The Bear & Ragged Staff	Michelmersh, Romsey	156
The Eclipse Inn	Winchester	158
The Fish Inn	Ringwood	159
The Foresters	Church crookham, Fleet	160
The Forest Inn	Ashurst	161
The George Inn	Thruxton, Andover	162
The Green Dragon	Liphook	163
The Green Dragon at Brook	Brook, Lyndhurst	164
The Hare & Hounds	Charlton Down, Andover	165
The Kings Head	Lymington	167
The Luzborough House	Romsey	168
The Oak	Smannell, Andover	169
The Ship Inn	Bishops Sutton, Alresford	170
The Star Inn	Romsey	171
The Wheatsheaf at Braishfield	Braishfield, Romsey	172
The White Hart	Petersfield	174

Garden, Patio or Terrace

Live Entertainment

BUCKINGHAMSHIRE

The Watts Arms	Hanslope, Wolverton	40

OXFORDSHIRE

The Fox Inn	Tiddington	76
The Griffin Inn	Chipping Warden	80
The Morning Star	Cholsey, Wallingford	83
The Old Anchor Inn	Abingdon	85
The Red Lion Inn	Cropredy, Banbury	92
The Seven Stars	Marsh Baldon	95
Six Bells on the Green	Warborough, Wallingford	96
The Vines Restaurant & Country House Hotel	Black Bourton	99
The White Hart	Old Headington	101

BERKSHIRE

The Duke of Connaught	Windsor	127
Tally Ho	Hungerford Newtown	130
Ye Olde Red Lion	Chieveley, Newbury	131

HAMPSHIRE

The Forest Inn	Ashurst	161
The Green Dragon at Brook	Brook, Lyndhurst	164
The Kings Arms	Lymington	166
The Ship Inn	Bishops Sutton, Alresford	170

WILTSHIRE

The Cat Tavern	Salisbury	220
The Old Inn	Allington, Salisbury	227
The Riverside Inn	Bradford-on-Avon	230

SPECIAL INTEREST LISTS

Restaurant or Dining Area

BUCKINGHAMSHIRE

The Cock & Rabbit	Great Missenden	27
The Green Man	Eversholt	29
The Lowndes Arms	Whaddon , Milton Keynes	31
The Old Beams	Shenley lodge, Milton Keynes	32
The Old Bell	Wooburn green	33
The Old Red Lion	Great Brickhill	35
The Seven Stars	Dinton, Aylesbury	39

OXFORDSHIRE

The Bell at Charlbury	Charlbury	67
The Carpenters Arms	Witney	68
The Coach & Horses	Adderbury, Banbury	69
The Cricketers	Warborough, Wallington	70
The Fox & Hounds	Uffington	74
The Fox & Hounds	Watlington	75
The Gate Inn	Upper Brailes, Banbury	77
The Lamb & Flag	Hailey, Witney	82
The New Inn	Wroxton Heath, Banbury	84
The Plough Inn	East Hendred	87
The Red Lion	Islip	89
The Red Lion	Woodcote	90
The Red Lion Inn	Cropredy, Banbury	92
The Romany Inn	Bampton	93
The Seven Stars	Marsh Baldon	95
Sturdy's Castle	Tackley	98
The Vines Restaurant & Country House Hotel	Black Bourton	99
The White Hart	Old Headington	101

BERKSHIRE

The Bladebone Inn	Bucklebury	124
The Coach & Horses	Beedon, Newbury	125

HAMPSHIRE

The Barley Mow	Winchfield, Hook	155
The Fish Inn	Ringwood	159
The Forest Inn	Ashurst	161
The Hare & Hounds	Charlton Down, Andover	165

Restaurant or Dining Area

Places of Interest

Travel Publishing

The Hidden Places	Regional and National guides to the less well-known places of interest and places to eat, stay and drink
Hidden Inns	Regional guides to traditional pubs and inns throughout the United Kingdom
GOLFERS GUIDES	Regional and National guides to 18 hole golf courses and local places to stay, eat and drink
 **RURAL GUIDES**	Regional and National guides to the traditional countryside of Britain and Ireland with easy to read facts on places to visit, stay, eat, drink and shop

For more information:

Phone: 0118 981 7777   **Fax:** 0118 982 0077
e-mail: adam@travelpublishing.co.uk   **website:** www.travelpublishing.co

Easy-to-use, Informative
Travel Guides on the British Isles

THE HIDDEN PLACES OF
Northumberland & Durham

An informative guide to the more secluded and less well-known places to visit
■ Places of interest ■ Accommodation ■ Food ■ Drink

HIDDEN INNS OF
YORKSHIRE
INCLUDING THE YORKSHIRE DALES AND MOORS

AN INFORMATIVE GUIDE TO THE MORE SECLUDED
PUBS AND INNS OF YORKSHIRE

THE HIDDEN PLACES OF
Wales

Informative guide to the more secluded and less well-known places to visit
Places of interest ■ Accommodation ■ Food ■ Drink

GUIDE TO RURAL ENGLAND
EAST ANGLIA
Second Edition

Norfolk, Suffolk, Essex and Cambridgeshire
Fully illustrated with detailed directions and maps
■ Where to go   ■ What to see   ■ What to do
■ Where to stay   ■ Where to eat   ■ Where to buy

THE GOLFERS GUIDE
to Ireland

Packed with information on Golf Courses and where to stay, eat and drink
Dermot Gilleece

GUIDE TO RURAL ENGLAND
THE WEST COUNTRY
Second Edition

Cornwall, Devon, Somerset and Dorset
Fully illustrated with detailed directions and maps
■ Where to go   ■ What to see   ■ What to do
■ Where to stay   ■ Where to eat   ■ Where to buy

Travel Publishing Limited

7a Apollo House • Calleva Park • Aldermaston • Berkshire RG7 8TN

ORDER FORM

To order any of our publications just fill in the payment details below and complete the order form. For orders of less than 4 copies please add £1 per book for postage and packing. Orders over 4 copies are P & P free.

Please Complete Either:

I enclose a cheque for £ _____ made payable to Travel Publishing Ltd

Or:

Card No: _____ Expiry Date: _____

Signature: _____

Name: _____

Address: _____

Tel no: _____

Please either send, telephone, fax or e-mail your order to:

Travel Publishing Ltd, 7a Apollo House, Calleva Park, Aldermaston, Berkshire RG7 8TN   Tel: 0118 981 7777   Fax: 0118 982 0077
e-mail: karen@travelpublishing.co.uk

Hidden Places Regional Titles

Title	Price	Quantity
Cambs & Lincolnshire	£7.99	....
Chilterns	£7.99	....
Cornwall	£8.99	....
Derbyshire	£8.99	....
Devon	£8.99	....
Dorset, Hants & Isle of Wight	£8.99	....
East Anglia	£8.99	....
Gloucs, Wiltshire & Somerset	£8.99	....
Heart of England	£7.99	....
Hereford, Worcs & Shropshire	£7.99	....
Highlands & Islands	£7.99	....
Kent	£8.99	....
Lake District & Cumbria	£8.99	....
Lancashire & Cheshire	£8.99	....
Lincolnshire & Notts	£8.99	....
Northumberland & Durham	£8.99	....
Sussex	£8.99	....
Yorkshire	£8.99	....

Hidden Places National Titles

Title	Price	Quantity
England	£11.99	....
Ireland	£11.99	....
Scotland	£10.99	....
Wales	£11.99	....

Hidden Inns Titles

Title	Price	Quantity
East Anglia	£5.99	....
Heart of England	£5.99	....
Lancashire & Cheshire	£5.99	....
North of England	£5.99	....
South	£5.99	....
South East	£7.99	....
South and Central Scotland	£5.99	....
Wales	£7.99	....
Welsh Borders	£5.99	....
West Country	£7.99	....
Yorkshire	£5.99	....

Country Living Rural Guides

Title	Price	Quantity
East Anglia	£10.99	....
Heart of England	£9.99	....
Ireland	£10.99	....
Scotland	£10.99	....
South of England	£9.99	....
South East of England	£9.99	....
Wales	£10.99	....
West Country	£10.99	....

Total Quantity _____

Post & Packing _____

Total Value _____

The *Travel Publishing* research team would like to receive reader's comments on any visitor attractions or places reviewed in the book and also recommendations for suitable entries to be included in the next edition. This will help ensure that the *Hidden Inns Series* continues to provide its readers with useful information on the more interesting, unusual or unique features of each inn or place ensuring that their visit to the local area is an enjoyable and stimulating experience. To provide your comments or recommendations would you please complete the forms below and overleaf as indicated and send to:

**The Research Department, Travel Publishing Ltd,
7a Apollo House, Calleva Park, Aldermaston, Reading, RG7 8TN.**

Your Name:

Your Address:

Your Telephone Number:

Please tick as appropriate:

Comments ☐   Recommendation ☐

Name of Establishment:

Address:

Telephone Number:

Name of Contact:

READER REACTION FORM

Comment or Reason for Recommendation:

READER REACTION FORM

The *Travel Publishing* research team would like to receive reader's comments on any visitor attractions or places reviewed in the book and also recommendations for suitable entries to be included in the next edition. This will help ensure that the *Hidden Inns Series* continues to provide its readers with useful information on the more interesting, unusual or unique features of each inn or place ensuring that their visit to the local area is an enjoyable and stimulating experience. To provide your comments or recommendations would you please complete the forms below and overleaf as indicated and send to:

**The Research Department, Travel Publishing Ltd,
7a Apollo House, Calleva Park, Aldermaston, Reading, RG7 8TN.**

Your Name:

Your Address:

Your Telephone Number:

Please tick as appropriate:

Comments ☐   Recommendation ☐

Name of Establishment:

Address:

Telephone Number:

Name of Contact:

READER REACTION FORM

Comment or Reason for Recommendation:

READER REACTION FORM

The *Travel Publishing* research team would like to receive reader's comments on any visitor attractions or places reviewed in the book and also recommendations for suitable entries to be included in the next edition. This will help ensure that the *Hidden Inns Series* continues to provide its readers with useful information on the more interesting, unusual or unique features of each inn or place ensuring that their visit to the local area is an enjoyable and stimulating experience. To provide your comments or recommendations would you please complete the forms below and overleaf as indicated and send to:

The Research Department, Travel Publishing Ltd,
7a Apollo House, Calleva Park, Aldermaston, Reading, RG7 8TN.

Your Name:

Your Address:

Your Telephone Number:

Please tick as appropriate:
                Comments ☐   Recommendation ☐

Name of Establishment:

Address:

Telephone Number:

Name of Contact:

READER REACTION FORM

Comment or Reason for Recommendation:

READER REACTION FORM

The *Travel Publishing* research team would like to receive reader's comments on any visitor attractions or places reviewed in the book and also recommendations for suitable entries to be included in the next edition. This will help ensure that the *Hidden Inns Series* continues to provide its readers with useful information on the more interesting, unusual or unique features of each inn or place ensuring that their visit to the local area is an enjoyable and stimulating experience. To provide your comments or recommendations would you please complete the forms below and overleaf as indicated and send to:

The Research Department, Travel Publishing Ltd,
7a Apollo House, Calleva Park, Aldermaston, Reading, RG7 8TN.

Your Name:

Your Address:

Your Telephone Number:

Please tick as appropriate:

Comments ☐   Recommendation ☐

Name of Establishment:

Address:

Telephone Number:

Name of Contact:

READER REACTION FORM

Comment or Reason for Recommendation: